BEHIND THE FIGURES

BEHIND THE FIGURES

Addresses and Articles by Arthur Andersen

1913-1941

Foreword

ARTHUR ANDERSEN was under thirty when he founded the public accounting firm of Arthur Andersen & Co. on December 1, 1913. He was the managing partner of the firm until his death in 1947.

His ability to grasp and solve the problems of business in a practical way gave him a ready entree as a speaker to groups of bankers and businessmen. His emphasis was always on getting and interpreting the facts behind the figures.

These addresses and articles by Mr. Andersen have been assembled here in order to preserve his thinking, which constituted the basic foundation of the firm which bears his name.

ARTHUR ANDERSEN

1885 - 1947

About Arthur Andersen

(Contained in the Presentation of Arthur Andersen for Election to the Ohio State University Accounting Hall of Fame, May 21, 1953.)

The Board of Nominations presents Arthur Edward Andersen for the Ohio State University Accounting Hall of Fame.

Mr. Andersen, a native of Illinois, received the degree of Bachelor of Business Administration from Northwestern University. He was granted a certificate as a Certified Public Accountant by the State of Illinois in 1908. In 1909, the year after the School of Commerce of Northwestern University was organized, he was offered and accepted an instructorship in the accounting department. In 1912, at the age of 27, Mr. Andersen was appointed Assistant Professor of Accounting, thus beginning a twelve-year career with that institution which led eventually to a full professorship and the position as head of the accounting department. He also served as a member and later as President of the Board of Trustees of Northwestern University. He was an inspiring teacher and challenged students in his classes to think objectively. He had an unwavering faith in education as the basis upon which the new profession of accounting should be developed.

In 1913 he founded the accounting firm shortly after to be known as Arthur Andersen & Co., in which he was senior partner until his death in 1947. In his professional practice he continually stressed his profound belief that the Certified Public Accountant not only has a duty to serve his client on a high professional level but a serious social responsibility.

Mr. Andersen served as President of the Illinois Society of Certified Public Accountants during the year 1918-1919; he served on important committees of the American Institute of Accountants, including those on the Form and Administration of Income Tax Laws, and the Committee on the Definition of Earned Surplus; was Chairman of the Illinois Board of Certified Public Accounting Examiners; and was a member of important committees of the U. S. Chamber of Commerce. He was one of the charter members of the American Association of University Instructors in Accounting, which later became the American Accounting Association.

In recognition of his attainments and contributions toward the development of Accounting as a profession, he received honorary degrees from Luther, Grinnell and St. Olaf colleges and also from his alma mater, Northwestern University.

For his contributions as an educator and as an outstanding practitioner, the Board of Nominations is proud to present Arthur Edward Andersen for the Accounting Hall of Fame.

THE OHIO STATE UNIVERSITY
ACCOUNTING HALL OF FAME
Be It Known That
ARTHUR EDWARD ANDERSEN

having made distinguished contributions to the advancement of the accounting profession, has been elected to the Accounting Hall of Fame of The Ohio State University upon the recommendation of a board of nominations. In evidence thereof this testimonial is presented on this 21st day of May, in the year nineteen hundred and fifty-three.

W. A. PATON	WALTER C. WEIDLER
Chairman, Board of Nominations	*Dean, College of Commerce and*
HERMANN C. MILLER	*Administration*
Chairman, Department of	HOWARD L. BEVIS
Accounting	*President, The Ohio State University*

Contents

Addresses and Articles by Arthur Andersen

PAGE

1913 Behind the Figures *(System, The Magazine of Business,* January, 1913) 1

Comment of P. K. Knight (as reprinted in *The Chronicle,* June, 1946) 13

1917 Modern Accounting Methods (Convention of United States Independent Telephone Association) 15

1921 The Accountant, the Industrial Engineer, and the Banker *(Administration,* August, 1921) 23

1924 Industrial and Financial Investigations (National Association of Cost Accountants, First Western Regional Conference, Chicago) 29

1924 The Present Day Accountant: His Contribution to the Problems of Financing (The American Association of University Instructors, Ninth Annual Meeting, Chicago) 41

1925 The Accountant's Function as Business Advisor (American Institute of Accountants Regional Meeting, Chicago) 51

1925 and 1926 The Financial and Industrial Investigation (A Series of Articles Which Appeared Originally in *Manufacturing Industries)*—

Its Purposes and Problems 57

Scope of Financial and Industrial Investigations 65

Judging Organization and Personnel 75

Analyzing Net Worth 83

Judging Operating Results 93

Operating and Balance Sheet Ratios 101

Operating and Turnover Ratios 109

1926 Accounting and Business Analysis for Credit Purposes (The Association of Reserve City Bankers, Fifteenth Annual Convention, Atlanta) 117

1927 The Functions and Duties of the Office of Comptroller (American Petroleum Institute) 127

1929   Financial and Industrial Investigations (Published in *The Accounting Review,* Volume IV, 1929)   135

1930   The Possibilities and the Dangers Inherent in Mergers, Consolidations and Acquisitions (National Association of Cost Accountants, Kansas City Chapter)   143

1931   The Major Problem Created by the Machine Age (National Association of Cost Accountants, Detroit)   155

1932   The Accountant and His Clientele (A William A. Vawter Foundation on Business Ethics Lecture, Northwestern University School of Commerce, Evanston, Illinois)   165

1933   An NRA Enigma: What Constitutes "Selling Below Cost"? (American Trade Association Executives, Chicago)   179

1934   Duties and Responsibilities of the Comptroller (Controllers Institute of America, Chicago Control)   189

1934   The Future of Our Economic System (Northwestern University, The Contemporary Thought Series, Evanston, Illinois)   201

1935   Present Day Problems Affecting the Presentation and Interpretation of Financial Statements (American Institute of Accountants, Boston)   213

1936   Excerpts from Mr. Andersen's Talk Before the Annual Meeting of the Partners and Managers of Arthur Andersen & Co., Chicago   223

1940   Introduction to the First Issue of *The Chronicle,* October 1, 1940   229

1941   A Layman Speaks (Commencement Address at St. Olaf's College, Northfield, Minnesota)   231

Behind the figures

Published in *System, The Magazine of Business,* January, 1913

Right accounting is more than history. It is not enough to know what has been done; records should show what should have been done.

An unexplained shortage of $15,000 in the raw material account for the year just closed, led the general manager of a specialty concern through the sales, purchasing, cost and operating departments to the little registering device at the side of each finishing machine.

The product was sold by the lineal foot. The figures indicated that the material used exceeded by $15,000 worth what had been delivered to customers. No "bookkeeping errors" were found, but when the accuracy of the records had been checked and proved, the reason for the loss was found in the devices for registering the quantity of product turned out. These were out of order. For more than a year every customer had been charged for much less than had actually been shipped because the counters had "slipped." Since the gifts were of finished product the loss was nearly double the cost of the raw material.

Right figures check, guide and control any business. A suitable accounting system, matched to the size and needs of the business, throws to the surface significant facts. More—it brings to the man at the head of the business grouped and related details which otherwise would escape attention. A market man in Massachusetts learns from his records of what people are buying, when he ought to push fish instead of meat, or pork instead of mutton. He is getting behind his figures, just as is the manufacturer in Chicago who sets quotas of sales and output based on what has been sold and made in the past and asks "why?" when the monthly reports fluctuate either below or above the figures set. No matter what your business may be, you can set your accounting to watch the significant factors in that business.

Different managers have different methods

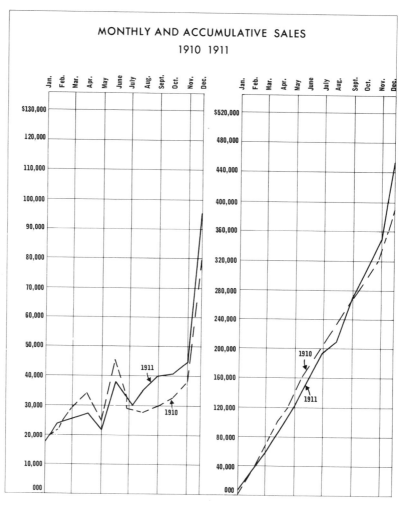

By going "behind the figures" here, the general manager of a large jewelry house was able to catch an unexpected slump in sales due to the failure of an advertising campaign to start on schedule and to put on pressure enough to correct and compensate for the falling off. The record for 1910 was charted later for comparison. In the right-hand section are shown the accumulative sales for both years.

of finding these significant facts. What some men sense by experience others get from tabulated and charted facts. A factory cost accountant put in a rather elaborate system for the superintendent. He collected the costs of steel for the blade, the wood for the handle, the labor and overhead expenses in making a kitchen knife. After he had collected figures for a couple of months, the superintendent of the plant took a note book out of his pocket and said that they agreed

pretty closely with what he had figured as the costs on the different grades.

The superintendent knew by long experience the average total cost of certain classes of orders. But when the cost man went over his tabulated figures and showed him the relative department charges for overhead expenses, he brought to the superintendent's attention a fact which he had not before realized—that he was losing money on certain classes of goods. Only by department comparisons could such a condition come to light.

A suitable cost system in a manufacturing plant may show one manager the significant facts in his business. Figures may prophesy in a merchandising establishment, when the records are planned to control the business. The sales manager of a large jewelry house with an extensive local and country business has a plan for knowing what is going on, which is adaptable to other lines. Like other executives, he has found that charts showing gross sales both in quantities and money values will enable him to know definitely what the sales department is doing in each line and will direct him to the weak spots in his organization.

Returning from a trip abroad, he found conditions in the business somewhat as indicated by the chart on page 2. A summary of sales by months and accumulative sales for the same period had been contrasted with the corresponding figures for the corresponding month or period of the previous year. At the beginning of January, 1911, just before the general manager left, quite an extensive advertising campaign had been prepared. He had looked for a large increase in sales.

But as the chart indicates, when he returned on the last of May, instead of an increase there had been a gradual decline in business for the current year. Investigation showed that the advertising campaign planned to start the first of January had not been begun until late in March. Had he not compared his sales he would not have learned at once the cause of the decline. As it was, the increase of business which is shown for the months of July and August on the charts was made possible by the prompt application of additional pressure on the sales and advertising departments.

Records of this sort reduced to a unit basis enable the managers of all kinds of businesses to watch their courses. State-

ments and charts which show the average price realized per ton, per pound or per barrel by steel, glue and brewing companies, enable the sales managers of these respective concerns to keep in touch with the results obtained by each salesman. Similarly the payrolls of large retail stores are watched. A record is kept of each clerk's business, day by day. Each week the percentage of salaries to the sales made is calculated. At any time the superintendent and department manager know what the payroll stands for in sales, and which clerks are efficient.

Whenever a business man, at the end of the year or the month, sits at his desk with the figures of the period before him, one of the obvious things he watches is the relation between expenses and the amount of business done. His records must be planned to show comparative statements and charts of sales, cost of sales, expenses and net profits. Unless the figures get to him in this form it is difficult to see how the outlay matches up with the amount of business done.

An interesting example which indicates how the vice-president of a wholesale house follows gross profits and departmental expenses is shown in the chart on page 4. Trade conditions had been poor and one of the department managers failed to compare his departmental expense with his gross profits. This condition continued until the month of August when, as will be seen, the gross profits were practically consumed by the departmental expense. Each month now this department head gets his comparative statements of gross profits and departmental expenses and does not wait for the figures to "push" him. He pushes the figures.

Tradition says figures do not lie. Yet, the wrong interpretation of figures may throw the head of the business completely off the track. Groups of facts must be considered with relation to the right groups of corresponding facts. Both sides of the question must be considered in the tabulated statistics.

3

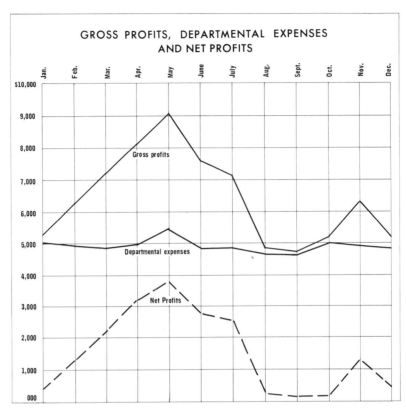

GROSS PROFITS, DEPARTMENTAL EXPENSES
AND NET PROFITS

A fine example of synchronous records of gross profits, departmental expenses and net profits in a wholesale grocery house, and the close interdependence of the three on one another. Note how the April-May-June increase in expenses affected the net, and how the failure to reduce expenses when gross profits began to decline, practically consumed the net profits during August and September.

A sash and door company began to scrutinize the records of its twelve salesmen, mostly young and middle-aged men. The low gross sales of one of the older salesmen at first led the president to believe that this older man was being kept on the payroll for sentimental reasons. But when he took the sales records of the various products and compared them with the profits obtained on each sale he changed his mind. He found that while the older man sold less in the aggregate than his fellow travelers, the total profit on his business was greater. Because of his experience, he knew the profitable and unprofitable lines. The comparison of the two sets of figures showed how the com-

pany had gone wrong and a new sales policy was inaugurated at once. Every salesman was instructed to concentrate effort on the profitable lines, and allow the low-profit lines to sell themselves or use them to push the more profitable specialties.

Look into any group of figures for the significant items; the records of one department compared with the others or of one branch compared with the next will often suggest a more uniformly profitable way of handling the business. Lumped figures do not show tendencies. A poor machine in one department may keep up the total relative cost of the output of that depart-

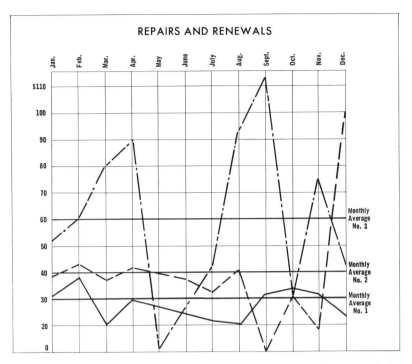

REPAIRS AND RENEWALS

Monthly Average No. 3

Monthly Average No. 2

Monthly Average No. 1

This graphic comparison of the repairs and renewals required by three mining machines brought to the owner's attention the abuse to which No. 3 was subjected and resulted in the hiring of another and a more careful operator for it.

ment. One slow line of goods may distort the figures of a store. It is better to individualize accounts wherever possible in order that each may stand on its own merits.

The president of a mining company suspected that his repair and renewal account was higher than it should be purely because of his general knowledge of conditions. Not until he had compared the expenditures for repairs and renewals on three machines, as shown by the chart above, did he realize that two of the machines had suffered unjustly for the faults of one. The three cutting machines were of the same general design and cost and were installed about the same time. When the facts came out that machine Number 3 had much greater repair and renewal expense than the other two, it was discovered that the man who had charge of this machine subjected it to much rougher

usage than the operators of the other two machines.

Figures that mean most to the head of a business must contain all the elements entering into a consideration of any particular item. Statements and charts of sales and expenses only without cost of goods sold may prove misleading. Business is done for profit, not for sales totals. Two concerns may be doing substantially the same gross business; one, however, may be doing its business at a much higher cost.

The Philadelphia and Baltimore offices of an electrical supply house had substantially the same volume of sales. Yet, when the annual statement came in it was found that much more money was made in one office than in the other in spite of the fact that the volume of sales was about the same in both. When the figures came to the general manager of the company, he saw at once

5

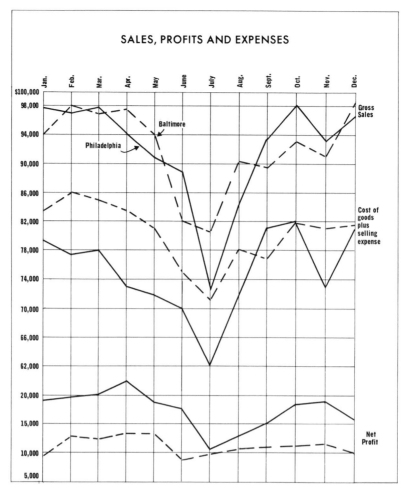

SALES, PROFITS AND EXPENSES

The "profitable parallel" as applied to the gross sales, the cost-plus-selling-expense of goods sold, and the net profits of two branch houses of a large manufacturing concern. The comparison was easy and fair because gross sales and field conditions were much the same for both. With a comparative analysis of vital figures like this, the owner or manager can find inefficiency and demonstrate it to the man responsible.

that the reason Baltimore netted less in profits than Philadelphia was due to two reasons: supplies were sold at too close a margin of profit and sales and office salaries were disproportionate to the amount of business done.

Often by matching department with department, branch office with branch office, machine with machine or clerk with clerk, a better understanding can be obtained of what the business is doing. It has been found in many businesses that comparative expense statements, furnished to branch managers with the comments of an executive officer, will do much to hold down cost. On the second Tuesday of each month, the manager of a soda-fountain business devotes his entire day to the study of statements and graphic charts. Sales, branch and departmental expenses and other elements entering into profit and loss accounts come under his supervision. One of the reasons why the company can do business at a low cost is because the manager knows how to use the figures in his business.

Studying a statement itemizing the expenses of one of the larger branches of the company, the head noticed that the wages of

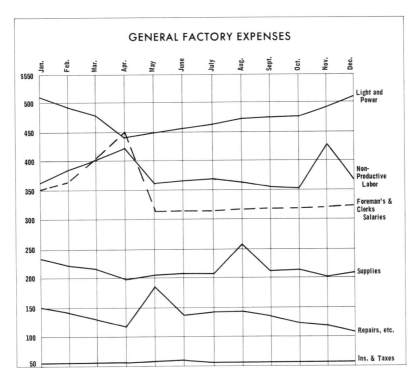

GENERAL FACTORY EXPENSES

Light and Power

Non-Productive Labor

Foreman's & Clerks Salaries

Supplies

Repairs, etc.

Ins. & Taxes

How unusual expenditures can be caught and corrected by a graphic monthly analysis is shown here. Notice how the April "peak" in foremen's and clerks' salaries was "ironed out" and kept at a more reasonable level thereafter.

the unloading and shipping department increased in the four months ending April 30th over a similar cost for the slack season of the previous year. Investigation developed that the manager of the branch had failed to cut, from eight to six, the men in his receiving department.

Receiving and shipping expenses at the Kansas City branch, greater than the average shipping expenses of the seven or eight other branches, drew attention to another condition which might not have come to the manager's notice. Inquiry showed that the receiving and storage facilities were inadequate, that it was necessary to handle material twice in unloading and storing, that the bins, shelves and general layout were poor. By spending five hundred dollars for the improvement of the storeroom, the company made an annual saving of sixteen hundred dollars in this particular item of expense.

Just as a sales manager may get from his records definite knowledge of his sales and profits, so the manufacturer can devise intelligent summaries of expenses that will show him the relative costs of his products. Overhead expenses often go up mysteriously. Unless the expenses are put on paper in comparative form, it is hard to get behind the totals and find out just what is causing the increase in expense. Non-productive labor, salaries of time keepers, order and shop clerks and supplies consumed, are all details which the head needs to group in such form that ready comparisons may be made.

Itemized, comparative figures make it possible to find the reason for high overhead expenses in the monthly statement of a business. Bulk totals, unless seen in relation to other figures, have little significance unless the man who watches the figures keeps the basic figures in the back of his head, and compares the bulk total with that.

PRODUCTIVE AND NON-PRODUCTIVE LABOR

To preserve the right ratio between productive and non-productive labor is one problem which every manager proposes to himself. This graphic record is the means by which a manufacturing chemist holds non-productive expense down.

Last year's figures may generally be taken as a basis for this year's total. Monthly quotas of expenses sometimes are best. Variations from standard can then be checked before a wrong policy is established. The cost of lubricants in one mine showed a marked increase over the corresponding period of the previous year. When the superintendent investigated he found that the machine operators were burning lubricating oil costing thirty cents a gallon in their torches instead of six-cent illuminating oil.

To check the previous waste, each machine operator was allotted two gallons of oil per day, although an additional quantity could be had by giving reasons. A second cause for the high lubricating cost was caught by watching the amount of money received for oil barrels returned. The credit item for returned barrels seemed smaller than the year before. It developed that the miners, instead of tapping a barrel, had been knocking in the head and filling their pails by dipping into the barrel. About six hundred dollars a year was saved by stopping this practice.

Comparative statements of factory expenses are always instructive. In one case when such figures came to the attention of the manager, an increase of $834.25 in miscellaneous materials and supplies uncovered an important source of waste. The foreman of Department A had in his charge a large stock of materials and supplies, many of which were used in Department B. Unknown to the former, the head of Department B had taken and used wastefully large quantities of material, thinking that the other foreman would have difficulty in explaining the large debit difference in his material account. Two little columns of figures brought

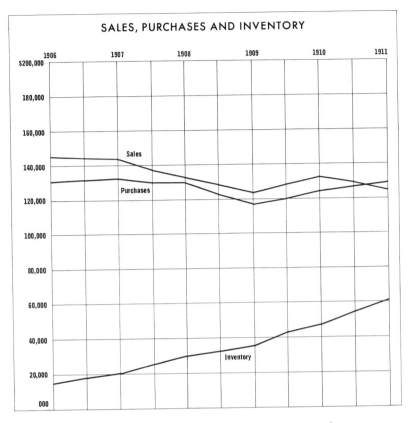

A serious leak in net income never fails to develop when a proper balance is not kept between purchases and sales and the investment in stocks on hand is allowed to become excessive. Here is the graphic record which first focused the attention of a wholesale hardware man on the question and helped him to frame his buying program to suit his sales and keep his inventory down to the minimum.

out this badly organized spot in the factory where inefficiency existed because of the jealous rivalry of these two foremen.

All sorts of items in overhead expense can be cared for if the totals come before the manager not in the form of bulk figures but itemized under separate headings. The electric-power-used item in one large manufacturing concern totaled $42,300 for the year ending December 31, 1911. In going over the figures, the manager of the plant thought here was an item which would cost more next year because he expected an increase in the business and power used would increase almost in proportion to an increase in production.

The totals stopped him. They looked big for the work he already did. He went out through the plant and made some rough estimates of apparent wastes in power here and there. Then he talked over the situation with his electrical engineer. He found that by overhauling his wiring, individual meters could be put in the different departments and so the expense of current used in each shop determined. The manager invested nine thousand dollars in these changes. And the first ten months of the current year indicate that in spite of an increase of fifteen percent in production over last year the total power cost will be, roughly, thirty-two thousand dollars. The saving in power alone the first year will pay for the changes made in the power equipment.

Just as properly displayed and grouped figures will show the rise and fall in manufacturing expenses, so they will indicate to the factory superintendent the interrelation between productive and non-productive labor —the totals watched most jealously in every manufacturing plant, since every manager knows the necessity of keeping down the ratio between non-productive and productive labor. The relative importance of these items escaped one manager until he plotted his figures in chart form like that shown in the chart on page 8. Put in this graphic way, the increase in non-productive labor for April, 1911, was apparent at a glance. When the foreman of the department was asked for an explanation it was found that two skilled workmen had been kept on the payroll during a slack period in order that the men would be available when business increased.

Such records are history. The money had been spent. But it was easy to establish a policy that thereafter the foreman should not settle such questions himself but should confer with the superintendent. In this case it was found that the particular men on this work could have been easily replaced, although in all instances this might not have been the case. In November of the same year, that chart shows non-productive labor in Department C increased one hundred dollars. In this case, the figures were prophecy, not history, for when the manager went behind them he found that they represented an increase in truckers to carry out a different method of moving and shifting merchandise which was not necessary.

"Let every dollar of capital invested or borrowed perform its full duty," is the way a prominent banker expresses the need of keeping inventories, customers' accounts, notes receivable, cash and working liabilities at the minimum and at the same time pro-

ducing the maximum earnings. These are conditions which the managers of a variety of concerns may look for in their statements. Just as records will show tendencies in sales and explain department outputs and machine efficiency, so the financial condition of a business may be watched.

Under normal conditions investment in working assets of such businesses as hardware, grocery, paint, shoes, jewelry, drug, dry goods, automobile and steel can easily be determined. Definite relationship must exist between capital represented in working assets and the annual turn-over. Records can be drawn from different sections of the business to show "lock-up in working capital" at the close of each month. Failure to keep this at the minimum necessitates borrowing and paying of interest otherwise unnecessary.

One manufacturer traced his uninvested working assets through his record of uncollected customers' accounts and inventories, as shown in the chart on page 11. Two branches in St. Louis and Omaha, selling belting, pulleys and other supplies, did substantially the same volume of business and operated under much the same conditions. The figures showed, however, that the Omaha branch had an investment in stock and accounts $30,000 larger than that of the St. Louis branch. When the situation was sifted down to its elements, it was discovered that the Omaha branch did not give the same strict attention to stock-keeping and the collection of accounts as did the St. Louis office. By installing a perpetual inventory and efficient sales records and revising the collection methods, the Omaha situation was brought up to the St. Louis standard.

In like manner the investment in the several classes of assets in various businesses may be profitably compared. Just as well as in sales and expense, the head of the business may see his figures in a "per unit" form. On this uniform basis, the relative investment in different branches can be

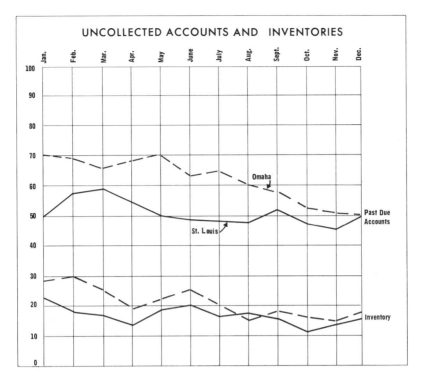

UNCOLLECTED ACCOUNTS AND INVENTORIES

"Past-due" accounts and inventories are difficult matters to control in many industries. By comparison of his Omaha and St. Louis branches, a manufacturer of belting reduced his investment, shown here on a scale of $1,000 units.

easily seen and the working assets kept at the lowest possible points in all.

Nor is it in the large business alone that this class of records is worthwhile. A printer doing an annual business of about $25,000, revised his storekeeping and accounting system and reduced his inventories by $1,500 and his uncollected customers' accounts by $2,000. This $3,500 has enabled him to pay off bank loans and save about $175 a year in interest. The plan by which he reduced his inventory should be of less interest to every business man than the fact that a basic principle in business is careful watch over the investment in inventories, customers' accounts, and notes receivable.

The inventory figure in any business is a worthwhile study, not only from the in-vestment angle, but from that of sales and purchases. Comparisons of sales, purchases and inventory from time to time will bring out facts in the business and help to maintain their correct ratios. Records that show when to buy will enable the purchaser to keep fresh materials and stocks on hand, as well as reduce capital tied up in inventories.

That definite figures, rightly grouped, will bring before the head of a business a better understanding of his whole business, these various experiences of other managers show. Any businessman may take a similar point of view on his figures.

Figures that prophesy mean the success or failure of men in business. For right accounting is more than history. It is not enough to know what has been done; records should show what should be done. The directors of a large eastern manufacturing concern, with inventories valued at ten million dollars, voted to pay an expert eighteen thousand dollars a year to devise means of giving them figures that would prophesy. By devising and installing a system of purchasing, receiving and storekeeping that would enforce minimum stocks of raw materials, goods in process and finished products without impairing the efficiency of the business, the money tied up in inventories was reduced by nearly two million dollars. The directors proved the value of right accounting.

Any businessman who looks upon his accounting as mere recording and not as a method of control for the details of his business misses the vital significance and use of the facts behind its figures.

Comment of the late Paul K. Knight when the preceding article was reprinted in The Chronicle, June 1, 1946

T HE basic idea presented by "Behind the Figures" answered for me the twin questions which everyone in the organization has been asked during his career (and which he answered for himself at one time) —"Why did you enter public accounting?" and "Why did you go with Arthur Andersen & Co.?" And back in 1917 when the firm was but four years old, the second question had point to it.

I had taken the available accounting courses at the newly organized commerce school at the University of Illinois and the emphasis then (as I fear it is today in too many of our schools) was on the bookkeeping technique of debits and credits, the principles of consolidated statements, vouching property additions, aging receivables, analysis of deferred charges, and the like. It was my impression that public accounting was an art of detail which would attract only the type of man who, as a hobby, might build miniature ships in bottles or carve proverbs on pin heads, and that the accountant's relation to a business enterprise was about that of a fly on a fly-wheel.

In my senior year, accounting majors were invited to a luncheon talk by a young Chicago accountant—Mr. Arthur Andersen. In his talk he presented the basic idea of the "Behind the Figures" article—look behind the figures to ascertain the factors that contribute to the operating results and form a business judgment as to how to improve the good factors and eliminate the bad. He gave us a new and broader picture of the function of the corporate and the public accountant and showed that with a constructive approach accounting and auditing can be a dynamic aggressive factor in business management. His ideas and the forceful leadership qualities he exhibited presented a notable contrast to the impressions gained from my visits to the older, long-established accounting firms in Chicago. Several months later, when I called on him and he agreed to hire me, I knew that I was on the right road and if I could make the grade, I had an exceptional opportunity ahead of me.

As the older men in the organization well know, the basic idea of looking behind the figures and applying business sense to their translation into terms of the contributing factors has been the solid foundation on which Mr. Andersen has built the firm of which we all are so proud. It should profit every man in the organization to study this article to broaden his understanding of the possibilities of greater service to clients, remembering that he will find therein not only the key to the success and growth of the firm, but also the key to a deep and satisfying enjoyment of his work in public accounting.

June 1, 1946.

Modern accounting methods

Before the Convention
of the United States
Independent Telephone
Association in 1917

*The first requirement for the
acceptability of telephone securities
is an adequate accounting system.*

ANYONE who is interested in a business desires to be properly acquainted with all of its essential operations, so that he may determine whether or not the business is being properly conducted and whether any further savings are possible. To do this he needs a statement summarized so that he can conveniently follow it and, at the same time, in sufficient detail so that all of the factors on which he may desire information will be brought out.

A man who is directly engaged in a business, is inclined to give most importance to those matters which have been engaging his attention in the very recent past. Such matters are likely to be magnified in his mind and made of first importance although they may be insignificant when compared with the entire operations. It is for this reason that the manager in direct touch with the business must have a summarized comparative statement.

Value of summarized statement

The insistence by bondholders or others who are financially interested in the company, upon regular monthly statements and in many cases upon the verification of the facts by an independent, outside auditor, is evidence that these individuals consider it of vital importance that they receive proper information as summarized from the books of account.

The directions of the Interstate Commerce Commission and other regulatory governmental bodies which define their requirements in complete detail, are simply another recognition of this fundamental necessity. The government has been forced to this disposition by the fact that it must have a means of intelligently analyzing and comparing all of the different businesses which come under its jurisdiction. The only means by which it could possibly accomplish the duties set before it, is to have correct statements which will make an intelligent comparison possible.

If the government has found it necessary to have a uniform classification of accounts so that it can intelligently analyze the operations of each of the different companies as well as to determine the general trend of the industry, how much more necessary is it to yourselves who are directly interested in the business?

There has been a tendency to regard governmental accounting requirements as arbitrary and as designed to serve the purpose of the government only. To the extent to which prescribed accounting systems represent approved methods of accounting, I think it is an error to regard them as primarily designed for the purpose of the government. They are designed rather to serve the purpose of all parties interested in the business.

It is true that accounting has now and will have a more important relation to government than has been the case in the past. Business is no longer individual and the next step is governmental control. The Interstate Commerce Commission, as we all know, controls the railroads, telephone companies, and other common carriers.

Relation of accounting to government

In the message of President Wilson to Congress, he asked the power to seize the railroads in the event of a strike. State commissions also exercise control over the utilities operating within their respective commonwealths. A more recent development is the creation of the Federal Trade Commission. Among the first acts of these regulatory bodies is to prescribe the form and manner in which businesses coming under their jurisdiction shall keep their accounts.

Governmental control is inevitable because the individual is no longer the sole party interested, as was the case in the individually competitive business. This necessitates not only greater care in the keeping of accounts, but also greater publicity to the financial operations of such businesses. Now, the interested parties are:

1. Stockholders, and administrative officers of the company who are the trustees managing the businesses.

2. Users of service.

3. Government, because of the development of income, capital stock, gross revenue and other taxes, and also because of the regulation of prices.

4. Investors in bonds and other securities.

Accounting defined

Accounting is too often thought of as the mechanical operation of recording financial transactions. Bookkeeping is mechanical, while accounting is analytical. Accounting will form part of the business training of future executives—the ability to read financial statements is now necessary.

One of the keenest businessmen in the Middle West and the principal stockholder in ten large corporations will not engage managers of his interests unless they have had some time during their business career in accounting training. Singularly, his corporations are better managed, as a whole, than most corporations with which I have been associated in a professional capacity. The ability to interpret facts brought out in the financial statements prepared from a company's books is essential to successful management. At no time in the history of American business has a greater need existed for a true knowledge of "costs."

Modern accounting is a product of the Twentieth Century. Increased competition, conservation of resources, greater caution in the issue of securities, and other factors have called for greater control over outlay and income. No business of any magnitude can long exist without the control afforded through its accounting. A properly organized accounting system, either for a utility or an industrial corporation, is but the instrumentality through which a management works. A chief measure of its strength lies in the information it yields.

Standardization of accounting

Commissioner Hurley, of the Federal Trade Commission, has stated that a very large proportion of manufacturers have operated their businesses without profit and that but a small part of the companies recognized depreciation in determining their profits. Undoubtedly the chief constructive work of the commission for the present will be in devising and installing uniform systems of accounting for those classes of businesses that require immediate help. In other words, in an intelligent survey and study of the requirements of particular industries, cost data must be obtained on a comparable basis, which can only be had through a standardization of accounting for those industries.

Endless references could be made to associations of manufacturers which have been formed to overcome unintelligent competition. The chief remedy has been found through the adoption of uniform accounting methods in order to determine the true cost.

It is not the purpose to discuss the merits or demerits of the classification of accounts promulgated by the Interstate Commerce Commission for telephone companies. History will record that it was one of the steps looking to the stabilization of the telephone industry. Any piece of constructive work must of necessity be subject to criticism and subsequent revision. The greatest good can only come through the cooperation of the telephone companies with the state and national commissions. In the long run I believe the chief benefit of modern accounting methods will accrue to the companies.

As I have suggested, the parties chiefly interested are:

1. The administrative officers and stockholders of the companies.

2. The governmental bodies which have control of rates or of taxation.

3. The subscribers who, under modern schemes of regulation, seem to be losing the opportunity to secure low prices as a result of competition and hence feel an increased interest in finances of the companies.

4. The investing public.

You, representing the progressive force of independent telephony, all realize the importance of proper accounting to the administrative officers. Many of you know by experience its importance to the stockholder. Surely, you cannot give a satisfactory account of your stewardship unless the books are kept so as to properly reflect the operating conditions.

Monthly financial statement

Businessmen, as a class, are keen to know the precautions they should take to obtain complete knowledge of their business and to strengthen their organizations. Those of you who have monthly statements of operations, appreciate the value of the check thus had on expenses.

Cost accounting has received far more thought in the past year on the part of American businessmen than at any previous time. Based upon my experience with companies whose affairs, under my direction, have been completely reorganized, I can safely say that the principal cause of inefficiency and unprofitableness in small manufacturing business is the lack of knowledge of "cost to manufacture." Managers of telephone companies must equally know the cost of rendering service and be able to detect inefficiencies in operations through cost analysis. The interests of the administrative officer and stockholder are essentially the same.

Modern accounting for the administrative officers and stockholders aims to show changes in costs of various steps in the conduct of the business by making possible comparisons between different operating periods. But the full purpose of accounting has not been fulfilled unless the officers are enabled not only to compare the costs of operation with corresponding costs for other periods, but are enabled also to compare the results which they have attained with those of other companies.

Making comparisons in costs

Modern accounting for public utilities should be not only analytical but uniform as well. A complete check on efficiency is not always afforded by a study of changes in the operating costs of a single company. The manager asks himself not only how his operating costs compare with those of previous months or years but whether they compare favorably with the results obtained by similar companies elsewhere.

The interest of government in telephone accounting is of rather recent development. There is a growing tendency to assess taxes on a gross revenue which theoretically finds its basis in the "ability to pay." As you know, under this method, as the gross revenue increases or decreases, the tax assessment is raised or lowered. It is obvious, therefore, that the existence of such laws in some states, and the increase in the federal income tax rate and the consequent additional burden from this source, makes it necessary to keep proper books of account.

The treasury department, in its decisions rendered from time to time, has taken the position that unless all deductions are actually on the books, they will not be allowed. In the case of depreciation, the treasury department has ruled that in addition to the requirement that the rate must be fair and reasonable the provision for accrued depreciation cannot be credited to the asset account but must, in order to be allowed, be carried to a reserve for depreciation account as a "liability against the assets."

The Interstate Commerce Commission's classification of accounts will undoubtedly result in marked improvements in telephone accounting. In general it meets the requirements of the industry although in some respects it seems to fall short of meeting the necessity for the determination of the costs by classes of service.

Cost of service

The "Cost of Service" theory, which was first applied in full by the Wisconsin commission in the St. Croix and Milwaukee cases, will, in my opinion, be generally applied. It is fundamentally sound and of course has, for many years, been recognized in industrials. It is unnecessary, however, to enter into any detailed discussion in this brief talk of the pros and cons of this method of analyzing the income account.

Somewhat as public utilities are now regulated by commissions, industrials will, sometime in the future, almost certainly be regulated. Those of us who can see the writing on the wall, feel that this is an age of both publicity and regulation. Regulatory bodies of the character of the leading state commissions, have earned a reputation for fair dealing and their standards can well be those of all commissions.

But in order that the powers of regulatory commissions may be fairly exercised, public utilities must expect to keep books and records on a basis which will give all of the information regarding all income and expenditures of every description essential to proper regulation. Excellent as the personnel of commissions may be, the commissions cannot perform their duties as they should unless the companies are in a position to furnish reliable data as to their operations and costs.

Proper accounting

I have known of instances where companies made application for an increase in rates when, as a matter of fact, they were making a fair return on their investment, but where their books did not show such a condition. Expenditures for betterments had been erroneously charged to operation. Other cases were those of companies whose management thought they were being conducted at a profit when, as a matter of fact, losses were actually incurred. Failure to provide for accrued depreciation as well as to correctly distinguish between construction, reconstruction, and repair and renewal expenditures tells the story in these cases. Any of these companies, if the accounting system had been properly kept, would have known the true conditions.

Whether we like the idea of regulation or not, it seems to be a settled governmental policy. Experience seems to show that those companies have fared best which have adopted the most progressive policies not only in construction and operating methods, but in the accounting means of showing the results of their operations.

Telephone men often are led to feel that subscribers will always be critical of a rate above the minimum which has generally prevailed. We hear a great deal about the dollar rate. Subscribers see neighboring companies giving dollar service and do not understand why their company cannot do so.

Subscribers do not know what it costs to furnish service. In the past, a group of subscribers, who were dissatisfied, would often go over in a body to another company or form the nucleus for a new company. Now that that remedy is largely taken away by legislation, subscribers sometimes discontinue service in a group, but such boycotting is not usually long-lived. The necessity of service brings them back.

Education of subscribers to an understanding of the cost of service is not easy, but publicity, when backed by the indisputable facts shown by modern accounting, has often been a factor in establishing better relations. There used to be a general belief that public utilities, as a class, were making exorbitant profits. Their case before the public can best be tried on the evidence—and the accounting system which records the uncontrovertible facts in the company's operations furnishes the evidence.

Answer to dollar rate problem

The best answer to the clamor for the dollar rate, or for any other rate below the cost of service, is a statement of actual costs. One telephone company that I know of increased its rates from $1 to $1.15 per month for rural service. Subscribers held indignation meetings and threatened boycott. The company was unable to show from its books the actual cost and finally had to sell its plant to a company organized by subscribers.

The dollar rate will be restored. The company was obliged to part with a property which would eventually have become profitable when the rate and service situation had been worked out further. But the company was not the only loser. The subscribers are bound to lose eventually by attempting to run their own company below cost and by the poor service which is inevitable.

What is the interest of the investor in proper accounting? What is the company's interest from an investment standpoint?

If we invest in government or municipal bonds, we give little thought to the accounting system of the government or city, because we know that the taxing power is back of our investment. Investors in farm mortgages do not require the farm owners to keep any records, because the real estate cannot ordinarily be depleted to a point where the security of the mortgage would be endangered.

With a public utility bond the situation is different. Unless specific provision is made for keeping them up, the assets securing an investment may decline in value before the maturity of the bond to a point where forced liquidation would mean a loss to bondholders. One of the reasons why waterworks bonds have had a high place among utility securities has undoubtedly been that a waterworks is a long-lived property and its rate of depreciation is small.

Among the modern public utilities, such as water, gas, electric and telephone companies, the telephone companies are generally found to have the highest depreciation rate. During the life of a 20-year bond, most telephone company properties would probably have worn out practically all of their original equipment, except for land and buildings. The depreciated value would normally be much less than the cost new, even in well-maintained properties. Unless provision is made for maintaining the original margin of safety by giving recognition to depreciation and providing for it, the investors' security may be seriously impaired.

A comparatively new development in the drawing of trust indentures securing bonds, is the introduction of a provision which necessitates the deposit in cash with the trustee of a sum equal to from 10 percent to 20 percent (depending upon whether it is an electric, a gas, or a street railway utility) of the gross earnings.

This fund is available for repairs, renewals, replacements and depreciation. It can be withdrawn from the deposit on proper certification to the trustee upon the part of the officials and in some cases on an auditor's certification. In other words, depreciation, which has been frequently referred to as "bookkeeping," is now generally recognized as an element of cost and represents loss in the value of an asset through wear, tear or obsolescence.

A purchaser of securities is entitled to have the equity existing at the time of the issue of the securities maintained throughout the life of the bond. Moreover, ample restrictions should be placed around the issue of additional bonds under the same indenture. In other words, expressed in plain language, a bondholder is entitled to have as much in property or other assets at the maturity of bonds as was in existence at the time of issue. This is fundamental and the pursuance of any other policy but that of recognizing accrued depreciation in the books, must result disastrously.

Provision for depreciation

During my professional experience I have conducted investigations of seemingly profitable businesses in which, much to the surprise of the owners, the annual dividends received consisted not only of a return *on* investment but also a partial return *of* investment. This arose entirely through the failure to provide for the replacement of the property.

The art of telephony has probably developed more rapidly than any other with the possible exception of the steam generation of electricity. An industry of this character has the problem of depreciation to face in its most acute form in that it is difficult of ascertainment. Obsolescence is by far the largest of the factors in all elements of depreciation which complicates the basis on which it should be provided for.

No costs can be true costs unless depreciation is included as a part thereof, and security holders will more than ever demand that it be recognized. If the securities of independent telephone companies are to meet with the same favor as other utility securities, then it behooves the companies to put their accounting on a truly scientific basis with ample provision for the replacement of property.

A case comes to mind of an independent telephone company that actually deposited in a separate bank account the amount set aside for accrued depreciation in order to overcome arguments of competitors, seeking to weaken its investment position, that no provision was made for the all-important element of depreciation. Can you point to any other industry that was or would be compelled to resort to such means of protecting itself?

Independent telephone companies must recognize that the marketing of securities will force additional demands on the companies. Any reputable bondhouse would undoubtedly reject a proposed bond issue if a proper system of accounting were not in force, or at least provision made for its installation.

Investment banking firms take the position that a management cannot successfully conduct a business so as to afford protection to the investor without a full knowledge, in dollars and cents, of the elements entering into that business. These same firms also know that in the present day, accurate data are not available except through the medium of properly organized accounting system. Confidence in a property cannot be more quickly obtained than through a well-organized accounting and statistical organization. On the other hand, lack of confidence is always apparent where a company's accounting is not on a modern basis.

Investors, as a whole, are becoming much more able to analyze the proposition in which they propose to invest their funds. It is true, to be sure, that a substantial number must rely almost entirely on the bondhouse putting out the issues. But the bondhouses are exercising far greater care than ever regarding the issue of securities. Above all, however, there is a new and keen desire to see that the bonds are kept good after they are issued. It is not unreasonable to suppose that more time than ever will be spent in watching the issues.

There is a growing tendency upon the part of American corporations to publish financial statements reflecting their operations. Probably a pioneer in that regard is the United States Steel Corporation which from its inception has published an annual report in considerable detail. Moreover, throughout the year, monthly reports are submitted of unfilled tonnage and quarterly reports of its net earnings.

A liberal policy in this respect has gained the confidence of the holders of the securities of the United States Steel Corporation. Its security holders also know that the accounts of their corporation, if you please, are properly kept and reflect the results from operation and the financial position at intervals of a year or less.

In England, corporations are required by law to render annual reports, in the prescribed form, to their stockholders. Furthermore, these annual reports are certified to by public auditors appointed not by the directors, but by the stockholders. With the unquestioned future development in the scope of the powers of the Federal Trade Commission, what is more likely than legislation looking to the extension of virtually the same plan of publicity in corporation affairs in this country?

Given proper accounting as a guarantee for the maintenance of assets to secure investments, there are important reasons why telephone securities should hold a high place in the investment market.

One source of their strength lies in the fact that their earnings are but slightly affected by periods of depression. The growth of the business is so rapid that, even in dull times, there is seldom an actual decline in the business. The worst that happens is a temporary check in the rate of advance.

In this respect, public utility securities should be particularly stable. Furthermore, the diffusion of sales of service is such that total earnings are usually very slightly affected by variations in the requirements of a large subscriber. Even when reverses in the subscriber's business might force him to curtail his use of electric current, especially for power purposes, his requirements for the telephone do not usually decrease materially.

I recognize that independent telephony owes its growth to the spirit of competition and that competition is still a factor to be reckoned with. But one of the factors which is strengthening the position of the telephone bond as an investment, is the growing security, as marked by modern legislation, against destructive competition. Other factors are the physical connection laws which in some instances operate to improve the competitive status of the independent company, and the general recognition which has come to the independent business as a permanent and necessary part of its development.

These are conditions in the business. But even with the most satisfactory of such conditions, the fact remains that the acceptability of the telephone bond must be judged by the standards set by bondhouses and the investing public for securities of other utilities; and that the first of their requirements is adequate accounting to serve as a guaranty that proper efforts will be made to keep up income, that management shall be efficient and progressive; and that the security represented by physical assets shall not be exhausted through failure to provide for depreciation.

The accountant, the industrial engineer, and the banker

Published in *Administration*,
August, 1921

The banker practically becomes a partner in the business to which he advances money and he depends on the accountant and the industrial engineer to give him a complete picture of the strength and soundness of the company.

DURING the last days of the Peace Conference a great international financier was watching from his hotel window in Paris the kaleidoscopic scene on the street below. Civil and military officials riding about in taxis or talking in cafés made up a goodly portion of the crowd. Suddenly the banker turned to a friend with the remark—"Jim, do you know what is the matter with the world today? Well, I'll tell you. There are too many people spending other people's money."

"Yes," said his friend, "that's true, but the remark comes strangely from you. All your life you've been handling other people's money."

"But I have done it as a public servant with a full sense of public responsibility and of the consequences to me as a banker if I failed to exercise the painstaking care necessary to insure the money being wisely invested. Furthermore, as you know, I have in effect become a silent partner in every business which I have recommended to my clients, and have insisted not only upon proper financial and operating standards, but have seen to it that my standards have been carried out in practice."

The extravagance of the early peace days is a thing of the past; but in the difficult times which have followed, the public servant function of the banker has become more and more evident and it is the purpose of this article to outline how in this work, by reason of the growing volume and complexity of American industry, he has come to analyze more and more closely the internal conditions of the business organizations to which he advances money, and how this, in turn, has resulted in the accountant and the industrial engineer becoming with him, "silent partners" of industry, with beneficial

23

effect not only in the stabilization of financial conditions, but in raising the standards of industrial and commercial practice, as well.

During the 65-year period between the first census of 1850 and the last complete census of 1915 there has not been a decade in which the capital invested in industry has not increased 50 percent; and it will be noted in the following table that two decades witnessed a growth of over 100 percent.

Back of this, of course, is a fascinating story of machine tool design, of the growth of railroads and other means of communication; but the point in which we are now interested is the new capital which has been drawn into industry.

The work of wisely protecting the investment of this constantly increasing capital has been an herculean task. A modern business of any size involves not only successful utilization of large sums of money, but the coordination of many professions and crafts, and the management of increasing numbers of employees within a single business unit; and with this increase in complexity the determination of what was sound and what unsound has become exceedingly difficult.

Consider the problem of organization for a moment. A glossary of occupations of the logging operations of a large modern lumber company includes over 300 distinct operations or trades which must be welded into a working unit. Moreover, these occupations must be organized in a small way as well as in a large way. That is to say, the balance of men in each of the several stages of a series of operations must be carefully worked out.

Assume a crew of the following for felling, bucking, swamping, sniping, and rossing:

4 fellers	1 knotter
5 buckers	1 swamper
1 sniper or rosser	

A well-balanced skidding and yarding crew, to keep up with the output of the above, would consist of the following:

1 side boss	1 chaser
1 hook tender	1 signal man
2 choker men	1 spool tender
1 rigging slinger	1 engineer
1 watchman	1 fireman
1 landing man	1 wood buck
1 block maker	

In case the distance to be skidded necessitates a roader there would be added to this crew another engineer, fireman, and wood buck, with possibly another chaser and signal man. Road conditions might neces-

Year and Basis	Capital	% Increase over Last Census
1850—All ....$	533,245,351	... %
1860—All	1,009,855,715	89.4
1870—All	1,694,567,015	67.8
1880—All	2,790,272,606	64.7
1890—All	6,525,050,759	133.8
1900—All	9,813,834,390	50.4
1900—Factories only	8,975,256,496	...
1910—Factories only	18,428,269,706	105.3
1915—Factories only	22,790,979,937	23.7
Percent 1915 Over 1905		79.8

sitate one or more water bucks, a pump man, a water slinger, and a block man.

When it is realized that logging is merely one department of a great integrated industry which includes transportation, milling, and manufacturing units, as well, the intricate character of the organization problems of even such a comparatively simple type of industry becomes clear, and what is true of the organization of men is true in increased measure of the organization of machinery, tools, and materials.

Furthermore, as the operating nature of the business has become complex, so have the merchandising and financing. Markets have been expanded, variety and scope of territory have increased, distributing machinery has become intricate, and the length of time elapsing between manufacture and sale has been greatly extended.

The increasing size and complexity of operating and merchandising have of course involved an increase in volume and complexity of financing, and this in turn has meant an expansion in volume and detail of the accounting records, just as the increase in the sales and operating complexity has meant more numerous and more involved records and controlling devices.

With this in mind it is obvious that passing upon the conditions and needs of the modern business organization is a vastly different matter from what it was 50 or even 25 years ago. As long as the banker was dealing with small and relatively simple industrial units he could handle their financial problems in a personal way. The moral risk was the important factor. The manager of the small industry could be safely presumed to know the intimate details of his own business and, his statement, with respect to the condition of that business, could be readily checked. Today business units are so large and so intricate that first-hand detailed information of conditions cannot be presumed; nor can such information as is available be readily substantiated.

As a result, even in *normal* times, when business was running on a fairly even keel, the conservative banker was gradually led to safeguard his own position by making a more impersonal and extended examination of the condition and true needs of the businesses he was asked to finance.

The accountant was called in as an adviser very early, and the rapid development of accounting as a profession has been greatly stimulated by this need for accurate and impersonal knowledge of the status of large and intricate business units.

The banker in substance said to the investigating accountant: I want you to make an unbiased examination of the condition of this company; I want you to first verify the accuracy of the company's books and to bring them into line with good accounting standards; I want you to extend your investigation back for a sufficient number of years to secure a working basis for judging the *trend* of earnings, the past financial policy of the management, their policy in conserving their properties and in providing for lean years; I want to know the *trend* of their inventories, their working capital requirements, and the ratios during the years under review of current liabilities to current assets and other similar significant ratios. In short, I shall hold you responsible for giving me an accurate and practical analysis of the past and present financial condition of this company on the basis of which I can decide upon whether to stand responsible for recommending this as a safe investment.

The analysis which the accountant was at first asked to make was, of course, relatively simple—a certified balance sheet, and later a statement of income and profits—the main function of the accountant at this time being the verification of the accuracy of the books. The idea of establishing the *trend* of the business developed later, until today the range of the refinancing report made by the accountant is very broad as will be indicated by the following outline of a typical report:

I. History and Organization

1. Incorporation date, charter terms, and outline of original and subsequent issues of securities.

2. Changes in ownership, management, lines of product manufactured.

3. Name, position, salaries, age, length of service, and stock-holdings of principal officers and executives.

4. Trend of sales.

5. Manner in which present net worth has been built up.

6. Financial position of the company at various stages of its growth during the period under review.

II. Working Capital Requirements

III. Results from Operations

1. Net sales, cost of sales, gross profits, comparison of gross profits to net sales for each year under review.

2. Comparison of total profits and income to net sales by years.

3. Comparison of selling and general expenses to net sales by years.

4. Comparison of Net Profits to net sales before and after deducting taxes, by years.

5. Comparison of interest charges to net sales by years.

6. Comparison of surplus net profits to net sales by years.

7. Analysis of cost of sales by years.

8. Analysis of general selling expense by years.

9. Further miscellaneous analyses, as, for example, ratio of material costs and productive labor costs to factory overhead and prime cost, explanation of variations in profits as between the different years of the period under review.

IV. Detailed Analysis of Each Item Shown in the Balance Sheet

1. Inventories

2. Notes and Accounts Receivable

3. Cash in Bank and On Hand

4. Deferred Charges

5. Subsidiary Company Stock

6. Land, Building, Machinery, Plant, Equipment, etc.

7. Current Liabilities

8. Bonds, etc.

9. Funded Debt

10. Capital Stock and Surplus

V. Summary of Insurance in Force

Reliable and impersonal information of this character obtained through independent sources gave the banker exact knowledge not only of the present position of the company, but of the policies and methods instrumental in bringing it to this position. Granting that a fairly typical period has been covered by the report, it gave him a further indication of what the management was likely to do in future similar periods.

From this point it was an easy step for him to call in the industrial engineer and say to him:

"It is all very well for me to know what the company has done, but I am practically becoming a partner in this business for the life of this advance of money and I am asking my investors likewise to become partners. I want, therefore, to know what the elements of strength and weakness are in this company, so that I may gain a notion of how it may be expected to operate for the period of this loan. I am not asking for a prophecy but for careful and scientific judgment, based on detailed analyses, of the soundness of the operating organization upon which this management depends for promptly carrying out its orders; suitability of its buildings and machinery for the manufacture of this particular article and the ease with which these buildings and this machinery can be converted to other lines of manufacture in the event of serious curtailment in the sales of the product now being made. I also want to know how stable the market for this product is apt to be, based on its present market distribution, and the stability of its relations with its principal customers. Furthermore, I want you to find out how promptly the management will receive information with respect to changing conditions of sales, financial position and operating methods, and to what extent this information can be depended upon for accuracy. This means that you must find out the adequacy of its systems for controlling sales, production, costs, and finances. Finally, in doing this, I want you to work in close cooperation with the accountants. Your work is supplementary to each other. Together it gives me a complete picture of the strength and soundness of this company."

As a result, the refinancing report has gradually grown to include:

VI. Comments on Commercial Relations
  1. Favorable or unfavorable character of purchases and unshipped sales orders.
  2. Sales methods and policies
    (a) Sales organization and system for controlling sales.
    (b) Trade channels.
    (c) Advertising methods and policies.
  3. The market position of the company
    (a) National position.
    (b) Geographical distribution.
    (c) Continuity of sales relations with principal customers.
    (d) Potential market.
VII. Comments on Industrial Status
  1. Organization plan and personnel.
  2. Systems for controlling materials, labor, production, equipment, costs, and accounting.

  3. Strength or weakness in present location in respect to raw materials, market and labor supply.

  4. Physical conditions
    (a) Buildings.
    (b) Layout of equipment, etc.

It must not be understood that the banker is demanding perfection in these matters. The standards in different industries vary greatly and requirements must be based on practical knowledge of these conditions. He is, however, saying to the management of the company to whom he is advancing funds: "With certain exceptions, your business measures up to what I have set as a satisfactory standard for a plant of this type. There are certain important weaknesses, however, which you must guarantee to correct and we will advance these funds subject to your definite agreement to make these corrections. Furthermore, I feel entitled to know at stated periods just what your financial and operating condition is and what progress is being made toward meeting our criticisms."

In this way, the banker is actually entering into a semiexecutive relationship with his clients for their mutual benefit and satisfaction. It is not difficult to understand that, with the broad experience of the successful banker in many industries, this insistence upon safe and practical standards is having an important and wholesome effect upon the general level of business methods and policies in use in our industries. The manufacturer is given the benefit of a broader experience than his own; the investor is being protected as never before, and industry is being developed along rational lines by placing capital only where it will do the most good. In this sense, the banker is tending more and more to become a public servant, a director and coordinator of the financial, industrial, and commercial resources of the country.

Industrial and financial investigations

Before the National
Association of Cost
Accountants, First
Western Regional
Conference, Chicago,
February 7, 1924

*This form of investigation
safeguards industry, finance and
the investing public in the
job of financing industry.*

THE subject of industrial and financial investigations is an intensely interesting one to me, because I believe that anyone who is engaged in that kind of work is pioneering. Some ten years ago I had the idea that accounting was not in itself an end, but rather was one of the means to an end, and that the sooner public accountants developed that bigger and broader viewpoint, the sooner they would place their services on a professional basis.

I incline to think of the balance sheet and the profit and loss accounts as the resting place of completed transactions. To be sure, the recorded transactions of past experience should always be a guide to the future; yet they should have only a relative value in guiding one in the future. They are not altogether complete or conclusive.

That there are other methods of mapping the future has become very evident in the past few years. Within the past ten years you have witnessed an increasing responsibility upon the part of investment bankers with respect to securities which they buy and offer to the public. Investment bankers today are infinitely more careful than they were ten years ago, not only as regards the type of securities which they buy and sell, but also as regards the probable future history of each issue. You can see throughout the United States a decided tendency toward financing businesses on a long-term basis and with that a tendency to assure the public—as nearly as the future may be pictured—that principal will be repaid and that interest obligations will be met as and when they fall due.

One of the more recent methods used in safeguarding the future of a security issue is through the industrial and financial investigation preliminary to refinancing. Of course, there are many specific purposes for which industrial and financial investigations may be made, but I propose to address myself to one only—and that has to do with safeguarding the purchase and sale of securities in connection with the financing or refinancing of a business.

Elements of business

An industrial investigation is the study and analysis of the three elements of business in their relationship to each other. These three elements are:

1. The equipment of business which includes buildings, machinery, personnel, product.

2. The mechanism for controlling and directing the use of this equipment, which is broadly termed management.

3. The conditions under which this equipment must be used by management in order to result in earnings. These conditions are competition, markets, location, demand, transportation, general prosperity or depression, etc.

Management—the real security behind stock and bond issues

Anyone who has made a study of business realizes that the real security behind any issue is not the cash in the bank, not the accounts receivable, not the inventories, not the plant, or any of these tangible assets. But the real security that is behind any property is the more intangible factor of management. In other words, that type of management which permits or causes earnings to flow from the use of the assets.

So, when you are financing for a period of years, it is altogether important that the principal safeguards should be taken at the outset. In other words, if a situation is unsound from a managerial point of view at the outset, you have introduced the largest possible risk that you can at the very beginning, and unless that is remedied the investment banker is infinitely better off without that issue.

While management is always the most vital single element in business, it assumes even greater importance when refinancing is contemplated, because within the loan period of ten, fifteen or twenty years the conditions of any given business may change greatly. Patents and copyrights may expire; public favor may change many external conditions; local labor, transportation, sources of material supply may be subject to wide variations. The most striking example, of course, would be that of a business engaged in the manufacture and sale of a specialty or luxury. That introduces all the risk and hazard which is possible.

If management does not compensate for these changing conditions by changing the equipment or policies of the business, profits may disappear. Yet even though management is the principal point to be studied, this analysis will be incomplete unless all of the facts of equipment and conditions are also known, since these facts set up the standards for judging the effectiveness and the requirements of management.

Limitations of audited statements and accounting analysis

Now, there is very little of this type of analysis which would be brought out in the ordinary, everyday audit or accounting analysis, and I therefore believe that the day should be past when securities are bought and sold on the basis of audited statements and nothing else. There are exceptions to that, of course, for you have other questions —such as magnitude—but you have a right to hold your breath even though it be the United States Steel Corporation or General Motors which may be involved in a piece of financing.

The effectiveness of management in the past may be partially gauged from the results shown by correctly audited statements and statistics, but even here conditions must be known, for profits sometimes flow from patent monopolies, from distribution monopolies, or from favorable labor and material markets, in spite of laxness in management.

Present conditions and the trends of conditions, however, are infinitely more important than the balance sheet and the profit and loss account. Unfortunately, these more vital points are the more intangible points, it requiring experience, knowledge and practiced analysis to draw conclusions of the trend of public favor, the trends of the industry as a whole, the trend of the economic cycle, the status of the company in the industry, the arrangement of organization and personnel, etc.

There is no definite and set routine for the investigation. There can be no method of procedure according to the yardstick. The element of judgment is the largest single factor in it. Yet, as a starting point, it is well to consider the proposed financing. Has this been forced upon the company by past ineffectiveness of management or is it a demonstration of good management in providing for future expansion or protection?

Conditions that lead to financing and refinancing

This brings up the question as to just what conditions may lead to financing and refinancing. First of all, there is the financing of an entirely new business, introducing probably all the elements of risk which attach to business. Yet if you eliminate faith and risk and hazard from business, you have no business. Whether it is a new business or one that is to be expanded and developed, the very life of business is the risk and hazard which is injected into it. Nevertheless, the financing of such a new business is not the part of the investment banker. Risk is so pronounced that the financing no longer has the aspects of investment, but becomes speculation.

Secondly, there is financing to refund bank loans, where it is unwise from a credit point of view or a financial point of view to have the company go along and carry as much in

the way of short maturity obligations as it may have. Of course there was a great deal of that type of financing following the deflation period of 1920.

Third, to refund prior issues—issues which have been out for many years and are about to fall due, and are therefore required to be refunded, yet which cannot be paid off because the company has in the meantime developed to the point where it has probably absorbed that capital and needs some more also.

Fourth, to obtain additional working capital, presumed to be required in connection with the development and growth of the business.

Fifth, in connection with the acquisition of other companies, in order to tie into a particular situation other units, to create a more balanced unit as a whole, which would make for lower costs and larger profits. Right in this connection it is probably safe to predict that in the next ten or fifteen years we are going to see combinations and mergers on a far greater scale than any of us can now realize. American industry is absolutely headed in the direction of organization on the basis of larger manufacturing and distributing units. It is inevitable. It must come.

We have gone along all these years on unlimited natural resources and have wasted millions—yes, billions of dollars—without it making any impression on us; and that, perhaps, has played the largest part in the development of American industry. The future, however, is going to call for a more intensive use of these resources, and that is the reason why there will be more opportunities in business in the next ten or fifteen years than there have been in the last ten or fifteen years —but for an entirely different type of man; the *organizer* rather than the inventor.

Sixth, there is financing forced by the familiar frozen inventories. We had quite a jolt in connection with such inventories following the deflation of 1920, and we are going to have other jolts from inventory losses as time goes on. My own feeling is that we will be going through a continuous period of deflation for the next ten, fifteen or twenty years. Probably no wise or prudent businessman will have his house in the condition it was in 1920. The bulk of businessmen have undoubtedly profited by their disastrous experience of that year and inventories will be more carefully guarded than ever before.

There are, of course, certain types of industry where it is impossible to forecast just what the conditions are going to be. I have in mind particularly the leather industry. My own feeling is that every man in this business is a gambler—not as a matter of choice, but of necessity. He does not know. He buys hides under one set of conditions and passes out leather six months later under an entirely different set of conditions. If the pendulum has swung the right way, he can consider himself lucky.

Seventh, financing in connection with new and additional plant and equipment, implying expansion and frequently resulting in the necessity for public financing.

Eighth, in connection with the sale of a large interest, where the chief stockholder wishes to retire, and may sell out to other stockholders or may pass on a part of the proprietorship to the public in one way or another, generally through a stock interest.

Ninth, the type of financing very fashionable in the years 1922 and 1923, where reorganization in connection with Section 202 of the Revenue Act permitted the withdrawal of substantial sums of money under a minimum tax.

Tenth, financing for the purpose of placing a large part—not necessarily a major part—in the hands of the public. This is a case of looking ahead to the time when the public will hold large interests in all industries and such financing at this time, in connection with the sale of stock to the public, is often

for no other purpose than the creation of a market for the stock.

Eleventh, policy financing. This is the result of the effort of certain interests who may have concentrated their holdings in one business, to sell a portion of their investment to the public and place the proceeds received therefrom in other types of business. The older I become and the more experience I have, the more it is impressed upon me that the placing of all one's eggs in one basket is a fatal mistake. Since the first part of 1923 my attention has been drawn to several striking examples of this sort, and the list of disasters is pathetic. The necessity for diversification of investments is one lesson I have drawn from my public accounting experience, and I only wish that this lesson might be forcibly impressed on my fellow men.

Thus there may be many reasons for refinancing. Fortunately, there are not so many different methods of financing. Just what form any financing will take is dependent upon the internal conditions of the business in conjunction with the general status of the stock and bond markets. Thus 1923 was one of the poorest bond market years in the past decade and many of the smaller bond houses have had considerable difficulty in making ends meet. The period of bond market depression extended for a longer time than had been true at any time within the last ten years. So the market conditions have a very decided influence upon the type of financing which may be resorted to and may even determine whether or not financing should be postponed.

Forms of financing

The most immediate form of financing is that of bank loans. Next to this form of shortest term financing comes notes or debentures—usually short-term or serial. During the war we were faced with unusually high interest rates and it was folly to finance on a long-term basis. It was too expensive. So there was a flood of short-term financing during that period such as probably none of us will witness again unless, of course, we have another great war.

The various types of bonds which generally fall in the class of mortgage bonds may run for ten, fifteen or twenty years, although recently in connection with public utility financing, thirty-year bonds have been issued. My own feeling is that if you get much beyond twenty years, it is too long a time. It certainly is too long in the case of the average industry. Really a fifteen-year limit on industrial bonds is the most desirable, because the success of the industrials is dependent almost entirely upon the quality of management. To go beyond the fifteen-year limit is gambling on the future management, and even within that limit the risk should be minimized by certain specified sinking fund requirements. There should be a substantial reduction of the debt so that even if the time comes when the property must be liquidated to protect the bondholders' interests, they will come out whole. In other words, a straight maturity running for a definite number of years in the case of an industrial is, in my judgment, extremely unsound.

Mediums of financing

Independent of the necessity for financing and to some extent of the form of financing, there are certain mediums of financing. The first consists of internal financing, in which the new securities are absorbed by present stockholders. This method is used quite frequently, but generally only where there is no market for the company's securities on the outside and where there really is no other means of financing except through the channel of the stockholders.

Secondly, there is financing through the private sale, where there is more or less canvassing and sales effort to place the securities among a selected group.

Third, placing through a small circle of direct stock and bond brokers, where the issue is not underwritten, but where they merely agree to sell the issue if, when and as they can, and at a stated rate of commission. That method is resorted to only in such cases where the issue does not measure up to the standards usually set for such issues.

Fourth, the most usual method of placing the issue with bankers who underwrite it, buy it outright at an agreed price, take all the risk of market conditions, and pass it on to the public.

These forms and mediums of financing have been briefly noted because they have a direct influence on the scope, purpose and form of the industrial investigation. At the present time this form of investigation is used chiefly by the investment banker, in connection with underwritten securities. This is true for several reasons, but chiefly because that method of distributing an issue leads to a concentration of responsibility.

Responsibility of investment banker

The investment banker has first of all a responsibility to himself. The security purchased is his stock in trade. It is no different than the dry goods handled by Marshall Field & Company or the stock handled by any other retailer or manufacturer. So he must buy goods for which there is a reasonable assurance of ready market and which can be disposed of at a profit.

He has in addition the responsibility of reputation. He must sell goods which stay sold and give entire satisfaction over a period of years. Therefore, the time for him to give serious consideration to the fundamentals upon which the security rests, is before it is sold rather than after. Even if he satisfies himself on this point and places the issue with the public, his responsibility is just beginning. The modern investment banking house which is properly organized and is sincere in its work, has a keen desire, as a matter of definite policy, to everlastingly protect the securities which it has offered to the public. It sees to it that the security is good, not only at the time it is offered, but that it is kept good after it is sold.

These responsibilities to himself and to the public are the major ones. There is also a responsibility to the company being financed. Nothing could react so unfavorably on a company than that its issue should fall down. That would have a boomerang effect which it would take years to live down. So the banker must avoid this danger of failure to finance, even to the point of refusing to undertake the underwriting unless he is reasonably sure the issue can be sold.

This assurance in a way links with the banker's responsibility to the public. If it appears that the investment has ample security back of it, that interest obligations will be met, and that the loan will be retired at maturity, then all responsibility is reasonably covered.

The banker has various means of securing the vital information relative to any company or any issue. His first point of approach on a bond issue is that of security, so an appraisal gives him in part the assurance of ample tangible assets underlying the loan. From the audit he can secure a correct record of past operations which serves as a partial basis for analysis and also permits making certain representations to the public with respect to the earning power of the business, assets and so forth. From the legal report he is able to properly set up the deal from its legal aspects, so that there will be no technical loopholes, thus protecting the security holders from this viewpoint.

Industrial investigation superior to the audit

While the above investigations are more or less usual and routine and have often served as the bankers' only protection, they are more and more being supplemented by the industrial investigation. It is this latter analysis which scrutinizes those more intangible elements of personnel, conditions, policies, status of the company in the industry, and generally the broader questions which in the end lead to earnings, more directly than do the very tangible elements of plant and equipment. It is this analysis which really determines whether it is a good issue or a poor issue. My personal judgment is that in the matter of final analysis, the audit findings may not have nearly the weight of the findings of the industrial investigation. The audit deals with history—but the industrial analysis deals with fundamentals and so may be used in forecasting the future.

Elements of the industrial investigation

Let me briefly comment upon the various elements which enter into such an analysis and you will see why I attach such importance to its determination of the worth of an issue.

First, it deals with inception and capitalization. It points out the conditions under which the business was founded, its operating history, and how and why of its growth in capitalization. You can get a tremendous amount of information from a statement of this sort. One which clearly reflects cash and more cash going in—unless perhaps there is a surplus which has never been capitalized, and which is seldom the case—would indicate immediately that something is wrong somewhere. If, on the other hand, its net worth has been built up out of earnings, over a period of years, there is a distinctly favorable reaction, if this result is in line with some other important elements.

I always like to see net worth built up from earnings, because men and business may both be judged (on the financial side) by what they have saved, rather than by what they have earned. This is dealing with the fundamentals of life. Not that a man or a business should be niggardly or parsimonious in his dealings, for every business and every individual must spend in order to get certain returns. But there must be a sense of values and a sense of balance, and this is often indicated by the relationship between earnings and savings.

The habits and instincts which are reflected as earned net worth are formed as the result of having developed the saving idea. So we may reasonably judge a man or a business, financially, by what he has saved. That is one of the fundamental things about an industrial investigation, because one cannot be one thing for one purpose and another thing for another purpose, if one is acting naturally, as most of us have to be on the average over a period of time.

As a second point, the investigation deals with products. Do they class as luxuries or necessities? Is their usage dependent upon the status of some other industry? Are they monopolistic or are they in a highly competitive field? Is distribution limited by transportation costs on a material of large weight and bulk but low value? Is their usage universal or is there a very limited market? These and other questions must be satisfactorily answered and then the situation as regards products must be correlated and analyzed in combination with the past history of the company and the probable trends of outside conditions.

Third, what are the facts of properties and operating conditions? It must be known what properties are owned and leased; their age and condition, adaptability to this business, convertibility to other businesses in the event of sale or liquidation; location with respect to raw material, labor, transportation and product markets. Is the business one of merchandising, assembling or manufacturing, and how does this affect the requirements of equipment? Have there been operating or labor difficulties in the past, and what steps have been taken to prevent recurrence of such conditions? Such are the factors which set up standards for judging the past and future effectiveness of management.

Fourth, personnel and control. That is another interesting study. For if the success of any business is dependent upon management and management is a product of men, then the real story of any business goes back to the men who have been, are, and may be in control of the business. The greatest asset of any business is its manpower. For that reason we like to know much about the directors, executives and subexecutives of the company. Not only do we want a man's name, position, age, salary, length of service with the company, percentage of stock ownership; but also we want his previous working experience, his reputation among fellow workers, his personality, his instincts and his hobbies. It is important also to know whether or not in connection with his compensation he has a bonus, profit-sharing or percentage arrangement with the company.

Suppose you should study the personnel data of a company and find that two men drew $25,000 a year, while the next highest man drew only $6,000; and suppose that each of the $25,000 men was away six months of the year—on vacation. Suppose, as in another case, you found one official drawing $40,000 a year, while the next highest drew $12,000. Are not these factors significant enough to lead to a very close study of the entire personnel and future policies of control? Furthermore, it should be carefully noted whether the executive positions are filled by men whose chief claim to ability is the fact that they are relatives or descendants of the founders of the business. With such a personnel policy the incentive to achievement, real interest and advancement is stifled and the development of executives within the organization ceases.

Consider the element of stock ownership. If the management is in the hands of people who have no particular financial interest, the situation may prove fundamentally weak. It has been true from the beginning of time that the easiest way to reach a man in connection with financial transactions is through his pocket. So it is logical that if a business is well managed and reaping good profits, you will generally find it to be under the direct management of the owners of the business. If, on the other hand, 85 percent of the stock is held by an estate and only 15 percent by those actively running the business, there is a fundamental weakness which should be corrected before financing is warranted.

Effective use of personnel

Even though personnel and control may be satisfactory, there is the further question of the effective use of this personnel. This may be called organization. From the investigation you wish to know whether there is a definite organization plan, whether each man knows his duties, whether the responsibility placed on any man is equaled by the necessary authority; whether the various sections of the business are properly correlated and whether a man's abilities are being fully used by placing him in the proper position. It is not unusual to find in the general manager's chair a man who would be far more effective as sales manager. It is not unusual to find a works manager who would make an excellent general manager. If the organization plan showed three general managers, or if it showed both a sales manager and a manager of sales, or if by no conceivable effort any organization plan could be outlined, would you not question the effective management of the business regardless of excellent individual personnel? Naturally, the larger the business, the more important becomes this question of organization.

Proper policies are vital

The policies of the management with respect to sales, advertising, service, credits and collections and purchasing are vital, not only by reason of their direct effect on the business, but also because it is in these points that the company has its direct contact with the public and the trade. Thus the public feels the company's sales policies in the matter of prices and stability of prices, and in the completeness of its line. The dealers or jobbers judge the business in part by whether the policy is that of forcing large quantities onto their shelves regardless of general price or demand conditions. Both dealers and public know whether the company stands behind its product, maintaining a quality policy rather than a price policy. More internal are the questions of whether sales are widely distributed or whether the company is progressive in developing an improved product, thus maintaining a freshness of demand.

In the matter of advertising the public directly feels the effect of a national program, while the dealers are concerned with the matter of cooperation in local advertising. Vital also are the policies determining the choice of advertising mediums and the "spasmodic" or "continuous" character of publicity. Internally there is the question of definite control over advertising expenditures, whether as a definite percentage of expected sales or on the basis of a budget.

Service is always a matter of definite policy. Some companies steadily lose their standing because of lack of service in disposing of their product or lack of accommodation to customers and dealers. Other companies have built their reputation on prompt deliveries, prompt and equitable adjustments and prompt and efficient service repairs. Very often a good service policy is the saving grace, enabling a business to carry on in the face of trying conditions, for it has built and preserved goodwill.

The policies maintained in the matter of credits and collections have an importance difficult to overemphasize. Thus some businesses have been built up on the "cash and carry" policy. Others are notable for their installment or long credit sales. Very striking are the matters of personnel attitude in handling credit or of making collections. Yet whatever the broader policies of the business, it is vital that there be a close coordination of the credit and collections departments; that policies once set should be adhered to rather than the subject of whim or "special" cases; and that collections be prompt within the limits set, rather than so lax as to lead to excessive bad debt losses. These points often indicate the relationship between the company and its customers.

On the other hand, the purchasing methods and policies indicate the relationship between the company and its suppliers. Broadly, of course, the purchasing may be of the speculative or of the protective type —if the former, then it is not in accord with the basic principles of business. In more detail we have the questions of prompt payment, of the attitude on price, of the means adopted for insuring deliveries when and as specified, and the personal attitude of the purchasing agent.

These are some of the points which are given close scrutiny by the industrial investigation, for not only do they serve to explain many of the facts reflected in the accounting statements, but also to illuminate the qualities of management and personnel, forming a distinct basis for judging the future attitude of the company under normal or abnormal conditions.

Records and control systems

Supplementing all else, and corresponding to a large degree with the nervous system of the human body, are the records and control systems of the business. They are the means whereby management preserves a correct and complete record of past actions and results, and they are the means for carrying out present operations and policies. It is essential that records and systems be complete, effective, clearly understood, not cumbersome or wasteful of personnel. All of this will be revealed by the industrial investigation, and from this analysis one can judge whether management is alive to modern business methods, has studied its own necessities, and is properly equipped.

If records are complete and well kept, there will be little difficulty in making an analysis of sales and earnings. As to sales—it is often desirable to know more than merely the total values by years. If the geographical location of sales is known and currently studied, it may be possible to develop hitherto unprofitable territories. If sales by class of

product are studied, it may be found expedient to push some lines and drop others. If earnings are analyzed in the same classification as sales an untold wealth of information is available to the management. Too often management does not use the information which is available, and the results of an industrial survey are often eye-opening to the executives.

Analysis of the balance sheet must not be neglected. Often the balance sheet comments of an audit are routine and perfunctory. From the industrial viewpoint, however, the figures assume a new significance. Thus there would be a specific inquiry into the bad debt policy; into credit terms; into the relation of the balance of uncollected accounts to sales; a careful segregation of officers' and stockholders' accounts, that are not customers' accounts, from other accounts or notes receivable; and probably an inquiry into the channels of large sales.

Perhaps more than the usual attention will be paid to an analysis of surplus—from the company's inception if this is possible— while all reserves will be closely scrutinized. Current liabilities will be closely inspected, as will current assets in general, to determine just how current they are. Contingent liabilities must be clearly defined, to insure that they are contingent rather than actual. Deferred charges and intangibles are subject to more than the usual analysis, while investments in other companies need a sound assurance as to their value. In other words, the usual balance sheet is subject to the closest possible scrutiny and analysis, and no values can be taken for granted.

Emphasis of industrial investigation on inventory and plant accounts

It is, however, upon the items of inventory and plant accounts that the industrial investigation concentrates. These principal assets are vital where financing is proposed. The plant accounts have a tremendous bearing upon the elements of surplus and bond security. The inventory accounts bear directly upon the questions of management and earnings.

The subject of inventories warrants considerable comment. Frankly, I believe that accountants generally are not capable of verifying inventories. Their training is such that they know very little about the subject. Their conception of the responsibility involved has been very limited. Usually it is considered sufficient to check a few prices, check a few extensions, check a few footings, then ask the management for an inventory certificate. If later some trouble develops the certificate forms something of an alibi or bomb-proof shelter.

Then consider the attitude of the industrial engineer on inventories: to him the elements of inventory balance, inventory control, basic valuations, obsolescence and condition are fully as important as the elements of correct quantities and strict pricing. In our own organization we have come more and more to depend upon the industrial engineers for the various elements of inventory verification, even in connection with annual audits.

Analysis of inventory

An inventory should be analyzed from the point of view of the relation of unfilled sales orders; or uncompleted production schedules; of the peaks and valleys of production, and of the effect on current liabilities, working capital and notes payable. For example, it may be that the financing is being applied at the low point of operations, which would result in satisfactory ratios. But when the peak of operations occurs the situation will become entirely different. Therefore, the analysis of the inventory should be made from the point of view of balance sheet effect at the peak and not at the liquidation point.

The inventory analysis must also include the effect of purchase commitments. To me, from a going-business point of view, the inventory is made up of goods on hand, in transit and on order. You may have just

as much loss on goods which you have contracted to buy as you will on goods actually on hand. Since it is a basic law of business accounting that profits shall not be anticipated and all possible losses provided for, the effect on the inventory situation is actual. I might even go so far as to say that in this respect our present income tax law should be modified, so that a manufacturer would have the right to take a loss on purchase commitments just as he has a right to take a loss on his inventory.

The accountant's viewpoint on plant accounts is comparable to his viewpoint on inventories. Verifications are liable to be made in a mechanical way, largely for the purpose of determining whether or not there are charges in the property account which should have gone to maintenance or to the depreciation reserve. Usually small attention has been paid to retirements. That is, the accounting analysis has been rather from the point of view of effect upon the profit and loss account than from the point of view of correctly stating the plant accounts.

In the event of financing, appraisals are usually applied as a basis for determining the plant values. The appraisal value is the present depreciated reproductive value—that is, the economic value—as compared to the accounting values of depreciated cost. Thus two distinct bases of valuation are set up, which I may designate as the economic and the monetary. That is analogous to the market and cost bases for inventory pricing.

I do not at this time wish to enter into a lengthy discussion of the subject of plant valuations for the purpose of financing, yet perhaps a few of the basic points will serve as showing the analysis necessary in an industrial investigation; we have had a war inflation of inventories and a war inflation of plant accounts; we also had a war inflation of capitalization in many instances. Inventories have been restated and tremendous losses incurred, yet in only rare instances have the plant accounts been restated, and in no case have the plant accounts been placed upon what may be termed a "depreciated normal postwar replacement cost" basis. Therefore at this time many businesses are carrying inflated values in their balance sheets.

Yet is that attitude economically or ethically sound? What is going to happen in these cases where there has been a war inflation of capitalization? Is it correct to show the present-day value as being the real asset value back of the securities? For example, picture this situation—of an entirely new plant built at the peak prices of 1920, which in 1930 may show on the balance sheet at a depreciated cost value of $5,000,000. Yet in 1930 the actual depreciated replacement cost may be only $3,000,000. Can the accountant continue to certify the balance sheet on the basis of including the 1920 costs, or should he write off that loss of $2,000,000? And is he correct in certifying the balance sheet at the present time on the basis of 1920 costs, or

should he set up a reserve for loss of plant assets just as he sets up a reserve for anticipated inventory loss?

These points will serve to show the attitude which must be taken in making an industrial investigation. To my mind, such an investigation is one of the highest developments of our modern methods of analysis. It uses the practical experience and technical knowledge of the engineer; it involves the highest development of the accountant; it rests upon the most fundamental facts and theories of economics, and it demands a broad-minded business viewpoint in the final analysis and determinations. It serves as an instrument in the biggest job we have before us in the financial world for the next twenty-five years—the job of financing industry. It is an instrument for building, because it safeguards industry, finance and the investing public. It maps the channels through which capital flows to industry. It is the revealer of facts, the builder of confidence and the guardian of the future.

The present day accountant: his contribution to the problems of financing

Before the Ninth Annual Meeting of the American Association of University Instructors, Chicago, December 10, 1924

An accountant cannot remain merely a high-grade technician if he is to occupy his rightful place in business.

FEW MEN do anything without first making some semblance of investigation. That is the basic rule resulting from the fact that man is a thinking creature. After *investigation* comes analysis, and after analysis judgment and decision. Yet all men have different qualifications for thought, both in their type of mental equipment and in their experience. Therefore have developed the specialists. When a man is sick he consults the physician, who investigates, diagnoses and prescribes. When he is rich he consults the tax expert, but when he is poor he may be able to consult only himself since, in the main, *thought* is a valuable commodity and the specialized thinker commands a price for his services. Advice is a plentiful commodity, often freely given, but usually worth only what it costs, since free advice is seldom based upon careful thought or intelligent analysis.

These remarks are of course very general and may have many applications. The specific point I wish to make is that the modern accountant is primarily a specialized thinker whom men employ in the study and analysis of various financial conditions. Too often, however, business men do not realize how broad may be the field of the accountant, and possibly just as often accountants themselves do not appreciate the depth of their responsibility nor the scope of analysis properly lying within their field of endeavor.

The broadening field of public accounting

My conception of accounting today is very different from what it was ten years ago, but I frequently hear people say "Mr. So and So? Oh, yes, he is just an accountant or "an auditor." I realize that we, as accountants, must live down that reputation and that our ability to do so depends upon our ability to develop a breadth of viewpoint. An accountant cannot remain merely a high-grade technician if he is to occupy his rightful place in the field of modern business. Business itself has changed and is still changing at a tremendous rate. The one-man business is practically as obsolete as the dodo and in its place have developed huge organizations of multiplied and coordinated manpower. The man who prided himself in handling business on a cash basis has been replaced by the corporation whose life blood is credit. The little local industry which was once hereditary from father to son has become the commercial giant whose activities span continents and oceans.

The public and commercial accountant must keep pace with this development in business. His viewpoint must be beyond the mere gathering or checking of figures. He must understand more than purely the technique of accounts. The thoroughly trained accountant of the future must have a sound understanding of the principles of economics, of finance and of organization, which are the three fundamental factors underlying any successful business. It is recognition of these necessities which led Mr. George F. Baker to endow the Harvard Graduate School of Business in the sum of $5,000,000—recognition of the fact that such a school is making tremendous strides in the development of the science of business. For business is a science notwithstanding the arguments advanced by those who face backward to the history of the past rather than forward to the newer industrial conditions.

In the past, business in this country has not been scientific. We are a new country. We have had unlimited resources to draw upon and we have wasted billions of dollars. We have had large margins and it has not required a particularly shrewd man to make a profit under such conditions. It has been the era of the inventive type of intellect and the man who had a certain sense of values, certain trading instincts, could under any reasonable conditions make money almost in spite of himself. Now we are coming to the point where conservation of resources plays a part; where the organizing type of intellect is predominant; where success is attained not so much through monopolistic opportunity as through the successful direction of huge manufacturing and merchandising structures.

It seems to me that there are even larger opportunities in the business of the future than there ever have been in the past, and this is especially true for those individuals who elect the field of accounting for their life's work. If accountants as a whole will catch the true vision and will be something more than accountants and something more than auditors, the business world in the next decade will draw more upon this profession in the filling of their chief executive positions. In the past it has drawn upon men with either legal or engineering training. The properly trained accountant should have more to offer in the way of broad fundamental training, now that the modern financial tendencies of business are such as to place him in a position of tremendous influence.

This applies not only to the commercial accountant, but to the public accountant as well. To me there is no profession which offers the opportunities for individual growth that public accounting does today, in its broadest possible sense. Public accounting as a lifetime profession cannot, of course, hold all of the men who enter that profession. Some will qualify as partners, more may qualify as managers, but many men will pass through a public accounting experience to find their real reward in general business. They will become not merely cost accountants, chief accountants or auditors. They will attain more and more to the highest level of business executives, in fields broader and more diverse because they have had the training and experience which gives them a true perspective and understanding of the science of business.

The investigative function of accounting

The development of modern business along the lines of mergers and consolidations, of horizontal and vertical integration, has imposed new necessities in the way of finance. Up to the last decade or two much business financing was confined to a small circle of investors, or was effected through the retention of profits or bank loans. More recently, financing has been general and widespread, with the public participating as partners in the enterprise, as holders of either stocks or bonds. The function of the investment banker has assumed a tremendous importance, since only through this medium could the large volume of small investors be reached.

In the past the accountant has played a certain part in the providing of money to industry. The banker contemplating a commercial loan or a line of credit felt more secure if he was able to study and analyze a balance sheet (although many loans have been granted without even that degree of investigation). If the balance sheet were certified by a public accountant the banker probably felt even more comfortable, since here was a species of investigation made under a certain degree of responsibility. If the loan were of considerable size, or if it involved the issuance of securities which might be publicly offered, the banker possibly requested a more complete audit of the business, including profit and loss statements and some analysis of the more important accounts.

Too many securities in this country are bought and sold on audited statements and nothing else. The time should be past, and the time *is* past, when securities will be bought on audited statements and nothing else.

Now it has been the viewpoint of accountants up to this time, and the viewpoint perhaps is still held by the majority of public accountants, that their responsibility begins and ends with the certification of the balance sheet and a statement of earnings. I maintain that the responsibility of the public accountant begins rather than ends at this point, in connection with the investigation for the purchase of securities. That is, if the accountant is to assume a real responsibility in connection with the issue of securities and is to be of real service to the investment banker, he should as nearly as possible place himself in the position of the banker and try to answer the questions which may be raised in his mind. He cannot merely provide an array of figures and leave it to the banker to make whatever analysis he can. The accountant must possess the experience and qualifications which will enable him to assume the responsibility for making an analysis and submitting final conclusions as to the soundness or advisability of the issue.

By far the most important feature in connection with many investigations lies in the general business analysis of the particular situation that is asking to be financed. Perhaps this is not accounting. But I know it does involve that all too uncommon thing —common sense—just good sound business sense.

I feel very strongly about this whole matter and that is largely responsible, I suppose, for the development which has taken place in my own organization, particularly with respect to the degree of responsibility assumed in connection with the making of investigations for the purchasers of securities.

There are, of course, investigations for a number of different purposes, but my discussion today will be confined entirely to the making of an investigation in connection with the purchase of securities of an industrial since the factors involved in investigating a public utility are fundamentally different.

The basis for investigation

I wish first of all to emphasize the thought

that such investigations are not by any means a routine or standardized procedure. To be sure, there are definite fundamentals common to all investigations; yet the nature and scope of the particular investigation as outlined places a considerable responsibility upon the investigator and demands that in addition to being a good technician he must take a broad business viewpoint in interpreting conditions and drawing his conclusions. He must, for example, secure complete information from the purchaser concerning the background of the securities. For this purpose the basic questions are: is the financing that of a new business; or is it for the refunding of a prior issue; or is it for the purpose of securing additional working capital; or is it concerned with the acquirement of stock of other companies which are needed in order to work out a condition of balanced, economical operation as a whole?

Probably the finest example of this last point, and illustrating the modern trend of American industry, is shown in the accomplishment of the Ford Motor Company, which starts with basic natural resources and carries them through the various stages of processing to a finished product. This is a case of vertical integration in industry and involves a definite program of acquirement and development upon the broadest type of business analysis in conjunction with many detailed phases of investigation.

On the other hand the background of the proposed securities may be frozen inventories, or inventory losses; or the acquirement of additional plant facilities; or the sale of a substantial part of the stock-holdings—the withdrawal of certain interests and the introduction of other interests; or reorganization in connection with tax laws; or in connection with creating a market for stock as a matter of policy financing, merely to get a better balanced ratio between loan capital and contributive capital.

Clearly these determinative factors will go a long way in shaping the nature and scope of the investigation and the investigator must have a sufficiently detailed discussion with the purchaser to give a clear understanding of the different phases of his contract. Once it is understood what end is proposed, the investigator is in a position to determine, as the work progresses, whether there is a reasonable chance of the situation's working out in the way the purchaser pictured it at the time he entered into the contract.

Having these points in mind, it is sometimes possible for the investigator to determine quickly that there is no basis for the issue. The result of analysis of four or five fundamental conditions may show it is impossible for the company to do any financing, and that there is no need to spend the client's money and the purchaser's time in pursuing the matter further. This illustrates the difference between a mere audit and a true investigation. Thus a straight audit could be made in such cases, presented to the banker, and after all this work had been done he would find after a few hours' analysis of the figures that the proposed financing was impossible. Or it might even be that the regular audit compilation of data would not show basic conditions, tending to mislead the purchaser or to make him overlook factors which would have been obvious under a true analysis, and so leading him into a situation which would later be bitterly regretted.

The investigator also has a duty in looking ahead to future conditions. A financing scheme may be worked out today which in a few years' time will become wholly inoperative. An example of this is seen in the Palmolive Company which grew from an insignificant concern to one of national importance in a comparatively short period —a situation where these problems were multiplied—yet it is now one of the strongest organizations in America from the viewpoint of financial stability. This end was only accomplished by reason of passing through several distinct stages of financing, each of which had to link correctly with the past while it looked intelligently forward to the future.

The broad elements of an investigation

There are four basic phases to any investigation made preliminary to refinancing:

First: the legal phase, which deals with the tangible factor of the laws and the more intangible factor of the interpretation of these laws.

Second: the appraisal, which definitely fixes the value of the tangible fixed assets.

Third: the audit, which determines the tangible values and the results from operations.

Fourth: the industrial engineering and general business analysis, which deals with the determination of the intangible factors and the interpretation of facts.

The legal phase I am, of course, not qualified to discuss, yet the legal elements often require careful coordination between the lawyer and the accountant, especially as regards certain elements of taxes and stock ownership. Not infrequently the experience of the accountant-analyst is of great value to the lawyer, and the accountant cannot overlook the opportunities afforded to improve his knowledge of the legal safeguards which may be thrown around an issue.

The appraisal also occupies a specialized and technical field, but here also coordination of effort is necessary. The appraisal date must correspond with the audit date and the accountant must be fully informed as to the basis for appraisal valuations. Discrepancies between appraisal values and book values must be accounted for and thoroughly understood, while not infrequently the appraisal figures must be rearranged if they are to be set up in accordance with book classifications and carried into the accounts. It may happen also that the accounting analysis of plant and equipment accounts will form a check upon the completeness or accuracy of the appraisal, especially where certain fixed assets are the result of construction by the company itself.

The features of the audit and of the industrial and general analyses are, of course, the elements I wish particularly to discuss today. At this point I may say that accountants generally have not the broad training or experience necessary to this type of analysis. In our own organization we have made our greatest development through use of the combined efforts of accountants and industrial engineers, neither one of which could accomplish the work alone. It took the mixing of the ability and talents of these two different types of men to produce what is probably a crude result—if one looks ahead to ten or twenty years from now. Yet the ground has been broken, and even if the present type of analysis is incomplete it has proven far superior to the mere audit, or the mere industrial engineering investigation. The greater progress will come as engineers and accountants develop the faculty for coordinated effort and as their findings are tempered by sound business sense and business experience.

The fundamentals of business analysis

In any investigation preliminary to the purchase of securities the accountant has a large responsibility. It is absolutely essential to have a correct statement of the balance sheet. This implies that all assets are correctly valued and that all liabilities are correctly stated. This is easy to say but involves the highest development of accounting, in that merely a placing of book figures in proper relationship is not sufficient, but rather the accountant must get down to the fundamentals of valuations and must use sound judgment in the determination of liabilities.

Thus it is not unusual to find that inventories are greatly overstated, per books, by reason of incorrect physical quantities, or because of incorrect unit pricing, or due to the inclusion of obsolete material or material which is spoiled or in poor physical condition. In some cases the incorrect statement of inventories will be found intentional, while in others it merely reflects poor managerial control. Somewhat the same factors may be found in connection with receivables, where the bad accounts are obviously greater than the reserves provided or where claims are in dispute. Investment securities also may be incorrectly stated, not so often because of physical inaccuracies, but occasionally by reason of incorrect pricing and sometimes by reason of misstated ownership. Fixed assets likewise must be analyzed from a practical viewpoint, since it may be found that actual physical retirements have not been carried to the accounts, or that items such as jigs, tools and fixtures are either insufficiently depreciated or have no real values once the specific job is completed for which they were made. Patterns and drawings may have been capitalized which should have been charged to the particular job for which they were prepared. It may be found that repairs and replacements have been capitalized or it may be found that actual construction has either not been capitalized or has been excessively depreciated.

There are lesser possibilities of error in the statement of liabilities, the main elements of analysis consisting in the possibility of concealed liabilities, in a correct viewpoint on contingent liabilities — which may be understated or may even be actual rather than contingent—and in the soundness of basis for deferred liabilities.

If assets and liabilities are both correctly stated, it follows that net worth is correctly stated. This is an absolute essential. The very basis for credit or for an analysis of credit always has been and will continue to be the balance sheet. There is no getting away from that.

The accountant is also responsible for the conventional statement of profits—unfortunately in the past few years it has been more frequently a statement of losses. In combination, the balance sheet and the profit and loss statement form one fundamental element. They show the history of the company and the present financial position. They are the tangible evidences of what a particular management has been able to do or not to do with a particular business.

Yet in many cases of analysis preliminary to financing, these two financial exhibits have played the least important part in the study of the situation as a whole. The factors of cash in bank, accounts receivable, inventories, plant assets and the liabilities are too tangible. You can put your hands on them. You know exactly what you are dealing with. Therefore they may be given too much weight in an analysis. For they are at best only the "still" photograph of a business, and security is the by-product of a going business. By security I mean not the safe return of your investment from a liquidated business, but rather the safe return on your investment for a going concern; in other words, the assurance of earnings in such amount as to discharge in full the incurred obligations of interest and return of principal. After all no business is any stronger than its ability to produce and distribute in sufficient quantities at a sufficient profit to show a net result that is satisfactory.

The profit and loss statement is the resting place of completed transactions. As such it is an index to the future, yet only a true index if we assume that all conditions of the business, the management, the industry and the world in general will remain the same in the future as in the past. By detailed analysis of the profit and loss statement, however, in conjunction with a parallel analysis of past conditions, it is possible to arrive at something resembling the general rules which have governed the past and may be expected to govern the future. It is at this point that the accountant must depart from the principles of accounting analysis, and must be qualified in business analysis and have a thorough understanding of the fundamental conditions upon which any industry must rest.

That, of course, opens up a very broad field. It will be found that there are many industries which an investment banker has no business to finance at all and, further, there are many companies within any one industry which under no circumstances should be financed. Where the purely audit figures may indicate a prosperous past and a still financially sound present, business analysis may indicate a most unsound future. This has been particularly true in the postwar period, where security issues have gone wrong in the year or two years following their sale to the public. Therein lies the responsibility of the investment banker, who becomes ethically bound when he states to the purchasing public, "We recommend these securities for investment." Thorough business analysis, founded upon sound accounting investigation and analysis, is his only safeguard when he advises a man whether or not he should buy a particular issue.

It has been shown that accounting analysis is something more than good audit technique. The next step is to show the fundamental questions upon which anyone must depend in order to pass on the main question of whether the issue is a good one or a poor one. These are questions of fundamental business knowledge, based upon a true and complete history of the business. They involve a broader analysis of business than the average businessman makes today.

First, the strength of an industrial situation for the future lies mainly in the strength of its manpower—in the strength of its executives. Secondary to this, yet closely woven to it, is the matter of organization—the control of manpower. In the past era of industrial history there was the regime of the one-man executive type of organization. Here one strong man knew the business from roof to cellar and was burdened with all of its multitudinous problems and details. In the present, and even more completely in the future, will be found the functionalized organization. Here one executive —much stronger than the former one-man type—will be found surrounded by five or six men. Through the coordination of their activities he attains a complete control over the diversified functions of the business. Obviously the requirement is for a higher degree of executive ability all down the line than has ever been true heretofore. The coordination of manpower through proper organization results in management, and analysis of management provides the first indices as to industrial security.

To me, the strongest single factor behind any issue is the quality of the management. You may have assets, you may have a strong balance sheet, but unless you have a type of management which through the employment of those assets can produce earnings, then those assets will gradually disappear over a period of years. Management is the most intangible factor to analyze, yet the study of management plays perhaps the largest part in the final determination of any particular situation which is concerned with the issue of stocks, bonds, notes or any other form of commercial security. For this reason I feel, generally speaking, that maturities in the case of industrials should not extend much beyond ten or fifteen years. There are exceptions, to be sure, yet since the real risk and hazard is in management there must, in these cases, be some compensating factor to make up for a possible change in management before the securities mature.

The next vital point concerns the industry in general and the place of the particular business in that industry. That is, the economic status of this particular business. Here are involved such questions as whether the product is a necessity, a luxury or a specialty, or one for which there is no real demand. Is this industry dependent for its activity upon some major industry as, for example, the tire industry fluctuates with the automotive industry, or the farm implement industry is governed by the prosperity of the farmers? Can it be determined whether the whole industry is on an upward incline as is true of gypsum production, or whether it is on a declining basis as has been true of carriage making? If the conditions of the general industry are satisfactory, you are led to consider the status of the business in the industry. I recall one company in which the officials proudly stated that they were the dominant factor of the whole industry—yet careful analysis showed that their sales were less than 2% of the total for the country. Other concerns have been found which provided from 40% to 80% of the sales for the particular industry, so their position was truly dominant. In yet other cases, certain companies are noted which stand out in their industry because of a policy of unvaryingly high quality of product or of absolute adherence to a policy of service to their customers. On the other hand it may well be that the company under consideration is completely dominated by competition and therefore has no control over the selling prices or specifications of its product.

As an example of the influence of competitive conditions in an industry, let me note the transition which has taken place in the automobile trade. Many small motor companies, today, are finding it difficult to operate successfully in competition with large manufacturers, though there are exceptions to this statement. Broadly speaking, however, the large unit is able to manufacture at lesser cost and to distribute at a lesser cost, without any essential sacrifice of quality and with a far greater opportunity for service. This same condition is, to a lesser extent, to be found in many other industries.

A third broad point is closely related to the work of accounting analysis and concerns the financial and industrial history of the company. It is desirable to show the inception and capitalization, the growth of net worth, the growth in value of sales and production in units. Things worthwhile do not grow up over night, but as a matter of gradual development. If people could only realize this there would not be so much in the way of losses from stock speculation. For instance, if you were analyzing an individual from the point of view of determining his place in the community you would want to know something about his history; you would want to know something about how he handled himself under different conditions; you would want his financial background—the way he handled his bank loans, his credit standing, what his savings had been; you would be interested in his family conditions, his social status, and most of all his reputation for honesty and sincerity. Over a period of time every one of us has to act naturally, and there is no one so clever or ingenious that he can hide basic dishonesty forever. As such things are significant in a man, so are they significant in a business, which has been called "the lengthened shadow of one man!"

I mentioned savings as one measure of an individual. The very basis of individual growth, the very basis of business growth, is the ability to save. That does not mean that a man needs to be niggardly or parsimonious, because every thinking man realizes that one must spend in order to make; but it means that an individual or a business must have a sense of values and a sense of balance which will carry him through fair weather or stormy weather with a firm hand on the wheel and a clear eye on the compass direction of a predetermined course.

For these reasons you study a business like a thing alive—not as a mass of dead figures. Analysis of net worth is an accounting function only as regards its basic accuracy; primarily it is studied as an index to the fundamentals upon which this business has been built over a period of time. As one grows older in business experience and absorbs the experience of many and varied situations, the fundamentals of business analysis come to have almost the exactitude of laws; and relative comparisons, even of intangible factors, take on almost the accuracy of yardstick measurements.

The details of business analysis

I have stated that the best results from investigative work come through a combination of accounting and engineering analysis. Evidently both factors must supply the detailed information upon which the general analyses just discussed are based. From an engineering viewpoint you must answer the questions:

Is the product meritorious?
Has it a definite and continuous market?
Is the company marketing it properly?

The engineer also provides the full detail of buildings and equipment, their adaptability to current production or their possibility of conversion to other uses. He discusses the location with respect to raw materials, labor, and market for the finished product. He studies the organization plan; the cost, the production and general record systems; and provides the basic data on the industry as a whole. In cooperation with the accountant he verifies the physical condition, quantities and utility of the inventory and provides the means for price verification. Similarly he checks any questionable data upon the plant assets. Using data furnished by the accountant he is able to chart and analyze sales as to geographic distribution, as to products or principal customers.

At the same time the accountant is carrying out the detail work of the audit and probably also making subsidiary analyses. For example, if the company is of any reasonable size, it is important to know the systems of internal check, which are really the principal safeguards any institution can throw around its cash and other transactions. There is at present a wave of embezzlement and defalcations that is beyond anything the surety companies have ever known. Possibly this is an aftermath of the war brought about by new standards of living based upon higher salaries and wages. Subsequent deflation has brought about the tendency to use some other fellow's money in an effort to maintain the previous standard of living. In any event such a condition cannot be too carefully watched.

It is the accountant's function to secure data relative to stock ownership and control. This does not come out in the ordinary course of an audit. But where the purchase of securities is contemplated, management is the vital factor; and if management has practically no stock interest, the incentive to highest effort is lessened. If management has no stock interest, there is practically no guarantee that those responsible for present success will remain to insure future success.

Closely linked to the analysis of stock control is the analysis of personnel. The investigator should learn, as regards the principal executives, their lengths of service with the company, their ages, and even their salaries. All points of stockholdings and personnel are of tremendous importance to the investment banker, for while he cannot disclose them in his circular they nevertheless must be analyzed before the circular is drawn up and may even regulate some provisions of the mortgage.

The accountant is responsible for a careful analysis of the surplus account, not only that he may have assurance of the correctness of profit, or loss, but also for clearly establishing the earned surplus. He also will study closely the question of return on investment, possibly developing the ratios of operating conditions by years and analysing such factors as the profit percentage to sales, the fluctuations and form of total investment, the ratios of loan capital to paid-in capital, the relationship of plant assets to sales and the relationships between inventories by seasons, or between inventories and bank loans, or any other particularly significant factors.

Just as important is the comparison of the present balance sheet with the balance sheet after giving effect to the proposed financing. The banker must be in a position to determine whether, after financing, the company will occupy the financial position necessary, in view of projected future policies.

The results of analysis

The purpose of the entire work is to determine whether a particular issue is advisable or inadvisable. This may almost be covered by the answer to a single question: is the security there? But security has a broad meaning. First, there is the actual, physical, liquidation security as indicated by the correct statement of assets—fixed assets, current assets, net worth, and the relationship between current assets and current liabilities. This is in some respects the security of a dead business. Second, there is the security of a going business, the determination of which has been the real function of the investigation. All of the questions of personnel management, product, economic status—are wrapped up in the one word, "security." It is for this interpreta- tion that the investigator is responsible and for the securing of which he must step far out of his old-time role of technical account- ant.

Such findings are vital to the investment banker. Should they not also be vital to the management of any business, regardless of whether or not it contemplates refinanc- ing? Should management be content with any lesser knowledge of the business, or with any lesser degree of analysis, than is de- manded by some outside interests?

These questions indicate my viewpoint upon the position which must be held by accountants in the future. Where the public accountant may investigate and analyze a business in the service of the investment banker, the commercial accountant, the comptroller, must accept the same view- points and the same responsibilities in the service of the management. Whether or not the accountant will accept these responsi- bilities of broader service to industry de- pends upon whether he has the vision and the willingness to see opportunity and to labor for a real position in the business world.

The accountant's function as business advisor

Before the Regional
Meeting of the American
Institute of Accountants,
Chicago, November 17, 1925

*In filling the function of
consultant to management
the accountant is entering
fields of investigative work
which mark a distinct advance
over the earlier conception
of the scope of his work.*

THE TIME when the accountant was viewed by businessmen as a necessary evil is not entirely past. Yet it is true that in the last decade businessmen have learned that the accountant is more than a compiler of figures and a detector of defalcations. In the experience of the past ten years the businessman has found that advice from an accounting viewpoint may have a high cash value in the form of taxes saved or refunded, war contracts liquidated, in recapitalizations and refinancings effected advantageously. These tangible "money" results the businessman can recognize as constructive work—which is entirely natural, since the final analysis of his own business lies in the figures reflected in balance-sheet and income account.

Having arrived at the point where he admits the tangible worth of some phases of accounting effort and advice, the businessman is predisposed to study, as having a constructive value, some phases of accounting work to which he has hitherto not given even a serious thought. This is true in the detailed as well as in the broad phases of accounting service. The present-day accountant who is alert will grasp every opportunity to foster this attitude by increasing the constructive value of all normal work and seeking newer and broader fields of service to business management.

Constructive features of audit work

The public accountant has an opportunity for direct service to management even in so routine a procedure as the annual audit. The average business executive has no real conception of what an audit is. To him an audit is an "audit." A "balance-sheet audit" and a "detailed audit" are merely technical names to him. And many accountants fail in their duty by not spending the time, effort and thought necessary to make sure that the chief executives clearly understand the scope of work covered, the reasons therefor and the results accomplished. The executive is prone to assume that an audit includes a complete check and verification of the entire accounting transactions during the period covered.

In addition to educating management to the real scope and meaning of audit work, the accountant should take every opportunity to improve the working methods of the company's own organization. The methods of internal check should be subject to as close scrutiny as are its results. Weaknesses in internal check should be discussed with the management at the time of the audit and all recommendations made a matter of record in the audit report. Internal check is only one phase to be considered, however. The tangible advantages of clean-cut accounting methods as applied to receivables, payables, credits, order procedures, perpetual inventories, etc., should receive equal emphasis. Personnel reductions effected either through revisions of method or the use of machines will be reflected in tangible savings. Provision for the summarization and interpretation of operating results through the proper form of executive reports furnishes the accountant with another opportunity for service.

These constructive contracts are natural outgrowths of audit work, but can be realized only if the accountant has more than an auditing vision and feels the responsibility for constructive service to management.

Advisory relations with management

The service which may be rendered from this somewhat detailed internal viewpoint is only one small sector of the coming field of the accountant. The accountant may aspire to a field of business vision which is almost broader than that held by management itself. The possibilities in this direction have been indicated in the recent past in matters of refinancing and reorganization.

In the past quarter-century business has been forced into a new era of operations. The scope of distribution has broadened, the size of businesses has increased and there have been vertical and horizontal integrations of astounding size. Moreover, increasingly greater amounts of capital have been required and have been provided through the agencies of banks and investment bankers, involving new financial relationships and obligations. Questions of funded, paid-in and temporary capital and their interrelationships have arisen which were previously unknown.

The accountant has had a large place in the consummation of these financings. The actual audit work has been only one of his responsibilities. Representing the banker, he has needed more than a banking viewpoint, since he has been charged with formulating conclusions as to the operating, merchandising and organization possibilities of the proposed mergers or consolidations. This step beyond the audit which has involved broad and practical analyses of these situations has come to be known as the "financial and industrial investigation" and the results of these investigations have often been far-reaching in their effect. No policies, changes or recommendations can be suggested which are permanently advantageous from the investment banker's viewpoint unless they are truly beneficial to the business as an operating organization. In the long run, no steps can be taken to protect senior securities unless they consider the interests of junior securities as well. The accountant must therefore have a complete understanding of the viewpoints of both bankers and management. He therefore has come to have an advisory relationship with management which sometimes has been attained independent of immediate financing and which often extends past the first contacts made at the time the consolidation was being effected. His field of consulting relationship may embrace problems involving freights, international credits and exchange, foreign agencies, branch-house control, sales budgets, national advertising, tariffs, patents, plant location, merchandising policies, operating controls, etc.

Scope of analysis

In filling the function of advisor or consultant to management the accountant is thus entering fields of investigative work which mark a distinct advance over the earlier conceptions of the scope of his service, and which deal with the broad aspects of business as a whole. One of the principal subjects of study is the personnel of the company and the functioning of this personnel as a unified organization. First, the reorganization plan must be studied; then each man in any position of importance must be studied in the light of his effectiveness in the particular function. These functional standards are naturally flexible and somewhat indefinite, being set as the result of experience and by the results shown. This study of personnel is only one of the elements included under this type of business analysis. There is also the examination of balance sheets and earnings statements from the business as distinguished from the theoretical accounting viewpoint. The total of the inventories is less important than the relationship between inventory and sales, or inventory and receivables, or inventory and fixed assets. The current assets may be important by reason of their makeup rather than their value, or by reason of their relationship to current liabilities or to bank loans. The ratio of contributive capital to loan capital is important. The makeup of net worth is far more vital than its amount. The trend of earnings is more significant even than their relation to net worth, which is in turn more important than their actual amount. Earnings in certain years, such as 1921 and 1922, are extremely significant, as furnishing an indication of the soundness and stability of the enterprise.

In the analysis, the geographical distribution of sales may possess great significance as bearing on the future trend of total sales, while the distribution by principal customers may indicate a potentially dangerous condition. The position enjoyed by the company in its own field of industry and the position of the type of business with reference to industry as a whole are also to be considered.

A business analysis of this character embraces also many special side investigations which ordinarily have no place in the work incident to the preparation of audited financial statements. In this class may be mentioned analysis of the distribution of stockholdings; the makeup of the board of directors (with even the personnel analyses of these directors); studies of the variations in stock control or voting trusts over a period of years; the investigation of principal executives as to age, length of service, salaries, stock interest, prior working experience, etc. These matters usually receive consideration only when the matter of refinancing is involved, but here they may attain a vital importance. The financing may practically hinge upon the question of extent of stock interest by the president or general manager; and a study of salary range and scale may reveal a poorly balanced executive organization.

Realizing the function as advisor

The abilities required for analysis must be supplemented by the ability to draw conclusions which will be sound and constructive. This means that the accountant of the future will possess not only a logical mentality and a broad viewpoint fortified by varied experience, but also resolution and decision. Possessed of these qualities and abilities, the accountant of today will find that he can scarcely avoid the role of business advisor. Bankers, on the one hand, will seek his outside view on matters of financing, and management, on the other hand, will consult him regarding the best interests of the business.

It is in bringing a balanced view to bear upon the problems of the undertaking and in assisting management in matters of business analysis that the accountant will have his greatest opportunities for service. The public and the commercial accountant must keep pace with the large developments in business. Their viewpoints must go beyond the mere gathering or checking of figures. They must understand more than the pure technique of accounts. The thoroughly trained accountant of the future must have a sound understanding of the principles of economics, of finance and of organization, which are the three fundamental factors underlying any successful business. It is in recognition of these necessities that George F. Baker has been led to endow the Harvard Graduate School of Business in the sum of $5,000,000.

Public accounting as a lifetime profession can not, of course, hold all the men who enter that profession. Some will qualify as partners; more may qualify as managers; but many men will pass through a public-accounting experience to find their real reward in general business. They will become not merely cost accountants, chief accountants, or auditors; they will attain more and more to the top rungs of the ladder and will be charged with broader and more diverse responsibilities, because they have had the training and experience which gives them a true perspective and understanding of the science of business. Where the public accountant may be called upon to investigate, analyze and advise, it is axiomatic that the commercial accountant, the comptroller, must accept the same scope, viewpoints and responsibilities in the service of the management.

In closing, let me leave you with this thought in mind. The acceptance and adoption of new ideas does not necessarily mean progress nor does holding fast to the old always mean conservatism; it may mean stagnation. It is my profound conviction that the accountant of the future will prosper and consolidate his position in the business world in proportion to his breadth of vision and willingness to accept these responsibilities of larger service to industry.

The Financial and Industrial Investigation

*A series of articles which appeared
originally in Manufacturing Industries
during 1925 and 1926*

Subtitles	Page
Its Purposes and Problems	57
Scope of Financial and Industrial Investigations	65
Judging Organization and Personnel	75
Analyzing Net Worth	83
Judging Operating Results	93
Operating and Balance Sheet Ratios	101
Operating and Turnover Ratios	109

The financial and industrial investigation, its purposes and problems

First of a series of articles which appeared originally in Manufacturing Industries during 1925 and 1926.

THE success of a business depends upon the ability of its management to take action based upon sound decisions. This is most true from a long-time viewpoint, as over short periods it is possible for an element of luck to enter in which results in earnings independent of the qualities of management.

Sound decisions can be reached only as a combination of good judgment with a knowledge of the *true and complete facts* of any given situation. In business, as in all forms of human endeavor, it is the securing of facts which proves most difficult. In modern business, with its marvelous size and complexity of individual units, this difficulty is far more pronounced than it was some decades ago, when business was done in very much smaller individual units.

When one man runs a business small enough to be run effectively by one man, he may know it so intimately and in such detail that no essential facts remain long concealed. When this business grows in size, acquiring greater operating facilities and covering greater sales territory, the one man will no longer be able to exercise his former intimate control. Instead, there is a passing on of responsibility to others and a more or less definite assignment of functions. The one-man control will necessarily be replaced by the control through organization. Unfortunately an organization is composed of individuals, and only rarely can the efforts and viewpoints of several individuals be so well coordinated that they even approach the coordination inherent in a single person.

Modern aids to management

The result, therefore, is liable to be one of overemphasis in some points, gaps of information or ability in others, and a general lack of vision for the business as a whole.

Even the chief executive may be biased by experience, training or inclination, so that his viewpoint is narrow or distorted. It is true that management is sometimes aware of its own shortcomings. It realizes a possible lack of ability in the technique of business, but seldom admits inability in matters of decision because it overweighs the factor of judgment and underestimates the danger of insufficient or distorted knowledge of facts.

Because management realizes possible limitations in the technique of its internal organization, and because its problems are becoming every day more complex, it has in the past few decades resorted to many special technical services as an aid to its own functioning. In matters of incorporation, of reorganization, of patents, of contracts, or of technical liability it has long had recourse to legal talent and now few large corporations fail to include their legal counsel in the directorate. In matters of finance, of reorganization, of recapitalization, bankers are by necessity and custom called upon in an advisory capacity. In the preparation of correct financial statements, and in matters involving correct accounting procedures and methods, special technical ability is called for from the ranks of accountants. In matters of property valuations or of perpetual plant and equipment records the appraisers contribute their quota of skill.

Some of these services are primarily concerned with the determining of salient facts and some are concerned with the supplying of judgment along certain special lines. Yet it remains for the management itself to coordinate all of these specialized viewpoints so that they will bear upon the single problem of the best interests of the business as a whole. Aside from the management, the only interests who are directly concerned with such a viewpoint, are those financially involved in the business—stockholders and bankers. But often the stockholders are the management, or else place their trust in the management, rousing to action only in the event of unsatisfactory earnings. So it may broadly be said that bankers as a whole (and this is increasingly true) incline to view a business in its broader aspects and to be concerned with the same problems that concern the management. The banker often represents the holders of senior securities in much the same sense that the management represents the holders of junior securities.

Because bankers see many businesses, because they cannot of themselves know the intimate details of a given business, and because of their responsibility in the matter of securities issued, they have gone a step ahead of management in the use of a recently developed technical aid to business. This aid is known as the financial and industrial investigation. One of its principal uses has been to lay before both bankers and management a broad collection of salient facts on any particular business—so arranging these facts that they represent an analysis of the policies which have regulated that business, thereby judging the effectiveness of management.

The banker uses this investigation as a preliminary to financing. It reveals the true facts of past operations from a comprehensive viewpoint and gives some basis for forecasting the future of the business over the life of the security issue. Even in this usage the investigation becomes an aid to management, if it convinces the banker of the soundness and necessity of the proposed financing.

Definition of financial and industrial investigation

This form of investigation may be described as being a study and analysis of the three elements of business, in their relationship and coordination within themselves and one with the other. These three elements are:

1. The equipment of business, which includes buildings, equipment, machinery, personnel and product.

2. The mechanism for controlling and directing the use of this equipment, which may be termed management.

3. The conditions under which this equipment must be used by management in order to result in earnings. These conditions include competition, markets, location, demand, transportation, general prosperity or depression, monopoly, etc.

Such a definition is extremely broad, and a simpler expression is to state that the investigation is an effort to determine all of the salient business facts of a given situation, to analyze these facts and to present conclusions which will be of a constructive nature.

If the investigation is made for purposes of internal guidance—at the request of the company officials—it may be of a more detailed character than if it is made at the instigation of bankers and in connection with financing, but fundamentally the points considered and the data used will be much the same in either case.

A similarity to this form of analysis is found in the "commercial research" departments now maintained by a number of the larger companies. Such departments, however, usually carry on work which is only a portion of that covered by the investigation, since it is seldom their function to analyze the internal financial conditions of the company or in any way to be concerned with the specific financial structure or the characteristics of outside financing. They do, however, go rather deeply into the analysis of sales, the various economic factors of the industry and the relative position and course of the company in the industry. There is no need to go any further into this question of commercial research departments than to point out the basic fact that management thereby admits the necessity for information related to economic trends and positions, and also to emphasize the further fact that economic principles must be kept clearly in mind during any financial and industrial investigation.

Two fundamentals may be laid down in connection with these investigations, economic experience and common sense. It is hard to say which is the more important. Of course, the heading of experience must be amplified to include knowledge, a knowledge of economics, of organization, of accounting, of engineering, of manufacturing, of men, of businesses in general and of the qualities of management. And the heading of common sense must be understood to include a large portion of vision or imagination.

Types and sources of information

As has been stated, the investigation is based first of all upon the collection of correct basic data. This may be drawn from many sources, but probably the greatest bulk of it comes from the past records of the company. It must not be inferred that this class of data is the most important or most significant, but at least it is tangible and in it should exist not the least trace of inaccuracy or uncertainty.

For example, it is often necessary that the investigation make use of unit figures on sales, etc. It may well be the case that such unit figures are different from the sales values appearing in the audited profit and loss statement. This is due to several reasons. Either they may not include returns and allowances, or they may include consigned goods, or they may contain clerical errors, or they may not be tabulated for exactly the same period as the audit values, or the unit classification of the sales department may differ from the value classification of the accounting department.

Careful analysis must be made even of audited statements which may be available, in order to insure an exact correlation of the statistics as to quantities or tonnage with the audited dollar values and to make certain that the accounting policies followed have been consistent over the period of years considered and have resulted in statements of earnings and financial condition that are correct.

Another class of information is that gathered relative to conditions in the given industry, possibly involving an analysis of the trend of prices, costs, production, sales, labor rates, investment, etc., over a period of years. This is secured from government files and publications, from trade associations and trade publications and from published results of industrial research.

Features which must be studied and judged during the course of the investigation involve such questions as whether the company is properly located with respect to its supply of labor and raw material; whether it is favorably situated with respect to its markets for finished product; whether the buildings are well or ill adapted to the particular type of manufacturing; or whether its equipment and its methods of processing are up-to-date, economical and practical.

Points of analysis

One of the principal subjects of study is the personnel of the company and the arrangement of this personnel to form an organization. First, the organization plan must be studied, then each man in any position of importance must be studied in the light of his effectiveness in the particular function. These functional standards are naturally flexible and somewhat indefinite, being set as the result of experience and by the operating results shown.

This study of personnel is only one of the items which form an important part in this class of business analysis. There is also the studying of balance sheets and earnings statements from the viewpoint of the business rather than from that of accounting technique. The total of the inventories is less important than the relationship between inventory and sales, or inventory and receivables, or inventory and fixed assets. The current assets are important by reason of their makeup rather than their value; or by reason of their relationship to current liabilities or to bank loans. The ratio of con-

tributive capital to loaned capital is important. The makeup of net worth is far more vital than its amount. The trend of earnings is more significant even than their relation to net worth, which is in turn more important than their actual amount. Earnings in certain years, such as 1921 and 1922, are extremely significant, as are also the makeup of debits to surplus in these same years.

In the analysis, the geographical distribution of sales may hold a large significance as bearing on the future trend of total sales, while the distribution by principal customers may indicate a potentially dangerous condition. The position enjoyed by the company in its own field of industry and the position of the type of business with reference to industry as a whole are also considered.

Then there is the study of many special bits of information which do not ordinarily appear in any financial statement, such as the distribution of stock holdings, makeup of the board of directors (with even the personnel analysis of these directors), variations in stock control or voting trusts over a period of years, analysis of principal executives as to age, length of service, salaries, stock interest, prior working experience, etc. These matters are usually of importance only where the matter of refinancing is involved, but here they may attain a vital importance. The financing may practically hinge upon the question of extent of stock interest by the president or general manager, and a study of salary range and scale may reveal a primary indication of poor management.

Classification of investigations

That the investigation may be made for two distinct purposes has already been noted. The investigation made at the request of the management may be classed as "internal" and is usually called for because of some specifically disturbing condition. The investigation made primarily for bankers may be classed as "external" and is called for either as a preliminary to financing or because of unsatisfactory operating results subsequent to financing.

The internal investigation is usually of a special and detailed nature while the external is broader in scope and purpose, though exhibiting many of the methods and much of the data which is demanded by the former.

The internal investigation is usually made for the direct and immediate purpose of *assisting* the management, while the external investigation often has as its primary reason the *testing* of management. The internal is called for because certain things are known to be, or suspected of being, faulty. The external is made to ascertain whether the policies of management are correct in principle and application and whether the future is likely to be such as to result in the continuance of earnings.

Conditions leading to internal investigation

The conditions which lead to internal investigation may be many and varied. For example, the management may note a decrease in sales, which the sales department cannot satisfactorily explain, or it may be that profits are decreasing even though sales are being maintained in normal volume, or inventories may be increasing out of normal proportion, or some one department may be showing unsatisfactory production or increasing costs, or monthly statements may be slow in coming in, or there may appear to be too large a clerical force for the volume of business, or perhaps there is a condition of confusion in credits, collections, or accounts receivable records. In fact, any one or several functions of the business may be showing signs of weakness.

Thus the internal investigation partakes of the nature of diagnosis and usually follows a failure on the part of management to find a remedy, for usually the business has been trying all sorts of homegrown remedies for the condition before it will admit its inability

to effect a cure and feels impelled to call for an outside diagnosis and treatment.

It is evident from this that the internal investigation is primarily a diagnosis which is intended to be followed by corrective action. But often it is difficult to make the management see the necessity for investigation before the corrective work is commenced. The investigation is, however, very distinct from the corrective action, which may be termed an "installation." For example, a company may request a "cost system," expecting to have put into effect a completely cut and dried plan, with a few new forms, and to secure in a few weeks' time accurate costs on all products. As a matter of fact there is seldom any such thing as a cost "system." There are certain basic theories for securing costs, but these are different from the actual clerical methods necessary in securing costs, and these methods are usually different in each business, due to the modifying factors of operating methods, organization, size, personnel, present records, etc., which are the individual part of a particular business.

Therefore the investigation must be made first. By it are determined the actual present conditions existing in that particular business. Thereby it is possible to lay a finger on the faulty or incomplete points. And with the investigation are combined the theory, economics, and long experience with similar problems necessary to produce a sound program of correction. This corrective program is usually not worked out in detail as a part of the investigation, but all of the broad, directive principles will be there. The reasons for not going into full detail are three in number. First of all, management may not wish to go ahead with the complete constructive program, so that the inclusion of details would merely represent wasted time, effort and expense. Secondly, after the corrective work is begun there may frequently be brought to light some further modifying conditions which would tend to change the actual details of the plan. And finally, the inclusion of too much detail tends to obscure the basic theory and plan of the corrective program.

Conditions leading to external investigation

Usually the external investigation is not made at the request of the management, for the financial investigation has by no means as yet attained the recognition given to the audit. Few businessmen would ever think of asking for permanent financing unless it was possible to carry to the banker an audited balance sheet. Yet practically no businessman ever thinks of carrying to the banker the report of a financial investigation. The banker, however, is beginning to realize that on loans covering from 10 to 20 years he needs to know more about the company that can be obtained from its audited statements.

This is truer of the larger banking institutions, of course, than of the smaller ones, because greater values and greater responsibilities are involved. It is because of these responsibilities that many of the larger banks are beginning to stipulate that the company desiring financing shall provide both completely audited figures and a complete financial and industrial investigation report.

Difficulties of external investigation

It may happen that because of the findings of the investigation, the banker decides to turn down the security issue. Then the company must pay for the work which has made its financing impossible and for a report in which the management itself may be rather severely criticized. If it is of a type subject to criticism it is very possibly narrow visioned and unprogressive enough to fail to grasp the justness of the criticism or to make any of the constructive changes recommended. Even under the best conditions it is difficult for the company management to see any necessity for the investigation, since it feels that an audited statement should furnish all of the information vital to the banker.

This is not a universal attitude and occasionally a business contemplating financing calls for such an investigation, using its findings either as a basis for corrective work preliminary to financing or as a basis for better terms of financing. In this way an internal benefit accrues from an investigation which was made primarily for external purposes.

It sometimes happens also that the bankers stipulate that certain of the investigative recommendations be carried out by the company as a prerequisite to financing, so that a purely involuntary benefit is obtained by the company, which may or may not agree with the soundness of these recommendations.

The confidence placed by the bankers in the results of the investigation is not, as a rule, shared by the company officials. The banker has learned by several experiences that the investigative findings, conclusions and recommendations are sound. But the company has had no such experience and every statement is subject to the closest scrutiny, comment, study, and demand for proof.

It is this "show me" attitude that makes it difficult for the investigator. By reason of his experience he may know that certain things are wrong, yet he must first show that certain conditions exist, must show what they mean and the dangers they may lead to. He is in the position of having to prove not only the work, but all of the theories back of it. And if the report contains even a minor misstatement—due possibly to receiving incorrect information from some official, or to overlooking some item —it may be seized upon as an evidence that everything in the report is unreliable. The report has to be practically perfect. Everything stated must be correct and provable. It must be complete, yet without anything unnecessary or irrelevant.

Future uses

It is evident that the financial and industrial investigation makes use of all of the data which may result from other specialized forms of service to management, correlating this material to give a complete analysis of the business as a whole. In view of the increasing tendency toward combinations and mergers, aided by greater public participation in offerings of industrial securities, such an analysis is of increasing importance to the investment banker. It enables him to pass upon the worth of a security issue with greater assurance in discharging his moral obligation to investors.

Similarly, the formation of these large operating units entails new management obligations. The larger units are less subject to special or local conditions, but more influenced by basic economic principles and by the large trends of industry. Management problems thus are of broader concept. At the same time, the details of operation are tremendously magnified and the possession of true and complete knowledge of the business requires uniformity and completeness of records and systems.

Management will find in the investigation one of its most comprehensive aids to judgment and control, just as the banker will find it the best means of marshalling the essential business facts.

The work done along these lines today is far in advance of the tentative analysis, largely based on accounting, of 10 years ago. The analytical investigations made 10 years hence will make present-day efforts appear feeble and tentative. But management itself is in much the same state, for each day sees management becoming more scientific and more highly organized as the increasing size of industrial units brings new problems of administration. Competition increases as all manufacturing and merchandising methods become more nearly standardized. Profit margins are decreasing. Success is the reward of management rather than the result of chance in invention, discovery, or exploitation of natural resources.

Scope of financial and industrial investigations

Second of a series of articles which appeared originally in Manufacturing Industries during 1925 and 1926.

IN the past few decades the conditions of industry have been greatly changed, principally through the perfection of labor-saving machinery which often can produce more units of a certain product in an hour than could formerly be produced in a week. This tremendous mechanical change has given rise to various industrial and economic changes. In the first place it has tended to decrease the number of men required by industry, and so has led to the development of new products, new industries and new uses for existent products. In the second place it has demanded a far wider distribution of all products, an increased market.

Fortunately mechanical advancement itself provided the means for greater distribution, giving improved instruments of transportation and communication. The steam and electric railroad, steamboat, automobile, truck, airplane, telephone, telegraph, radio, printing press, all have been developed or improved to aid in the nationalization and internationalization of industry. But as markets have broadened, and as all mechanical devices have been continually bettered, these very factors have, in turn, placed a new pressure on industry, demanding greater and greater production facilities and larger and larger industrial units, thus creating a regenerative cycle of growth.

Larger industrial units have led to a multiplication and magnification of all of the problems of financing, purchasing, manufacturing and merchandising. Mass production is possible only if there is an assured and steady supply of raw material; it is possible only when all manufacturing departments work to controlled standards and in a coordination of time and quantity; it demands a balanced relationship between sales demand and production schedules; and it requires the closest attention to finance as related to the producing and selling programs.

Change in ownership

In the matters of finance, industry is changing from sole proprietorships and partnerships to corporations, and these corporations are continually demanding a more widely contributed capital. The increased capital requirements have led to more public financing, greater bank loans and continuous refinancing. This process leads in turn to the relationship of management with bankers, lawyers, appraisers, accountants, engineers, stock and bond brokers. It necessitates audits, statements, improved accounting, budgets, perpetual inventories. In the matters of sales and distribution the large industrial unit is involved in problems of freight rates, ocean freights, international exchange, international credit, foreign agencies, branch house control, sales budgets, national advertising, tariffs. On the production side there are problems of engineering research, design and development, patents, processes, materials, sources of supply and mechanical improvements.

All of this merely presents a picture of things as they are and gives some idea of the modern trend toward greater size and complexity of the industrial unit. Recently there have been some striking examples of the growth of particular businesses. This growth may be by reason of expansion from within—as was at first the case with the Ford Motor Company—or by the acquisition of supplemental businesses and industries to form one "vertically integrated" structure—as is the present policy of the Ford business. Or it may result from the combination of similar industries to form a "horizontal integration," as was the case with General Motors, International Harvester Company and the Standard Oil Company. In any event the tendency is more and more to combinations and mergers and it is useless to attempt a forecast of what may eventually come about in the way of huge business structures. An ultra-modern effect is seen in the recent efforts of the Stinnes interests, which became international in their program of combination and acquirement.

This means that the problems of business also will increase and will attain a complexity and variety even greater than they have at present. It is possible to see that the purchasing functions of a great business may become those of divisional coordination rather than of merchandising. That is, one industrial structure may own and operate its coal and iron mines, its palm, cotton or olive plantations, its timber tracts and sawmills. It may carry the raw materials so produced on its own railroads and vessels to the points of fabrication or distribution. It may operate intermediate processing plants such as refineries, blast furnaces, rolling mills, planing mills and spinning mills. Its warehousing facilities may be tremendous. The final manufacturing units may draw on all of these preliminary processing elements and may feed a multitude of sales products to an international merchandising organization. It may operate banks and insurance companies, newspapers and printing plants, may administer communities of employees with the infinite details necessary to everyday life. Many of these elements already exist to a greater or less degree, marking the first steps toward a true industrial socialism.

Place of the financial investigation

With the expansion of industrial units the matter of outside financing has assumed a continually greater importance in the affairs of modern business. The past ten years have witnessed also an increasing degree of responsibility upon the part of investment bankers with respect to securities which they place before the public. This responsibility not only concerns itself with the immediate history of the issue, but also with its probable future in terms of interest and principal obligations. At the same time there has

66

been a decided tendency throughout the United States toward financing businesses on a long-term basis. The natural consequence of these trends has been to develop such methods of analysis as may, to some extent, be used in forecasting the future of a security issue, and also, to some extent, in suggesting safeguards which may preserve its soundness.

These methods of analysis have in a way been forced upon management. It is to be expected that management will be an unintentionally *biased* party and will be itself convinced of the necessity for a security issue, will believe that the proceeds of the financing are to be correctly applied, and will see no real need for any extensive analysis of conditions. On the other hand the investment banker has seen too many instances of business failure to accept at face value the opinions of the management, even while retaining also a certain *bias* in favor of the issue. Therefore, the day is practically past when the company's statement "per books" is accepted as a basis for long-term loans. The audited statement is both the bankers' protection and the managements' own instrument for internal control. Its position is so well defined and its use so customary that the yearly audit or the audit preliminary to refinancing attract no more than passing attention.

Place of the appraisal

Still other forms of analysis are, however, neither so well established nor so well understood. Recently because of the wide fluctuation in fixed values and because of past lax handling of plant accounts, the appraisal has begun to attain a standardized place in business analysis. The financial and industrial investigation is still somewhat immature in development and uncertain in its use and status, yet promises to be one of the most effective methods of analysis in the event of refinancing, especially where there is to be a public offering of securities.

Anyone who has made a study of business realizes that the true security behind any issue of securities is not the cash in bank, not the accounts receivable, not the inventories, not the plant, nor any of these tangible assets; but the real security behind any issue is the more intangible factor of management which is the cause of the flow of earnings from the use of assets.

While management is always the most vital single element in business, it assumes a broader importance when refinancing is contemplated, because upon this factor rest the expectations of bankers and security holders. Within the loan period of 10, 15 or 20 years the conditions of any given business may change greatly. Patents and copyrights may expire; public favor may change; new inventions in that or in other lines may influence many external conditions; local labor, transportation and sources of material supply may be subject to wide variations. If management does not compensate for these changing conditions by changing the equipment or policies of the business, profits may disappear. Yet even though management is the principal point to be studied, the analysis will be incomplete unless all of the facts of equipment and conditions are also known, since these facts set up the standards for judging the effectiveness and the requirements of management.

The effectiveness of management in the past may be partially gaged from the results shown by correctly audited statements and statistics, but even here the conditions must be shown, since profits sometimes flow from patent monopolies, distribution monopolies, or favorable labor or material markets, in spite of laxness in management.

Present conditions and the trends of conditions may be infinitely more important than the balance sheet and the profit and loss account. Unfortunately, these more vital points are the more intangible points. Experience, knowledge and practiced analysis are required to draw conclusions as to the trend of public favor, trends of the industry as a whole, trend of the economic cycle, the status of the company in the industry, the arrangement of organization, personnel, etc.

Differences between external and internal investigations

The external investigation is always largely concerned with past operations as a basis for judging the future, but the internal investigation, on the other hand, is usually concerned with some defect in present operations or present methods. The external proposes to indicate the future course of the business in a broad way, but the internal proposes detailed corrections in order to give generally better future records and operations. The external is broad in scope and most of these investigations cover the same general outline of points, but the internal is usually more detailed, confined to a relatively few points of procedure, with each such investigation very distinct in itself and different from all others. Even if the internal investigation covers a fairly broad field it will do so in the form of a general preliminary survey, to be later supplemented by individual investigations of each important section, which are often intermingled with considerable "installation work."

Thus the scope of an internal investigation may extend from a broad survey of the business as a whole, to determine the causes of existing weaknesses, to a study of some very minor point, such as the best method of setting up a certain card index, or the proper form of inventory record in a small warehouse.

Fundamentally, the difference between the two forms of investigation is that the external discusses conditions with a third party for *protective* purposes, while the internal discusses conditions with the management for *corrective* purposes.

Points for internal investigation

Since the internal investigation covers usually the present operating conditions it will only rarely touch such points as markets, condition of the industry, position in the industry, financial policies, etc., which so often are vital and significant points in the external survey. If it does touch these points it will usually be as a part of the problem of investigating budget possibilities, or of developing a new sales product, or correlating sales with production. These, however, are the more unusual subjects for analysis.

The more usual points are those in connection with:

1. Organization
2. Materials control
3. Labor control
4. Production control
5. Cost control
6. Accounting records
7. Sales records
8. Miscellaneous records

Of all of these, probably, costs call for more investigation and installation than any other one problem. This is because cost of sales which, next to sales, is the largest and most important item in the operating statement is, at the same time, the most complex; yet the cost department is of necessity a hybrid, tied on one side to the shop operations and on the other to the books of account. Not infrequently there is no definite supervisory responsibility over the cost work, which may or may not be tied into the books.

Moreover, any investigation of costs must include an investigation of labor, material, production and burden controls, as well as some study of the accounting systems and records, which makes a cost investigation just about as broad a field as one could wish to cover in complete detail.

The internal investigation is so special and so detailed in most cases that very little standardization of data and methods is possible. The external investigations usually follow basically similar lines, and certain sources of data must always be taken into consideration. The following sections therefore apply particularly to investigations made for purposes of financing, although many of the same points may arise in the course of internal analysis.

Data used in investigations

The data gathered in the process of making an investigation varies and has varying importance according to the particular situation. It varies not only by reason of the internal condition of the business but also by reason of the type of security issue which is proposed.

Thus in an issue of bonds one of the first factors to be considered, though this does not mean the most important factor, is that of property values. Here it is probable that considerable dependence must be placed upon an appraisal. Because of the difference in property values from a "going business" viewpoint and a "liquidation" viewpoint the banker is used to setting up a certain margin or factor of safety between the amount of the bond issue and the apparent value of the property.

Data from appraisal

The facts brought out by the appraisal, however, cannot be accepted blindly by the investigator who must first study and weigh the appraisal in order to grasp its true significance. The appraisal, for instance, may have been made at a time of low dollar values, such as we have at the present time and had to a greater extent in 1919 and 1920. This may mean that a property which cost new $1,000,000 will be appraised at $2,000,000. This in effect represents the market value of the property. But it is only the market value in case you have a willing or eager buyer. Also, it is a present market value, and if the value of the dollar should change as it does almost continuously this value will change. Thus the commodity index by Babson was as high as 297 in the year 1920, whereas now it is close to 170. This means that something which had a market value of about $3,000,000 in 1920 now has a value of about $1,700,000. The consequence is that plant values as set by appraisal in 1920 have already suffered a great value deflation which has similarly reduced the safety factor of any bond financing predicated on these appraised values.

On the other hand, it cannot be assumed that book values, or cost, are always a safer basis for determining plant values, since it may well be the case that construction was carried on during a period of inflated values and that a subsequent deflation has left an unreal book figure.

It would appear then that almost any data used by the investigator is open to question and analysis, and this is really the true answer, for no data can be accepted by him for the purpose of the investigation at its face value, no responsibility for actual facts can be shifted on to some other person or some other firm. So in the case of appraisal data the investigator checks it from several different viewpoints, regardless of whether or not it is used in the balance sheet.

It is checked first as to date which in turn correlates with economic cycles to indicate a period of abnormal, normal or subnormal dollar value. Then it is checked by comparison with the book figures, determining the years of principal construction and fitting them also into the economic cycle. If the case appears important it may be advisable to go back over a period of years to apply an adjusted basis of depreciation, or to inspect in some detail the property accounts for wrongly capitalized expenditures, or to inspect the maintenance and repair accounts for charges which should have been capitalized.

There are, moreover, other important items, especially as applied to the equipment account. The appraisal may set a high value on jigs, patterns or dies which are special to certain orders, which have no value unless there are continuous repeat orders, and which may actually have been charged into the cost of the original job. These values do not support a bond issue and must be separately indicated in any comment on plant and equipment assets.

Similarly much of the equipment may be in the form of special machines which show a high appraisal value, but which may have no sale value except as junk. They also do not support the issue even though they properly have a place in the accounts and in the appraisal as a value to the going business.

Even the buildings may not have a real liquidation value in the amount indicated by the appraisal or depreciated cost figures, by reason of a number of conditions. They may be of unnecessarily expensive construction, or they may be of a type difficult to adapt to any other line of business, or they may be located in some place remote from other manufacturing businesses—just some local industry which has grown up far from any industrial center and dependent upon local labor and local goodwill. Any of these conditions would act adversely when it came to selling the buildings.

From these facts it is easy to see why the bankers like to have at least a two-to-one ratio between fixed assets and the size of the issue. It is also easy to see why the investigator cannot merely *accept* the data which come from other sources. It is not sufficient to secure the truth; the whole truth must be known.

Legal data

Just as appraisal data are essential, yet must be tempered with information from other sources, so certain legal data are necessary yet must be used in a practical sense.

Situations of this nature arise in connection with the determination of whether a company has a direct or contingent liability for Federal or State income taxes. Even where the audit has been made by other accountants, and where legal advice has been taken in the matter there still remains a responsibility on the part of the investigator to determine whether the tax situation has been correctly handled.

It may happen that there exists an unstated liability great enough seriously to upset the profit figures for past years and to cause a weaker financial position than that stated. On the other hand there may be a possibility of reducing the stated liability or of securing a refund. It may also be that the assessment has been made and that the financing must be arranged to take care of fairly immediate cash payments.

At still another important point legal data enter into the investigation, this time in connection with the present situation. It may be that the company is suing or being sued, and the status of this litigation will have a bearing on contingent liabilities and possibly on the whole future of the business. Thus there was litigation on the basic Bell telephone patents during their entire life and an adverse decision as to their validity would have changed the entire history of a number of companies. Not only would it have affected the Bell company but it would have changed the course of the entire industry. A somewhat similar situation exists today in the radio industry, though probably in a more complex form, for not only are basic patents involved, but also a multitude of manufacturing and design patents. Various companies admittedly copy the product of others, and not merely on a "bootlegging" basis. Another striking example of an involved and serious patent situation is to be found in the patent history of the automobile industry, in which the Selden patent was declared invalid by the Supreme Court only after millions of dollars in royalties had been paid.

This legal patent factor comes up in many investigations. It has an effect in determining income, liabilities, future prospects and present policies. Thus some companies under strong patent protection lease their machines instead of selling them, getting a large rental income which will probably cease or be materially reduced after the expiration of the patents. Policies must be so shaped that the transition from a protected situation to a competitive situation may be made without undue loss of income.

There is another angle to this problem, in that patents may carry a large balance sheet value, which may or may not have been depreciated. If the value has been set up in an unreal fashion, through appraisal or excessive assignment of stock, and if adequate depreciation has been provided on the patents on the basis of their book values there may result an element of concealed earnings; or if the patents have not been depreciated, earnings may have been overstated and a write-off of the patent values against surplus may be required on their expiration. Or it may be that depreciation has not been taken in the past, but may be permissible, and may result in a reduction or refund in the prior years' income taxes. The whole question of patent depreciation and the possibility that expenditures for patents may eventually, with propriety, be merged *in toto* with goodwill is, of course, a question to be considered in each individual case. The answer depends largely upon the success of the company in building up goodwill during the protected period. In any event, the investigator must secure all possible legal and practical data regarding the patent situation and must digest and analyze it for its effect on the various phases of the business.

Research data

Still another class of data which must be gathered and used during the investigation may be called research data. This is of various sorts. Very often, as a preliminary, a study is made of all of the published financial data on the company, for which Poor's and Moody's Manual is the chief source. It may be necessary to go back in these volumes for 10 or 15 years, picking out essential data and having it transcribed for the working papers. Often it is surprising to find how much data may be so gathered on sales, on profits, on balance sheets, on history and financial reorganization and on personnel, much of which is useful in establishing a background for a true understanding of present conditions.

Sometimes this same source permits of gathering data on the company's principal competitors and gives a gage for judging whether this particular business is maintaining proper profit and expense ratios. Such data are of course incomplete, uncertain as to composition, and must be used with caution.

Again, there are industries and businesses in which tariffs are a vital factor and in such cases it is necessary to get not only the existing rulings but also some knowledge of contemplated legislation. For this class of research data one is led to government bureaus and trade associations. Just to illustrate the situation consider the cutlery industry. Here the American manufacturers are in direct competition with Germany. The war has not changed this condition appreciably. Germany excels in its tool steels and pays a price for labor so astoundingly low that often its products can be given a retail price in this country which is lower than the cost of production for American manufacturers. Tariff is at present the only prop which can possibly uphold this industry. Much the same thing has been true in the past in the dye and chemical industries, and is still truer than is comfortable to contemplate.

Data of this sort are vital, but often other data on the industry are essential even though not quite so important as the tariff condition just noted. For example, the growth of the industry, its total size (expressed in sales, investment, etc.) and its general history should be known if the particular business is to be assigned its place in the industry and if its problems are to be fully understood. For such information one goes first of all to the files of government publications. Usually such data are dependable, but very often are incomplete and care must be taken to sift out what is authentic from what is statistical. Thus the "Census of Manufacturers" now published each five years is probably as accurate as such information can hope to be, but the interim data by years probably will be based on partial or incomplete returns and figures.

One of the surprising things about such research is the great mass of often very detailed data which has been compiled by the U. S. Government on the major industries. On agriculture the information is not only complete and detailed but also very closely up-to-date. The same thing is true to a lesser extent of the iron and steel industries.

In many of the industries there are trade associations which have unusually complete information on file. The Rubber Association of America is typical.

The search for data is almost a profession in itself and there are firms which specialize in this type of service. A similar, yet basically different, source of information is that of the business forecast services, which deal with business as a whole, with certain specific industries in detail, with certain phases of industry (such as the labor question), and with general data on a number of industries. Primarily they supply data on the current situation or else attempt to forecast the trend for a year or more in advance. They have great value for this purpose, but must be used with discretion since facts must be differentiated from opinions and opinions may be based on incomplete facts.

The investigator must know how to make the best use of all such sources. Often data must be secured from all sources and then correlated, sifted and judged, to arrive at the true picture. Seldom can research data be accepted at face value and often great masses of non-essential data must be gone through in arriving at the significant facts.

Accounting data

Naturally a great deal of information must be drawn from the company's own records and it is often a question of what to get, how much to get, how much to omit and how to set up the data in the most forceful form. At first glance, it would appear that there is little sequence, logic or connection to the figures which can be secured.

However, the bulk of the essential and useful material is contained in a connected logical form, the profit and loss statement. By this is not meant merely the usual profit and loss statement, but one which covers a fair period, usually five, but sometimes as much as ten years.

This statement can first be set up in a very condensed manner, having the principal items of net sales, cost of sales, gross profit, other income or deductions, selling expense, general expense, special expenditures (such as federal taxes) and finally surplus net profit. In this form it usually appears as the principal profit and loss exhibit in the report. Supporting this summary statement detailed tabulations will be prepared analyzing the various sections. Probably sales will be shown by the more important classifications of goods sold and, if possible, cost of sales and gross profit. Then cost of sales may be analyzed as a whole in considerable detail, with particular reference to the items composing manufacturing burden. Another schedule will analyze in detail the items of selling expense while others will similarly analyze general and administrative expense.

Thus there is prepared a complete tie-up analysis of profit and loss over a period of years. In preparing this there is needed a large element of judgment in deciding just how much detail will be shown. Carried out to the extreme of original entries, this would of course result in the detailing of every transaction taking place in the business, and would then be useless. In other words, the purposes of these statements are summarization and analysis, which in a way are opposite qualities, so the final result is a balance between detail and final figures.

From these analyses one may determine the trend of sales as a whole and by products, gross profits by lines, trends of principal expense items, ratios of various expenditures to sales, trends of net profits, and one may uncover a multitude of other facts which have a distinct bearing on company operations and the qualities of management.

Use of balance sheets

In addition to this accounting data, setting forth the results from operations by years, there will also be required balance sheets, as at the end of the period, at the beginning of the period and preferably at the end of each year in the period under investigation. These will permit stating the trends of inventories, of current assets and liabilities, of fixed assets, of cash, and of receivables, loans and payables. Such analyses are usually best expressed as ratios, usually the ratio to net sales or net profits, but often to each other. The full discussion of the more significant ratios is reserved for later consideration.

From the above data also will be drawn off an application of funds statement which is often one of the most significant single items in an investigation, showing as it does the use management has made of the funds provided.

In some cases the accounting data may be carried a step further. All of the above compilations deal with past records, but it is possible to assume an expected sales volume and then, using the financial relations developed from past experience, to set up a forecast for the coming year. Usually this will be done where the cash position is a vital factor in order to show the bank loan or other credit requirements. Thus there might be developed what is practically a budget for the coming year, evidenced in monthly balance sheets and profit and loss statements. As has been stated, this is an unusual procedure, but very illuminating if the company appears to be in a dangerous financial position. It is more likely to be done where an issue has "gone bad" than where a security issue is contemplated.

All of this is what may be called routine accounting data. Undoubtedly, in most investigations, there will be a need of special accounting information and analyses incident to the compilation and verification of the results contained in the exhibits. These data take the form of comments on the handling of the accounts, with special reference to the deficiencies in procedure disclosed by the examination, classifications of receivables according to age and collectibility, studies of the company's depreciation policies, surplus reconciliations, etc., etc.

Relative importance of data

While a complete and detailed analysis of a given situation would result in a great mass of information, not all of this material would be pertinent or necessary for the purpose of investigation. A sense of discrimination and relative values must regulate the manner in which the analysis is made. Thus a hasty survey may indicate beyond a doubt the stability of the industry, generally sound policies of merchandising and manufacturing, satisfactory qualities of management. This throws greater importance upon the audit and financial findings, which may then compose more than three-fourths of the entire report, concerned primarily with the average earnings, the various values of assets back of the issue, the position after financing, etc. In short, the report may be concerned primarily with the analysis and interpretation of the facts disclosed by the audit.

On the other hand, the audit and financial data may be unusually complete and satisfactory, the vital questions being those of the industrial future of the business. An example of this latter type might well be found in connection with the financing of a brewery business in 1920 or 1921, when the effects of prohibition were problematical, when the future success of the business might be dependent upon the qualities and marketability of entirely new products, when an entirely new distribution system was being inaugurated, when even new operating processes and personnel were being developed. Here the report could briefly deal with the financial aspects of past performance and present position, but would be forced to give a lengthy and detailed analysis of the industrial problems of the present and future.

A somewhat similar type of report would be required preliminary to the financing of a rubber company in 1921 or 1922, when a tremendous overexpansion of the entire industry had vitally changed the previous industrial status, and when the rate of growth of the automobile industry became a dominant factor in determining when conditions might again approximate a pre-1920 normal.

Factors, such as those just outlined, might cause two reports to take entirely different forms, even though the broad scope of the two investigations was fundamentally the same. In this, the experience and judgment of the investigator come into full play, not only in setting the proper emphasis, but in so shaping the report that the necessity for this emphasis and the importance of certain conclusions is clearly conveyed to the bankers and the management.

Judging organization and personnel in the financial and industrial investigation

Third of a series of articles which appeared originally in Manufacturing Industries during 1925 and 1926.

THE normal expectation of most businesses is growth. This growth is attained through greater sales, greater operations and utilization of greater capital. It is almost invariably accompanied by increased personnel, by a greater specialization or functionalization of each man's work and by increasing difficulties in the supervision of personnel and the direction of work.

Very often the most critical time in the history of a business is when it reaches the point of being too large for one-man control and too small for effective functional organization control. At that time too little is known about the principles of organization, there is rarely a clean-cut definition of authorities or assignment of responsibilities, and the personnel has not been trained to handle the broader scope of work thrust upon it. For a long time thereafter the effect of the one-man regime will be felt and in many businesses of the present day there exist organization and personnel problems arising from the retention of old and privileged employees, from the handling of certain detailed and minor functions by the executives, from a tendency to disregard organization lines and from overlapping functions.

The perfect organization is unattainable because theory must always be modified by particular and usually personal conditions, and also because the business itself is always growing or changing, necessitating a flexibility and adaptability in organization plan. Yet the matter of organization and personnel is so vital and so influences the effectiveness of management that it becomes one of the first and most important points of study in either the internal or external investigation.

Broad tests of correct organization

The best organization form is that which

first recognizes a few basic principles and then is intimately adapted to the particular conditions of the given business. This adaptation may often at first glance make the organization plan appear faulty. Certain fundamentals are essential, however, and should be found in every sound plan of organization. Responsibilities and authorities must be clearly defined and must be equal. The organization plan should be functional rather than personal in character. It should be generally understood and definitely observed.

Since organization is the principal instrument of management, the correctness of organization and personnel may often be partially judged by the effectiveness of management. That is, the history of sales, history of earnings, and analysis of net worth, to a great extent, reflect the qualities of organization and personnel. If the accomplishment has been good, and there have been no abnormally favoring circumstances such as patent monopoly or distribution monopoly, it is fair to assume that the organization has been good.

This is the broadest kind of a test and is not entirely dependable. The only other broad test is that of *esprit d' corps*. That is an intangible thing but nevertheless very evident. If the workers as a whole appear satisfied and interested in their work, if labor troubles are rare, if there is an air of "being on the job", these are indicative of favorable executive organization and personnel.

Naturally, the form of organization and to some extent the choice of personnel is a reflection of the abilities, attitudes, characteristics and methods of the chief executive. A business has been described as the lengthened shadow of one man, and by studying the chief executive, or rather, the one person who is really vitalizing the business, a very fair conception may usually be gained of what to expect from the detailed analysis of the whole organization. Sometimes the characteristics of the organization are those of some dominant personality who has passed out of the picture, but whose policies still profoundly influence the business.

Detailed tests of organization

The investigative analysis of organization is made along standardized lines and necessitates the use of organization charts. The first step is to secure from the principal executives their conception of the plan, gradually combining and coordinating these ideas, modifying them by observation until a true plan of the executive level may be charted. The same process is gone through in each of the main sections of the business —sales, accounting and manufacturing— and then in each of the sub-departments, resulting finally in the production of a reliable chart of the complete organization plan as it actually exists and operates.

The preparation of such a chart is more difficult than would be expected, for it is only rarely that the organization has previously been charted or defined, and usually any existent charts are incorrect. Moreover, organization plans are usually so vague that a different conception exists in the mind of every person. Sometimes there has been a conscious effort to avoid defining the organization plan, on the theory that a definition of authorities would lead to discord and jealousy. Sometimes this theory is followed to such an extent that no definite titles of position are used on the basis that it does no good to call a man "General Manager," —that he should prove his authority by demonstrated ability. This is an extreme attitude, but one that has been found to exist.

Having prepared a complete chart of the organization as it exists at present, the next step is to subject this chart to an intensive analysis for the purpose of determining its principal points of strength and weakness. It must be studied to determine whether there is a fairly clear definition of functions or whether certain men are each charged with several working functions. It will also show whether the functionalization and centralization of authority and responsibility are laid out on a sound basis, whether certain executives carry too heavy a load, whether there is provision for carrying on the work in the event the "key" executives drop out, and whether there is tangible provision for the coordination of the various functions of the business as a whole.

Each of the foregoing considerations is vital to the proper organization of the business and merits thorough investigation. It will be found in many instances that certain survivals of the one-man business idea have seriously crippled the application of the theoretical organization plan. Certain men will be found actually responsible for a number of unrelated functions who have carried over these responsibilities from the old days when the business was so small that they could effectively perform these various functions. Other men will be found who are charged with certain definite duties under the company's theoretical plan of organization, but who actually do not possess the requisite authority nor shoulder the real responsibility. These men really perform the functions of clerks or assistants to the older men who have retained the real authority while surrendering certain of the titles.

Organization balance

Another angle of the investigation concerns itself with determining whether the organization is properly balanced. If certain executives are continuously swamped with work while others are normally carrying a light load it is a sign of weakness in the organization plan or in the executive personnel. Assuming that the fault is found to be entirely with the distribution and allocation of executive responsibilities, it is evident that steps should be taken, which, without destroying a true functionalization of the administrative and executive work of the organization, will serve to equalize the load.

The investigator will frequently find that although the principal executive positions are being effectively filled by the present incumbents, no real attempt is being made to train understudies who can take hold and carry on when the older men let go. Death is no respecter of persons and old age is inevitable. Unless provision for these eventualities is made in advance, an organization may be dealt a staggering blow at the very time the fortunes of the business are at a critical stage and the very best the entire organization can give is hardly good enough.

The analysis of a company's chart of organization may disclose the fact that, although each department of the business is run efficiently there is no effective coordination of the various functions into one harmonious, unified organization. Misunderstandings and petty jealousies among the several department heads may be nullifying the otherwise excellent work of the executives to a serious degree. If a chronic situation of this kind is found to exist, the responsibility therefor must be laid at the door of the general manager of the company. It is his duty to see that every department head is imbued with a breadth of vision which enables him to look beyond the walls of his own department and to work wholeheartedly in the interests of the organization as a whole. In addition to this cooperation of purpose there must be an effective correlation of endeavor as well. Production should be kept within the limitations of probable demand; and sales campaigns, on the other hand, should take into consideration the maximum production possible with the present plant facilities and factory organization.

Relations of organization and personnel

Although it is essential that there be a definite organization plan and that this plan follow certain basic principles, it is nevertheless true that organization is only the means of making the best use of personnel, and that incompetent personnel will result in faulty management in spite of a very high development of organization. Nevertheless faults in organization often produce faults in management which are improperly ascribed to faults in personnel. In the broad sense, an organization is faulty unless it gives every man a chance to grow and holds out to him a logical reward of bettered position as he develops.

If the executives hold their positions because of a family influence rather than because of ability, the ambitions of the sub-executive personnel will be stifled and really promising men will not remain long in an organization with that inherent handicap.

Similarly, if the higher executives do not deliberately try to develop the men under them by increasing delegations of responsibility and authority, these sub-heads will not develop fully of their own initiative.

If the management fails to analyze properly the requirements of various positions, or fails to analyze the characteristics of the various employees, it is almost inevitable that some men will be misplaced, that is, required to do a type of work for which they do not have the training, experience, mentality, personality or inclination. Thus a man who might be excellent as a statistician would probably be a failure as a salesman. Possibly a competent salesman would be absolutely misplaced as sales manager. A good accounts-receivable clerk might fail as credit manager, or a shop superintendent fail as purchasing agent. It is not unusual to find men misplaced in the high executive levels, for men have been made general managers because of excellent showings as sales managers or comptrollers; and men have been retained as works managers who should have been advanced to general managers. Not infrequently the influence of inherited stock interest has resulted in the filling of high executive places by incompetents.

The investigation of the executive personnel, therefore, is an essential corollary to the analysis of the organization plan. This investigation entails a study of the qualifications of each of the executives for the position he holds, with special consideration to the results he has accomplished.

Functions of committees

In making the investigation of organization it will usually be found that there are various committees or conferences, which are supposed to be made up of certain executives or department heads, and which are supposed to meet at fairly definite times for advisory or analytical purposes. In many cases however these committees have lapsed from their original intention. They either may not meet as arranged, or certain of the personnel are habitually absent, or their meetings may prove futile of constructive accomplishment. Cases have been noted where executive committees theoretically existed but actually had held no official meetings for years and kept no records whatever of such informal get-togethers as occurred.

For the purposes of the investigation it is essential that all existing committees and conferences be carefully identified and that any "theoretical" committees be studied as to their actuality and effectiveness. Furthermore, the organization plan must be studied to determine whether there is a lack of coordination which might be remedied by the creation of certain committees. If committees are recommended in the proposed organization plan, they must be fully specified as to personnel, time and frequency of meeting, purpose, functions of authority and responsibility, and relationship to principal executives.

If committees are worth having, it is worthwhile for them to keep full and accurate records of their meetings, in order that full value may be had from the subjects discussed and the suggestions and conclusions arrived at. It will be necessary that they have the power of appointing special sub-committees on problems requiring further investigation, study or assembly of data.

It sometimes happens that committees which were properly conceived and started have so changed their functions as to be actually a danger and detriment to the business. One example of this that comes to mind is that of an executive committee which gradually gained the ascendancy over the chief executive, until it actually absorbed the executive function, yet because of discord between individuals was always failing to come to absolute decisions, each individual assuming the right to issue orders or make decisions on any matter. Such a situation is sometimes the result of a normally conceived advisory committee system, but in other cases it results from actually setting up a committee form of organization.

The committee form of organization is usually found to be dangerous, since most such committees waver between the extremes of gross assumption of authority by some members and a disclaiming of authority by all members. This results in preventing both workers and outsiders from securing either quick decisions or effective action on questions of policy. Fortunately this committee system of control is becoming rare, but where it is encountered in the course of an investigation it must be subjected to the most careful scrutiny for its manner of operation and its effect on the business as a whole.

If the business is of any size it will be found that almost inevitably committees are the chief vehicle for producing teamwork and coordination of viewpoint in the organization. The larger the business, the greater is the need for such definite coordination, because the number and the physical separation of executives prevents the opportunities for personal contact and understanding which occur in the smaller establishments.

Properly directed committees are indispensable to the conduct of modern business. They serve as advisory bodies to the higher executives, tend to create broader individual viewpoints, and promote harmony, unity, tolerance, and understanding among the entire personnel.

Personal statistics

Preliminary to the study of personnel qualifications there must be secured a list of the executive and administrative personnel, giving position, name, age, salary, years of experience in the business, and sometimes the stockholdings. This list is analyzed from the viewpoints of: age, how long the executives may expect to remain active in the business and whether the subexecutives are younger; salary, whether compensation is adequate for the position or excessive and whether cheap men are used in responsible positions; stockholdings or bonuses, to indicate whether remuneration is based on effort and whether a financial incentive exists. Various minor analyses and conclusions may be made from such a list, and sometimes it is desirable to carry a similar analysis down to and including the workers, showing classifications of skilled and unskilled, age and service by groups, rates of hourly pay, men on day or piece work, number on pension list, and other equally significant groupings.

Personnel qualifications

Having secured the foregoing statistical data on the executive and administrative personnel, the next step is to size up the fitness of the individual for the executive position he occupies. The qualifications to be considered in such an analysis may be said to be comprised of the following:

> Character
>
> Mental capacity
>
> Judgment
>
> Experience
>
> Personality
>
> Education

The relative importance of these qualifications, of course, will vary with the position that the man occupies although it may be said that honesty and integrity of purpose are fundamental prerequisites for every responsible executive position. Mental capacity is a qualification that is of immense importance where original thinking and constructive work are required, but which may be almost a handicap to the performance of monotonous and routine tasks for any extended period. Mental capacity often varies largely by inclination or tendency, in fact this may almost be said to be the rule of life. Certain men may have great abilities along the lines of mathematics who are duds when it comes to things mechanical. A great lawyer may possess an inherent inability to understand the elements of double-entry bookkeeping. Similarly, a man may be so constituted that he can readily grasp sales principles, sales psychology and sales arguments and yet be hopelessly bewildered by problems of production planning or materials control. Experience and education represent acquired qualifications to a large extent although the benefit derived by a man from his training will be affected largely by his mental capacity. Judgment and personality, on the other hand, resemble mental capacity in being qualifications that are primarily inherent in the individual, although these qualifications also may undoubtedly be developed by intelligently directed effort.

Qualifications of education

In every position the matter of education must be given some weight. Thus a laborer in the yard gang needs so little that he may not be able to read or write, he need not even speak the language of the country. His educational requirements are practically zero. But unless he can read, write, speak the language and possibly have some knowledge of figures, he cannot normally hope to be made foreman. Generally, as the importance of the work increases, the educational requirement increases. This is true even aside from that class of work which is technical in character and is based on educational training or preparation. In the higher executive levels an education of a cultural type is a great advantage if not actually a necessity, since the position may carry with it distinct social obligations.

In analyzing the educational attainment of a person the mistake must not be made of gaging it by the extent of school, college or university contact. Many men are so absorptive that they acquire new elements each day from books, papers, or personal contact. Many others are so earnest in self-improvement that they are consciously and conscientiously increasing their education by means of night school, correspondence courses, or self-imposed routines of study. Nor must it be assumed that the more education a person has, the better he is fitted for his given job—rather, the job must be studied as to its educational requirements, then if the person measures up to these, that is all that is required.

Qualifications of experience

Experience and education are in some ways closely related, for specialized education may be acquired by experience in the particular type of work. It is hard therefore to draw the line between the requirements of education and experience in many positions. This is particularly true where education has been of the job-preparatory or trade school type. For example, men may come from automobile trade schools and work satisfactorily side by side with mechanics of 20 years' experience. So the job must be carefully studied as to the extent to which greater or specialized education may be substituted for specialized experience, or vice versa.

In positions requiring supervisory capacity experience is vital. There is, to be sure, a question of aptitude, for some men have such attributes of personality that no amount of experience can make them capable of departmental supervision, and this fundamental handicap usually is so potent that it blocks the acquirement of experience.

Some experience is indirect, since every man handles some types of work for the first time. Yet his ability in the job may be increased by experience of a related or supplementary type. Thus experience as a stock clerk is an aid to handling a clerical job in the purchasing or production departments. Experience as sales manager is of value in taking on the duties of general manager. Even experience as a top sergeant in the army may be an asset in many factory supervisory positions.

It is practically axiomatic that a man's abilities in any position are increased by the extent of his experience in that or in closely similar positions. The extent of increase is, however, problematical. Thus of two men with equal years of experience, one may have so much greater mental capacity, or so much more energy, or ambition, that he has derived several times the benefit from that experience that the other has.

There is a theory that the difference between the average man and the notably successful man is only two per cent—of either ability, desire or energy. This is debatable. But it is the slightly greater "drive" of some men which causes them to derive more benefit from all experiences, acquire more education, make greater use of their inherent abilities and becomes more outstanding in personality. It is intangible, but makes itself known in tangible results and therefore is always taken into consideration.

Personnel analysis

The problem of the investigator, therefore, becomes one of studying each one of the important members of the organization and of reaching a sound conclusion as to whether he is fit or unfit in the particular position occupied. Although the six qualifications mentioned above are important for every executive position, he will be governed in reaching his conclusions by the special requirements of the position under consideration. Thus the duties of general manager make such varied and exacting calls upon a man that the successful general manager must, as a rule, possess the first five qualifications, and preferably the sixth also, in a marked degree in order to measure up to the demands of his position. The prime essentials for the successful sales manager may be said to be personality or wide acquaintance with the trade, which is just a form of experience, and that combination of mental capacity and judgment which enables him to plan his campaigns with resourcefulness and daring while seasoning them with the essential modicum of common sense. The accountant must be a model of conscientiousness and business integrity while possessing sufficient technical knowledge of his work to enable him to make a true record of the company's financial transactions.

The foregoing cases are used only as illustrative of the varying standards the investigator will use in striving to determine the fitness of the individual for the position he occupies. In the course of his investigation he may find several executives who appear to fall far short of his minimum requirements. If engaged in a financial investigation for a security issue he may probably stop at this point, but if engaged on an internal investigation for the management, he will attempt to find the underlying reasons for the shortcomings in order that he may be in a position to make constructive recommendations.

Certain of these men who fail to make the grade will be found to be individuals who owed their positions in the first place to family connections or other influence rather than to any demonstrated capacity for the work. Other men will have succeeded to their positions, under the rule of seniority, through years of loyal and painstaking effort. Unfortunately, not every faithful employee, who has grown old in the company's employ is fitted for an important position and the promotion which was intended as a reward for years of loyal service may have spoiled a perfectly good shop foreman in

81

the making of an incompetent shop superintendent. Still other men will be found to possess real capacity and valuable preliminary training whose failure to meet the requirements of their positions is due to the fact that, fundamentally, they are better adapted for other work.

Having reached his conclusions in each case as to the underlying causes for the failures and shortcomings among the personnel, the investigator will bring his recommendations as tactfully as possible to the attention of the men who have ordered the investigation. In making these recommendations the greatest care must be exercised to avoid all pretensions to omniscience or infallibility, for it goes without saying that it is impossible for any man to step in and, in the course of a relatively limited investigation, diagnose accurately and effectively prescribe for all of the organization problems of a large corporation. On the other hand, there is no discounting the value of an outside viewpoint, especially when it represents the viewpoint of an investigator trained in the study and solution of problems of just this type.

Vital importance of personnel

With the industrial activities of our present day ever broadening and ever assuming larger and more complex structures, it is inevitable that problems of organization and personnel will more and more become of vital importance in determining the fortunes and, indeed, the continuing existence of any business enterprise. The days of profit margins sufficiently wide to absorb the mistakes of faulty management are rapidly drawing to a close. In fact, we already see many of the key industries of this country in the hands of a relatively small number of large and highly developed units which have achieved their strong position in their respective fields only through having developed a highly organized and supremely effective type of management.

To the solution of these broader questions involving corporate success or failure the investigator of organization and personnel problems should be prepared to make a real contribution.

Thus we see how in modern business, correct organization and capable personnel go hand in hand as essential factors to success. The investigator who delves into these problems, who attempts to place his finger upon the weak spots in the plan of organization or among the executive personnel and who undertakes to make recommendations looking to their cure, is charged with a most serious responsibility to sift and weigh the evidence until he is certain of his conclusions. Let him but sense the extent of this obligation and the weight of his responsibility, and then his opportunities for constructive service will be commensurate with the responsibilities he assumes.

Analyzing net worth in the financial and industrial investigation

Fourth of a series of articles which appeared originally in Manufacturing Industries during 1925 and 1926.

CAREFUL analysis of the net worth of a business will usually develop many facts bearing upon the financial policies of the management. Such an analysis cannot be made purely from the viewpoint of figures, but includes a study of the conditions which have produced given values of net worth, and even goes beyond this investigation into a study of the form of net worth. It may be said that this analysis supplements the audit of all other sections of the balance sheet, by which the various assets and liabilities have been evaluated; and it serves to paint a word picture of the manner in which these assets have been created and these liabilities incurred. It is frequently more important to know the steps by which these things have been done than to know the actual amounts of assets and liabilities.

Another purpose served by the verification of the net worth section is to determine, so far as possible, the financial policies that have guided the management over the life of the corporation, in regard to such matters as depreciation, dividends in relation to earnings, surplus in relation to capital stock, etc.

Sources of net worth

Net worth is acquired from the three primary sources of investment by stockholders, retention of earned profits, and capital profits. It is true in many cases, and inevitably so during the early stages of corporate existence, that investment by stockholders is the principal source of net worth.

An investigation of the investment by the stockholders in its broad sense, includes an examination into the inception and financial history of the company as well as analysis of its capitalization. The examination into the inception and financial history must be approached from two angles: from the financial aspect, and from the operating aspect. The examination from the financial angle should include the articles of incorporation, corporation minutes, entries opening the corporate general books, and other pertinent data relative to the inception of the present corporate organization. The result of this examination must be a clear and concise statement of the steps taken in the organization of the present corporation. Such a statement must show the properties acquired and the consideration given therefor, and must set forth this information in an orderly manner which will indicate the actual steps that were taken in the formation of the corporation.

Operating aspect

The operating aspect of this portion of the investigation is much broader in its scope and more fundamental in character. It approaches the problem from the business rather than the purely financial side. The analysis will show a history of the beginning of the business as distinguished from the inception of the corporation which may represent the consolidation of a number of independent companies. It is frequently found, for example, that a consolidation has been effected of a number of companies which were hitherto competing. Subsequent to the consolidation, the poorly situated plants may be discontinued and production centered in the better situated plants, provided their capacity is sufficient to take care of the combined requirements of the consolidated business.

The advantages arising from such a consolidation may be many, among which may be mentioned the possibility of producing a mechanically superior product through the combination of the best features of the hitherto competing products, the economies arising from operating plants throughout the year at a point which is near normal capacity, and the more skillful managerial control which may be secured by the consolidated

organization, which has sufficient volume to employ men of ability with large experience in manufacturing products of this character.

It may be, on the other hand, that the consolidation was carried through in order to secure the more efficient and economical production of a number of manufactured articles which, although not competing in themselves, are of a character such that they may be most efficiently manufactured under one central control.

It may prove necessary to outline from a business standpoint the beginnings and principal steps in the growth of the several predecessor organizations up to the time of the consolidation, and from the date of the organization of the present corporation down to the end of the period covered by the present investigation. Such an outline will show, among other things, the development of the patents used by the organization and the principal steps in producing and establishing on the market the principal products of the company over a period of years.

Analysis of original capitalization

Having secured a complete history of the beginnings of the company, both from the financial and operating standpoints, it now becomes quite desirable to make an analysis of the capitalization of the company from the date of the organization of the present corporation down to the date of the balance sheet. It is assumed, of course, in this connection, that the corporation under investigation has been organized a considerable period of years, so that a study of this character will furnish a real guide as to the manner in which the assets of the company have been created and the liabilities have been incurred.

In case the corporation under investigation has been in business for only a year or two, and it is desired to make a comprehensive investigation of the company for the purpose of a security issue, it will be necessary to go back of the date of organization of the present corporation and to make the analysis of the results from operations and the net worth section cover a considerable period for the predecessor company or companies. This is especially true in case the men responsible for the management of the present corporation were the guiding spirits of the predecessor companies. It will be assumed, however, that the corporation under investigation has been organized and has been in operation for a considerable period of years prior to the date of the investigation.

The analysis of the capitalization of the company should show the original investment of the stockholders, any additional investments made by the stockholders, the amount of stock dividends which have been paid and added to the capitalization, and finally the extent of the participation of the original organizers and present managers in the stock ownership.

Three major considerations

The original investment of the stockholders will be represented by stock issued for any one of three considerations.

First, the stockholders may have paid cash for their capital stock, and the liability for the cash investment of the stockholders may be carried in the capital stock account, or if a premium has been paid by the stockholders for the stock issued, the premium paid should be carried as paid-in surplus. It is clear that if stock has been issued for cash for a price at least equal to the par value of the stock, no investigation is called for except to make certain that no unfair discrimination was practiced between the stockholders and that the sale was duly authorized.

Second, stock may have been issued originally to the stockholders for fixed property or for other tangible considerations other than cash. Such considerations may include accounts receivable or stocks or material

and supplies, in case the owner of a small unincorporated business sells his property for capital stock of the new corporation.

Finally, stock may be issued for patents and goodwill. Stock so issued may represent an issue for actual and real consideration or may represent an amount taken by the original owners to reward themselves for having undertaken the enterprise. Profits in the flotation of the enterprise taken by the promoter are also frequently disguised and charged to patents and goodwill if stock is issued to the promoter in payment for his services. It is hardly feasible in this discussion to outline the steps to be taken in passing upon the validity of the issues of stock for property or other tangible considerations, or for patents and goodwill. In general, however, it may be said that if the issues have been properly authorized, and if no fraud or collusion is indicated, there is no occasion to question the actual value of the consideration given for the stock as issued. However, the character of the property acquired in consideration for the issue of stock should be plainly shown, and if it appears that no real value was acquired through the issue, the report should so state.*

Analysis of subsequent capitalization

Having analyzed the original investment made by the stockholders and having segregated the issues of stock between that issued for cash consideration, that for tangible property, and that for patents and goodwill, an analysis should be made of the additional investment by stockholders and segregated in the same manner. This segregation is important in the analysis of the additional issues for the identical reasons outlined in connection with the discussion on the analysis of the original issue of stock. As already

---

* A frequent method of indicating a qualification of this character is to show in parentheses after the words "Net Worth" on the balance sheet, the phrase "including intangibles." Such a phrase (immediately after the words "Net Worth") indicates that the value of the net worth is dependent to an extent upon the problematical value of the intangibles.

indicated, stock issues may represent original investments, additional investments, and stock dividends. Stock dividends consist of nothing more or less than permanently impounded profits and must be related to the sources from which these profits came. They need to be considered at this point only for the purpose of completing the outline of the company's capitalization.

The foregoing outline of the analysis to be made of the issues of capital stock, and which is intended to cover both the issue of preferred and common stock, should also be made having due regard to certain questions, the answer to which will throw a considerable degree of light on the policies of those most actively interested in the company's business. In making such an analysis, consideration should be given to the portion of the total stock investment owned by the original organizers. If the original organizers have parted with a large portion of their original holdings or if their original holdings in the first instance were relatively nominal, it may be that they do not have sufficient faith in the future of the business to invest their own resources in it to any material amount.

It is also well to have in mind the division of the stock investment of the original organizers between preferred and common stock. We frequently find the situation where the organizers have not put any cash or any real tangible property into the business, but have secured control of the company through the issue to themselves at time of organization of a large portion of the total common stock issued in consideration for patents, goodwill and other intangibles. It may be in such a case that the preferred stock, which was issued and sold for cash, actually represents the only real equity back of the business and, if the original organizers have made no cash investment whatever in the business, the question may well be raised as to the amount of faith they have in its future success.

The extent of the participation of the original organizers in the purchase of subsequent issues of stock is also an important consideration, since it indicates whether they have continued to support the company to the extent of their means, or whether they have drawn back and allowed outsiders to take all of the risk incident to the subsequent issues.

It is self-evident that the stockholdings of the active officers in charge of the finances and operations of the company furnish a most important guide as to the sincerity of the management in its protestations as to the success and future prosperity of the company.

Growth of net worth

The answers to any questions of this character, however, must be considered with due regard to the individual case in question. It may be, for instance, that the original organizers of the business were men of small personal means who possessed little beyond some valuable patents and some good connections which would be very useful in the operation of the company. It may also be true that the principal officers of the company are men with no private fortunes, who have invested as much as they consistently could in the securities of the company, although their aggregate investment may be relatively almost nominal. In such cases it is evident that the character of the stock investment by the organizers or officers may furnish no reliable criterion as to their sincerity of purpose or their faith in the future of the company. In general, however, these questions are important and should receive careful consideration.

Since some portion of net worth, and often a considerable portion, is derived from the retention of earnings, it will be necessary to summarize the net profits by years from the date of organization of the corporation down to the date of the balance sheet. These net profits, of course, should be audited for the period covered by the investigation, that is to say, the period for which an audited income account is to be submitted. For the period prior thereto, the net profits per books may be used subject to any large adjustments that may be indicated as the result of the general analysis of the property and depreciation reserve accounts for the years prior to the beginning of the period for which the investigation is to be submitted and also subject to all that may be indicated by the investigation of the years actually audited.

It may be assumed, for instance, that a company has been in existence for a period of 15 years and that a 5-year income account is to be submitted in connection with the investigation. In such a case it is desirable to make a general examination of the property and depreciation reserve accounts from the date of organization, even though the property values may be stated on the basis of an appraisal as of the date of the balance sheet. Large errors, which would affect the yearly net profits indicated by this general examination of the property and depreciation reserve accounts, should be taken care of in the summary of the net profits.

Now that a history of earnings from the inception of the company to the close of the period covered by the investigation has been prepared, it is necessary to consider the disposition of those net earnings. There should therefore be prepared a summary of all cash dividends paid year by year from the date of organization down to the date of the balance sheet. It is quite desirable to have the dividends paid year by year set out in a column parallel to the net earnings year by year. Such a statement will indicate whether the company has consistently pursued a conservative and provident course in building up its net worth through the retention of part of its operating profits in the business.

The dividends on preferred stock frequently represent a charge which must be met if the company is to continue in successful operation, and dividends on preferred stock paid out of accumulated earnings of prior years are a necessary incident in the experience of a company which has issued preferred stock and which has wide variations in its operating results from year to year. So far as common stock dividends are concerned, however, it would seem to be the part of prudence for a company to conform the amount of its cash dividends on common stock from year to year to the actual surplus net earnings available therefor, after making provision for preferred dividends and after leaving some residue of earnings to be retained in the business.

Net worth from capital profits

The third and last source of net worth is to be found in capital profits. Capital profits may be segregated into profits actually realized and profits constructively realized.

Capital profits actually realized arise from transactions not directly connected with the regular business and frequently in connection with the sale of real estate, whether this real estate has been held merely as an outside investment or has been used in the operation of the business. In either case, the profit arising from the disposition of the real estate should, if the item is large, be shown as a capital profit rather than as part of the profits arising from the regular operation of the business of the company.

An example of true capital profit is seen in the case of a company whose plant was situated on a piece of land that ultimately became very valuable as a terminal site for a large railroad. The price paid for this property under condemnation proceedings was sufficient to reimburse the company for the entire original cost of this property, including the buildings which had been erected on the site and had been in use by the company for many years. Since the company had never enjoyed sufficient earnings to set up any provision for depreciation, this sale made at a time when its manufacturing plant was pretty well worn out, furnished a happy solution to a problem that had become extremely difficult. A capital profit of this character which has been actually realized, may be included in the earned surplus of the company, of course. There is no question, however, that such a profit should be set out separately in any history of the earnings credited to surplus account during the period from the date of organization of the company to the date of the balance sheet.

Capital profits "constructively realized"

The situation is different, however, in respect to capital profits "constructively realized." Such profits may never properly be included in earned surplus, but should always be shown as capital surplus and should be designated by descriptive captions which will indicate the general nature of these profits. Such profits, when they do actually exist, represent, of course, the actual accretion in value of fixed assets through the operation of the law of unearned increment. If a building site purchased five years ago for $1,000 is adjacent to sites of similar size and identical in every way which have been recently sold at prices varying from $2,000 to $3,000, it is quite evident that the value of this site also has increased with the passage of time.

In general, however, any capital profits arising through the appreciation of fixed assets which have not been taken up on the books, should be supported by the results of an appraisal made by a reputable appraisal firm, or by some other definite and conclusive evidence that the appreciation claimed has actually taken place. Surplus credits arising from mere write-ups of the book values of the fixed assets should be reversed, if possible. Frequently, however, these write-ups have been authorized by the directors of the company who have adopted this method of improving their balance sheet. In such cases it may be likely that it will not be possible to reverse these write-ups. In such cases it is absolutely necessary to describe the item so clearly and definitely that no one can possibly be misled, or confuse such a write-up with actual capital profits which have been constructively realized.

Interpretation of stock dividends

Stock dividends do not, of course, either add to or subtract from the total net worth of a company, although their declaration may have an effect on the company's net worth as indicated by the market quotations of its stock. Actually, however, stock dividends furnish merely a means of transferring capital from one pocket to another. They represent a permanent investment of profits, rather than a distribution of profits, since the declaration of a stock dividend transfers a section of the net worth from surplus, where it is available for dividends to the capital stock account where it is not available. If a company is making large profits and growing rapidly it may be an indication of a very praiseworthy conservatism to declare large stock dividends which will have the result of increasing the stockholders' permanent investment and reducing the amount of the investment which is available for distribution in the form of cash dividends.

A question sometimes arises as to the capitalization of appreciation by means of a stock dividend. The legality of this procedure cannot be questioned; its propriety may constitute a very difficult question. It may be said, of course, that if the corporation were to reorganize and form a new corporation, it would be possible to issue stock of par or (in the case of no par value stock) declared value sufficient to absorb the entire amount of appreciation arising from the valuation of the assets. It may be argued, therefore, that the same result is being secured merely in another way by paying out the capital surplus in the form of a stock dividend.

In case capital profits created by an appreciation of the fixed assets have been paid out in the form of stock dividends, the fact that these stock dividends do not represent investment of actual earnings from operations, but rather merely the transfer of capital profits arising from the appreciation of fixed assets, should be set out clearly in the review of the company's net worth.

Analysis of capital stock

Thus a larger or smaller proportion of the net worth may be represented by capital stock and a considerable importance attaches to the form given to this stock and to the classes of the stockholders.

The position of the holder of preferred stock is largely that of a silent partner who has made his investment in order to secure a relatively high yield coupled with somewhat greater security than that possessed by the common stock. The common stockholder, on the other hand, frequently possesses the sole voting power and almost invariably the voting control. Eliminating the speculator who buys in order to profit by market fluctuations of the common stock, the investor in the common stock of an enterprise has put in his money either because of his active participation in the affairs and destinies of the business or because of his faith in its ultimate success.

Having outlined in a very general way the fundamental characteristics of each of the two principal classes of stock, it will be desirable to give consideration to the special attributes of each class. Preferred stock is preferred in the event of liquidation and in the payment of dividends; that is to say, the agreement under which preferred stock is issued ordinarily provides that dividends shall be paid on the preferred stock before dividends can be declared and paid on the common stock. In many cases this provision for priority of dividend payments attaching to the preferred stock is made cumulative. In the case of cumulative preferred stock, it is stipulated that in the event dividends are passed on the preferred stock in any year

or years, the preferred stock dividends in arrears shall be paid up in full before any dividends can be paid on the common. The stock agreement provides also that in the event of liquidation, voluntary or otherwise, the preferred stockholders shall be paid in full before any distribution of the assets of the corporation shall be made to the common stockholders.

Characteristics of preferred stock

Preferred stock, however, is ordinarily definitely limited as to the rate of dividend return which shall be paid its holders. Certain preferred stock issues carry participating stipulations which tend, of course, to cause the stock to partake partially of the character of common stock. Ordinarily, the rate of return payable on preferred stock is definitely fixed and will not be increased in the event the company enjoys great prosperity and earns a high return on the capital invested. Preferred stock is hedged about with various protective provisions. In addition to the dividend and liquidation provisions previously referred to, it is frequently provided that the corporation shall maintain at all times a certain ratio of current assets to current liabilities and also shall maintain a certain ratio of net assets to preferred stock outstanding.

Preferred stock agreements frequently carry a sinking fund provision which provides for the retirement of stock over a period of years. These stipulations may and should require the company to make provision for these sinking fund payments through the appropriation of surplus net earnings for that purpose. Another stipulation designed to protect the interest of the preferred stockholders is frequently inserted to the effect that no mortgages or other fixed liens shall be placed upon the property without the prior consent of a two-thirds majority of the preferred stockholders.

As indicated by the foregoing discussion, it is evident that preferred stock possesses certain advantages and certain disadvantages for the investor. As contrasted with bonds, preferred stock yields a higher return. Its principal disadvantage, as contrasted with bonds, is that it is very much less well secured since the preferred stockholder is usually somewhat impotent in the event of disaster. He cannot foreclose in the event of default, as can a bondholder, and by the time he succeeds to the voting power, providing the agreement under which he has purchased his preferred stock provides for the preferred stock to become vested with the voting power in the event of default, he is likely to find himself compelled to submit to a scaling down process through a reorganization in order to get anything out of the *debacle*.

The protective provisions which perhaps appeared to make the preferred stock extremely safe will all prove to be worthless in the event the company starts to suffer heavy losses from operation, since an industrial company losing money may frequently suffer terrific losses which wipe out a large portion of the stockholders' equity before the preferred stockholder can secure control. Unfortunately no restrictive provisions have yet been devised which will prevent a company from losing money. In the event a company loses heavily through operating losses and the preferred stockholder comes into the voting control through default in preferred dividends, he frequently finds that the company has such a large floating indebtedness to the banks that, if the business were to be liquidated, the settlement of the obligations to bankers and other creditors would absorb all the proceeds from the liquidation and leave him with little or no return on his original investment. In such an event he is perforce compelled to agree to the plan of reorganization designed by the creditors' committee, which perhaps provides for bonds to be taken by the principal creditors and for the preferred and common stockholders to make mutual sacrifices effected through reductions both in the amount

of their stockholdings and the dividend requirements of these holdings.

Comparison between bonds, preferred and common stocks

Contrasting the relative security of preferred stock with bonds, it should be remembered that mortgage bonds permit the investor, through his trustee, to step in and foreclose on the property in the event of default. When an industrial company already has a bond issue outstanding, banks will be very much more conservative and cautious about loaning the company money, and this situation tends to prevent a company from losing large sums and dissipating its entire net worth in operating losses before actually coming to a showdown. In case a company has no bonds outstanding, on the other hand, and has financed itself through the issue of preferred and common stock, banks may lend the company a considerable sum based on the security afforded by the capital investment of the preferred stockholders. In the event the sums advanced are dissipated through losses in operation, the bank can still fall back upon the capital investment of the preferred stockholders to secure payment of its claims and the preferred stockholders find themselves with little or nothing left of their original investment.

Preferred stocks

Contrasting preferred stock with common stock, on the other hand, the preferred stockholder enjoys greater assurance that his income will be steady and continuous and, in the event of reorganization, the contributions levied upon him are much less drastic. On the other hand, his return is fixed and limited except in the case of participating preferred stock, which has already been referred to, and he can entertain no hopes that he will share in the melon providing his company achieves great success.

From the point of view of the corporation, preferred stock has certain advantages and certain disadvantages. Its yield is higher than the yield enjoyed by bonds, but, on the other hand, there is not the danger that the preferred stockholder, like the bondholder, will step in and foreclose in the event of default. As contrasted with common stock, the issue of preferred stock is frequently a source of a weakness to the company since preferred stock dividends cannot be passed without impairing the company's credit seriously. This situation is accentuated in the case of a public utility that has sold preferred stock locally in considerable volume by virtue of a widespread customer-ownership campaign.

Contrasted with common stock, preferred stock has certain advantages and disadvantages to the investor. First and most important, it is more secure, there is less danger that the preferred stockholder will see his entire investment wiped out. Unless he is able to keep in close touch with the affairs of the company, or unless the company is nationally known and known to be extremely conservative in its management, it is unsafe for the small investor to invest largely in common stock, since he runs the very considerable risk of being wiped out in the event of disaster and is bound to suffer most severely in the event of reorganization. On the other hand, in the event of success, he can enjoy the full measure of his company's prosperity.

Advantageous use of preferred stock

There are certain types of enterprise which may properly use preferred stock issues as a means of raising additional capital. For example, this means may safely be used by old established companies whose earnings are relatively stable from year to year and who have large surplus capital represented by readily realizable assets. In the event a company does not desire to reduce its working capital to a narrow margin, but needs additional funds in order to carry out certain legitimate expenditures for the busi-

ness, and especially where the common stockholders have great faith in the future prosperity of their company and do not wish to admit outsiders to a participation in these large anticipated profits, it might be highly desirable to provide the additional working capital required by means of an issue of preferred stock. Preferred stock issues are especially satisfactory means of raising additional capital for public utilities or other companies whose business is of such a character that the net earnings are relatively stable from year to year and can almost definitely be relied upon.

Preferred stock issues are dangerous, on the other hand, to new companies not yet firmly established, and to companies whose business is of such a character that almost of necessity they must anticipate that years of large earnings will be followed by years of low earnings or perhaps by years of losses.

In connection with our consideration of the different classes of stock it may be desirable to touch upon the two principal advantages to the corporation in the issue of no par value stock. First of all, since it has no par value, it may readily be sold at a price attractive to the investor without the corporation's incurring the odium incident to selling stock at a discount. It is especially useful in the event of reorganization in permitting the corporation to scale down the equity of the common stockholders to absorb a deficit, and to permit the rejuvenated company to start business with a clean slate and yet accomplish these desired ends without reducing the number of shares of stock held by the common stockholders. This latter purpose may, of course, be secured by scaling down the par value of stock. For instance, stock having a par value of $100 a share may be scaled down to a par value of $10, or even $1 a share. It is not necessary, of course, to issue no par value stock in order to effect the rejuvenation of the corporation in the manner outlined, but no par value stock appears to be the favorite medium for this purpose.

Some states regulate the par values of stock which may be issued, but a minimum par value stock often has all of the characteristics of a no par value stock. The form of the stock may be influenced by the prevailing type of market, and a company may be better able at a certain time to sell common stock to the public than preferred stock. Recently there have been considerable issues of stock which are a cross between preferred and common, usually having no par value, with a Class "A" series preferred as to fixed dividends and as to equity in the event of liquidation, but participating with Class "B" as to dividends after certain definite distributions have been made to the Class "B" stock.

In any contemplated financing, the securities offered should be of the type which will be readily absorbed by the public, will provide necessary capital for the company at the least cost, will not close the door to future financing, and are so protected as to benefit the security holder without burdening or hampering the operation of the business. There is a mutual basis which may be worked out whereby all of the interests involved may be protected in case of trouble, with the security holder, however, occupying a position prior to the owners of the business in the event of a reorganization.

Judging operating results

Fifth of a series of articles which appeared originally in Manufacturing Industries during 1925 and 1926.

Usually an exhaustive analysis of a company's profit and loss statements over a period of years is necessary only in connection with financing. This may be preliminary to financing or may be called for because earnings after financing have not proven entirely satisfactory. Partial analyses of operations are sometimes made in connection with internal investigations, but these are more frequently of a specialized nature and are conducted to supplement the analysis of some operating problem. For the purpose of this discussion it will be assumed that the analyses of operations are being made in connection with financing of some nature.

Such an analysis accomplishes two distinct results: it shows the actual performance of the company and the reasons for this performance; and it gives the basis for passing upon the soundness of management policies.

It is not sufficient that a business has shown satisfactory profits over a past period of years, for these profits might have been greatly increased were it not for elements of extravagance, lack of sales initiative, careless servicing, or what not. The profits earned may result from patent monopoly, natural advantages of material or labor supply or overwhelming demand, and actually the business may have succeeded financially in spite of poor management. Such a situation gives no assurance of future earnings and the existence of these conditions would be indicated by the profit and loss analysis.

Earnings requirements

Beyond all else it is necessary that the business show a demonstrated earning capacity, for capital has a value only in proportion to the return from its use. Return, of course, is gaged almost directly in proportion to the risk involved. The return on federal and municipal securities is lower than the return on industrial bonds, which, in turn, is lower than the return expected from capital stock. If the type of enterprise is known, it is fairly easy to judge what should be the normal rate of return on the capital involved. Inversely, if the earnings of a business are known it is then possible to set up normal values for the various classes of stock that may have been issued.

A recent striking example of this principle was shown in the financing of the Dodge Bros. Motor Company, wherein the demonstrated earning capacity over a period of years led to the capitalization of intangibles in the amount of approximately $75,000,000.

A prime essential in determining the form of the capital structure of the new corporation is that the business shall be able to earn an adequate return on the new capitalization. If no additional capital is involved the task is fairly easy, but if the introduction of additional capital is based upon the acquisition of new facilities and upon expansion over past operations, it will be necessary to make some very careful forecasts, even in the detail of a complete budget of operations, sometimes over a coming period of several years.

In the consideration of return on capital, it is necessary to consider more than the senior securities which may be offered to the public. Each business has a complete financial structure which, if well laid out, is carefully balanced in its proportions of funded debt and contributive capital. The business as a whole is sick if its earnings can do no more than care for its senior obligations. The market value of common stock may be seriously affected by the issuance of a large block of cumulative preferred stock, and too great an obligation for preferred stock may destroy the initiative of the active operating management if it has large holdings of the common.

It becomes important, therefore, to analyze the ratio of the earnings to the capitalization and the probable margin of safety, after taking care of the interest and dividend requirements and after meeting the sinking fund requirements on bonds or preferred stock.

Determination of profits

Back of any analysis which may be made, lie the operating statements which must be used by the investigator. Upon the accuracy, completeness and comparability of these statements for the period of years covered, rests the worth of the analytical conclusions. It is, therefore, essential that for the vital period of time these statements shall be the result of an audit or audits.

Normally it is desirable to have audited statements for each of the five years preceding the date of the investigation. Very often an interim audit must be made to cover the elapsed portion of the current year, so the statements may cover four years and six months, or four years and nine months. There may be cases where the corporation has been in existence for only two or three years, making it desirable to secure audited statements of the predecessor or component companies.

Even where audited statements are available for a five-year period it is often desirable and always helpful to draw off at least condensed statements from the company records for a prior 5, 10 or 15-year period, as permitting a study of long-time trends. These data are particularly valuable where the industry is one of extreme hazard or is subject to violent cyclic fluctuations.

This emphasis placed upon the use of audited statements is necessary for several reasons: earnings must not only be accurate for the entire period considered as a unit; they must also be accurate for each one of the years covered by that period. It is essential that problems in connection with the appreciation or depreciation of fixed assets should be handled correctly and that the company's accounting procedures, in general, shall have been consistent from year to year. Unless inventories have been taken and priced on a single, consistent basis, it is probable that earnings have been distorted thereby as between years.

Unless the makeup of the accounts has been the same in each year and there has been a correct allocation as between capital and expense accounts, earnings may not only have been shifted as between years, but may also be appreciably over or understated. Unless depreciation has been charged off on a uniform basis each year the earnings may be tremendously changed.

Importance of depreciation and appreciation

Depreciation and appreciation have assumed an especial importance in the past few years, partly because of the necessities imposed by tax requirements and partly because of the extreme fluctuation in dollar values. In the past a concern may have taken depreciation in proportion to the year's earnings, that is, large amounts in some years and little or nothing in others. It may also have gone on the basis of writing off its properties as completely and rapidly as possible, with the result that the book values of the property accounts become meaningless, while at the same time profits were understated for one period and overstated for subsequent periods. If property values are later reestablished on the basis of normal and regular depreciation, a fairly true picture may be obtained, and the increase in net worth thus secured is in the nature of earned surplus.

But if property accounts are appreciated solely on the basis of the change in dollar value—for purposes of financing—a very different result will be attained. The increased property accounts call for increased depreciation. Thus net profits will be decreased and the former ratios of earnings to capital will be greatly changed.

Basic elements of analysis

Stress has been placed upon the accurate determination of earnings by years. It is important to know whether operations are normally consistent, or whether it is characteristic of the business or of the whole industry to have irregular earnings, as good years followed by bad years. It is important to know the exact effect of outside conditions on the business. Thus in some cases of excellent management there were *bona fide* normal earnings in the years 1921 and 1922 when the majority of business showed either losses or abnormally low earnings. In some cases such drastic inventory losses were taken in 1920 or 1921 that the business showed fictitious earnings in 1921 or 1922, giving a false impression of early recovery from the industrial depression. Similar effects may have been obtained by inequitable deferment of selling, general or advertising expenses in years of actually small profits.

The inequalities between years are of less importance where the results from operations are averaged over a 5 or a 10-year period, but the analysis by averages cannot be substituted for the analysis by years, since a different purpose is served. The analysis by averages should give an index as to the normal expectancy of return on sales and on capital as well as to show the normal proportions of different classes of cost and expense. This analysis has been difficult during the past decade in many businesses.

For example, some industries had a very substantial prosperity in the years 1915 and 1916 because of war work for the Allies. Some businesses were depressed in 1917 and 1918, while many others reached a high level of activity in war work for the United States Government. The years 1919 and 1920 were generally prosperous for all businesses and all industries, while 1921 and 1922, to less extent, were almost disastrous. These profound industrial inequalities, operating largely independent of the individual business, must be considered in arriving at the average of normal expectancy.

In some businesses it is possible to average the years 1922 to 1925, inclusive. In most businesses 1919, 1920 and 1921 must be totally disregarded. In many businesses no use can be made of the war years 1917 and 1918. Sometimes averages may be struck for several different periods and comparisons made of these periodic averages. Thus if the years 1913 to 1917, inclusive, are used, there may result a fair prewar average which may not be greatly at variance with that obtained by averaging the years 1918 to 1922, inclusive, or the years 1923 to 1925, inclusive. In each business individual judgment is necessary in establishing the bases which can safely be used for this class of analysis.

Sources of profits

Closely related to the study of averages is the study of sources of profits. It may be that favorable showings are made almost entirely by reason of low costs and a high gross, while much money is practically thrown away by reason of loosely controlled and extravagant sales policies; or a "sellers market" and correspondingly high prices may permit profits despite lax and inefficient operating. Conditions of easy profit were more common a decade or two ago than they are now, when improved processing, improved transportation, bulk production and national advertising and distribution are continually increasing the pressure of competition.

There are profits which are outside of the results from normal operations and which must be defined and segregated from operating profits. This includes capital gain, such as results from the advantageous sale of land, buildings or equipment. It also includes financial gain, interest on securities held which are not essential to the conduct of the business. Thus one business habitually held a half-million dollars' worth of federal securities, which was really surplus capital and which gave a return not to exceed 4 percent. In the analysis of return on capital it was necessary to deduct the half-million dollars from capital employed and the $20,000 from income before the normal results from operations could be judged. Such an existent condition is, of course, illuminative in judging the characteristics of the management.

In all of this analysis the predominant idea is to secure from the past some basis for judging the probabilities of the future. To findings on the particular business must be added findings on the general status and trend of the industry, and often the general economic status and trends of the nation and of the world.

The profit and loss statement

In a summary statement of operations there will appear 12 principal items in a natural sequence, as follows:

1. Sales
2. Returns, allowances and discounts
3. Net sales
4. Cost of sales
5. Gross profit
6. Selling expense
7. Administrative expense
8. Net operating profit
9. Miscellaneous income
10. Interest paid
11. Federal taxes
12. Surplus net profits

It will be noted that gross sales is clearly distinguished from net sales and that some prominence is given to deductions from sales. This is essential for purposes of investigation. Often allowances and discounts are merged with selling expenses, serve to distort the amount and percentage of such expense and give a false analysis of this phase of operations.

Back of the single items of gross sales and net sales it is always necessary to set up supporting analytical schedules in greater or less detail, dependent upon the importance of the sales situation in the whole analysis.

Almost invariably there are several sales products and it is important to show the volume of sales of each product by years. This permits a study of the trend and importance of each item of product, some of which may be on the increase and others on the decrease, to the point where it may be advantageous to withdraw some from the market. This is particularly true where there are various models of a general type of product and the older ones contribute such small volume as not to warrant the investment in machinery, patterns, tools, inventory, etc., necessary to their continuance. Sales by the different products in units is usually a valuable subsidiary schedule, since apparent sales trends in values are often the distorted result of price fluctuations.

A schedule showing geographical distribution of sales, either in units, values, or both, is often highly significant as showing undue concentration in some territories, lack of development in others, too wide a spread of sales effort, sales in sections where freight charges are prohibitive, or sales possibilities in virgin territory through use of water transportation. Sometimes this analysis will show a concentration of sales at a point so far distant from the factory as to indicate savings through branch production or through a jobbing connection.

Schedules showing the percentage of total sales by years to a few principal customers may reveal the dangerous situation of dependence on a single industry, or upon the favor of one, two or three customers. Usually security results from diversification, and this in sales analysis means diversification of territory, customers, and industries.

There must be applied to the results of sales analysis much the same modifying factors which were considered in connection with earnings. The effect of local and general economic conditions, intensity of competition and the protection afforded by patent or manufacturing monopolies, stage of development of the particular art or industry, all must be given full weight in judging the effectiveness of management control over sales in the light of results attained.

Consideration of gross profits and costs

If the cost of sales can be broken down exactly as sales have been analyzed, that is, by products, models, etc., it becomes possible to show gross profits according to sales classification. This becomes valuable material for analysis, since it often reveals many profit inequalities. For example, there are in many businesses certain products which are sold at low margin of profit for the purposes of securing volume and of introducing other and more profitable lines. It may well be that without careful control or without constant analysis these "leader" lines are sold at a loss or at no profit. Similarly, it sometimes occurs that lines supposed highly profitable, and therefore strongly pushed by the sales management, are yielding a low return.

A valuable form of analysis is a tabulation showing the percentage of sales which each line bears to sales as a whole, and which sets forth in a parallel column the percentage of gross profit contributed by each line. It has been found that one product which comprised 50 percent of the total sales contributed 80 percent of the gross profit, while another product contributed 20 percent of the sales and showed a 10 percent gross loss. Instances have been noted where a company would have had higher gross and net profits if it had discarded nine of its ten sales products.

Such inequalities indicate either a poor managerial control or else a pressure of outside conditions which is so severe that the issue might better be evaded by a complete revision of sales policies.

97

Standards for certain businesses

Long experience in the study of gross profits results in the setting of certain mental standards for certain classes of business. Thus certain types of industry are known to require approximately a 60 percent gross profit ratio in order to produce a satisfactory percentage of net profit, while other industries require only a 25 percent gross in order to show a proper net. It becomes possible by the law of averages to say whether a low net result is a primary product of ineffective manufacturing or of extravagant administrative and selling policies.

Naturally, the accuracy of gross profit determinations in yearly operating statements depends to a great extent upon the accuracy and consistency of inventory taking and pricing, while the accuracy of monthly gross profit figures depends upon the reliability of costs and perpetual inventories. This means that the investigator has a duty in checking the probable accuracy of the important elements of costs and cost of sales as a preliminary to the use of such figures for analytical purposes. Even if yearly cost of sales figures are correct, the current costs may be incorrect, the surest index to this condition being found in the amount of the discrepancies between physical and book inventories.

Since gross profit is a resultant of selling price and manufacturing cost, prices must also be considered in this analysis. It may be that sales volumes, and hence costs, are directly influenced by fluctuations in price. Often an attempt to establish prices on the basis of costs alone is a disastrous move, since too high a cost in the first place may lead to a prohibitive price, which reduces sales volume, raises costs, and thus leads theoretically to a still higher price. In some cases prices are worked out on practically a budget basis by anticipating a certain sales volume, calculating costs on the proposed volume and then adding a proper gross profit. In other cases it will be found that there is no flexibility to the price range, prices being controlled by the effect of dominant competition. In this latter situation the only chance of increasing the gross profit ratio lies in more economical manufacturing.

It is sometimes considered that gross profit is the responsibility of the manufacturing organization and that net profit is the responsibility of the administrative and selling personnel. It is evident, however, that this is not entirely true, since selling prices are usually in large part set by the sales organization. But once the gross profit has been made, the question of whether or not there is a satisfactory net is governed largely by the amount of and the control over general and selling expenses.

The simplest index to these classes of expense lies in the ratio they bear to total sales. If there were no selling expense except a direct salesman's commission the percentage would be absolutely uniform, unless the rate of commission were revised. This is seldom possible of attainment. Due to fixed charges for sales offices and equipment, advertising, clerical salaries, shipping expense, etc., a condition usually exists that causes decreased sales volume to result in an increased ratio of sales expense. An increase in sales may or may not result in an important decrease in this ratio, since increased sales may mean increased commissions, warrant increased salaries, call for increased clerical assistance, and be secured through increased advertising or promotional sales effort.

The ratio of general expense to sales will fluctuate almost directly with increase or decrease in sales, since it is usually fairly fixed and stable in amount. The important points of analysis, therefore, consist in a study of the items making up these expenses, to determine whether they are justified at all, whether they are too large, whether they betray an attitude of indifference or extravagance upon the part of the management, or whether some increase caused by additional records and systems might not be of far-reaching benefit in giving better executive control.

Factors based on sales dollar

It has been found possible in some businesses to study the history and actualities of selling and general expense so closely that they are currently controlled on the basis of so many cents per sales dollar, both as a whole and as individual items. Thus salary costs may be dangerous if exceeding 11 cents on the sales dollar, rental of sales offices must not exceed 2 cents per sales dollar, etc.

In addition to this type of analysis, a number of important indications as to the policies and attitudes of the management may be gathered from a study of certain items by years. Thus an increase in bad debt losses leads to inquiry as to the cause, whether due to laxness in the credit department or to a deliberate intention to increase sales volume by more widespread sales. A change in advertising appropriations will always lead back to a distinct change in policy, whether of changed advertising media or basic sales policies. Sometimes a decrease in advertising is attended by reduced prices, by greater quantity discounts, by the introduction of consignment sales, etc., and there the relationship is fairly obvious. Final operating figures must be studied as the resultant of management policies rather than as an end in themselves.

Operating and balance sheet ratios in the financial and industrial investigation

Sixth of a series of articles which appeared originally in Manufacturing Industries during 1925 and 1926.

SURVIVAL under conditions of modern competitive business necessitates a constant vigil over financial relationships and operating results. All businesses strive to obtain competitive advantages in industry and thereby secure an increased return on capital. This very effort tends to narrow the margins of profit and any business which is not alert to competitive progress soon finds itself facing elimination. Sales price levels are seldom within the control of a single business. They are set fundamentally by competition, so that the average concern will realize a reasonable return under average conditions over a period of time. The margin between sales and costs must pay operating expenses and costs of financing, and then yield a fair return on capital invested. The individual business must give its attention to those factors over which it has control, namely, costs of financing, rates of turnover and expenses.

One of the most significant indices to the condition of a business is that afforded through the use of ratios developed from balance sheet and operating statement figures. Some few ratios are commonly used, such as the ratio of net profits to sales, or to net worth, and the ratio of current assets to current liabilities. Other ratios of still greater significance may be only rarely used. The relationships of inventory to sales or cost of sales, of charge sales to receivables, of mortgage debt to assets pledged, of sales to total assets, all have a meaning if it be read.

Ratios as indices to operations

Ratios are valuable indices because they picture relationships uninfluenced by changes in economic values. The economic law of supply and demand is constantly exerting its influence on the general level of prices. In periods of high prices, commodities are

101

high and the purchasing power of money is low. In periods of low prices, commodities are cheap and the purchasing power of money is high. During times of general inflation, profits of business will naturally increase as the buying power of money will be diminished. During times of general deflation, profits will naturally decrease as the buying power of money will be enhanced. An enterprise may realize an increase in profits during a period of rising prices, but may find that there is an actual decrease in ratio or margin on net sales.

The true measure of profits is not the amount of profits realized, but the ratio of those profits to net sales, ratios constituting a measure uninfluenced by changing values. Business should be so conducted that it will yield, as nearly as may be, the same ratio of net profits, all other factors being equal, in periods of inflation and deflation as in normal times, and that ratio should be complementary to a reasonable return on the current value of capital employed. The point to be kept in mind is that the expression of sales values and other current items keeps pace with current economic conditions, but the expression of capital does not. Yet an intelligent study of ratios will aid materially in determining whether a business has kept pace with or perhaps even anticipated changing conditions, especially during times of marked instability, such as were experienced from 1914 to 1921.

Types of ratios

Profits are effected by management through three main sources, namely, low financing costs secured through balanced capital structure, rapidity of turnovers and profit margins which include control of expenses. Significant ratios concern the relationships in the same three sources: turnover ratios, operating ratios and balance sheet ratios. The more important ratios in each of these three groups are as follows:

Balance sheet ratios:

    Working capital ratio.

Net worth to total capital employed.

Mortgage debt to assets pledged.

Common and preferred stock equities to net worth in cases of preferred stock financing.

Earnings retained in business to total earnings.

Turnover ratios:

    Sales to total assets.

    Charge sales to receivables.

    Sales or cost of sales to inventories.

    Sales to plant.

    Net profits to net worth.

Operating ratios:

    Gross profits to sales.

    Selling and general expenses to sales.

    Operating profits to sales.

    Earnings available for financing to annual cost of financing.

    Surplus net profits to sales.

In the analysis of a business, these ratios are applied further in detail to the various elements of financial condition and operating results to the extent warranted by relevant information desired in each particular case. Each of the typical ratios noted above has significance from an analytical viewpoint.

Significance of ratio

Thus the working capital ratio is significant in the light of ability to pay current obligations. This influences credit standing and purchasing power. The company that can purchase at lowest prices has an initial competitive advantage. The ratio of net worth to total capital employed reveals the adequacy of capital investment as compared with borrowed capital and the policy of financing as to proprietary risk. There is a vast difference between a management that finances to acquire temporary borrowed funds and one that finances to have the public furnish most of the capital. The ratio

102

of mortgage debt to assets pledged reflects a measure of the security and assurance that the borrowed capital will be repaid. The ratios of common and preferred stock equities to net worth show the segregation of proprietary risk and are of particular interest in cases of preferred stock financing. The ratio of earnings left in the business to total earnings has embodied in it the elements of conservatism, normal expansion and gradual liquidation of liabilities.

The ratio of sales to total assets embodies the general efficient use of total capital employed. The ratio of charge sales to receivables is the fruit of an efficient or lax credit and collection system. The ratio of sales or cost of sales to inventory is the result of a quick turnover or the carrying of surplus, unbalanced or obsolete stocks. The ratio of sales to plant may show conservative policy or overexpansion. The ratio of net profits to net worth involves the turnover of investment and shows the earning power of a business from the viewpoint of stockholders.

The ratio of gross profits to sales represents the spread between the cost of goods purchased and their selling price or between manufacturing costs and sales. It is the margin of profit between sale price and cost by purchase or manufacture. The ratio of selling and general expenses to sales shows the relative cost of marketing the products and administering the business. It is the proportion of sales expended in selling goods and in administrative conduct of the enterprise. The ratio of operating profits to sales is one of the chief factors in determining whether the business is measuring up to standard in obtaining a fair return on capital. Operating profits are profits before earnings from extraneous sources, cost of financing and income taxes. The ratio of earnings available for financing to annual cost of financing is one measure of the degree of protection to borrowed capital. The ratio of surplus net profits to sales has its sig-

nificance in the light of rapidity of turnover of net worth to sales, the result of these two factors being the ratio of return on investment.

The working capital ratio is the one most frequently used, being the ratio of current assets to current liabilities, and sometimes known as the "bankers' ratio." It reveals the proportion of working capital which is furnished by the business and the proportion which is obtained from creditors, and is thus of prime concern to ordinary trade creditors in the usual course of business and to those making short-time loans.

Factors affecting the working capital ratio are rapidity of turnover of receivables and inventory, amount of credit utilized from trade creditors and the amount of working capital furnished by the capital permanently invested in the business as compared with the amount obtained on short-time loans. Receivables and inventory are major items in the working capital of most enterprises. Conditions which result in favorable or unfavorable turnover of these assets have their effect upon the working capital ratio. Rapidity of turnover of receivables is affected by the terms of credit, business conditions affecting customers' ability to pay and stringency of enforcing collections. Turnover of inventory is influenced by the character and price of the unit of product, its balanced relationship in accordance with production demands, the accumulation of slow-moving and obsolete stocks and the general volume of inventory carried in relation to sales.

Both receivables and inventory of a particular business will vary under the influence of change in these underlying conditions. The working capital ratio is affected directly by the amount of credit utilized from trade creditors. When bills are paid promptly, outstanding accounts payable are less and the ratio is more favorable. When enterprises find it difficult to pay creditors, accounts payable increase and the ratio diminishes. The working capital ratio is affected by the extent to which the necessary working capital is furnished by capital invested in the business. When working capital requirements exceed the amount furnished by the capital in the business, the excess is ordinarily obtained on short-time loans, usually through the medium of bank loans. As such short-time loans increase, the working capital ratio diminishes; as they are liquidated, the ratio increases.

Temporary financing for fluctuations

Nearly every business has seasonal fluctuations to a greater or less degree. Seasons of production, of consumption, and of intense activity place varying demands upon the working capital requirements. The normal working capital should be furnished by the invested capital or net worth of a business, but peaks within the year occasioned by unusual conditions or seasonal business may be financed by current bank loans. Fundamentally sound policy requires that current bank loans be virtually paid at least once each year in off-peak periods.

The working capital position and ratio are thus of vital significance and are under constant scrutiny by commercial bankers. The ratio is likewise of importance in connection with bond and stock issues, for no business can be conducted successfully without a sound working capital position.

The range of working capital ratios as between industries depends somewhat upon the characteristics of the industry. In business involving turnover of receivables and inventory, rapidity of turnover and purchase credit terms of the trade are dominant factors having their effect upon the ratio. An industry handling low priced commodities and giving short terms of credit requires less working capital and usually shows a higher ratio than one dealing in higher priced articles and granting longer terms of credit. Ordinarily, a ratio of at least 2 to 1 is required. This ratio has its inception, no doubt, on the theory that the enterprise shall have equally as much at stake as the creditors, if not more. Business not involving turnover of receivables and inventory does not require as high a ratio. Operators of office buildings, public utilities and professional lines frequently have ratios but slightly in excess of 1 to 1.

Ratio of net worth to total capital employed

The ratio of net worth to total capital employed reveals the relative proportions of invested capital and borrowed capital to the total capital employed in the business. Net worth includes earnings retained in the business, for they constitute a part of invested capital just as much as the original investment. Borrowed capital includes both long-term debt and current liabilities. This ratio is a measure which assists in determining the adequacy of invested capital and the security of borrowed capital. Fundamentally, the more capital the borrowing enterprise has at stake, the safer the loans. Ordinarily, except in the case of public utilities and other enterprises whose earnings possess a high degree of stability, invested capital should exceed borrowed capital. The function of borrowed capital is to finance reasonable requirements, either temporary or over a term of years. When borrowed capital exceeds invested capital, it is assuming the aspect of financing the enterprise, of sharing the element of proprietary risk, and must take added precaution as to its security.

The ratio furnishes a basis for determining the policy of financing. Sound and conservative business will borrow capital only to finance reasonable requirements which may be either temporary or over a term of years. It gives borrowed capital every assurance that it will be repaid and does not expect it to assume the least semblance of proprietary risk. The ratio of net worth to total capital employed in such business is usually high. There is another type of management that has limited invested capital and has ambitions in business beyond that warranted by the capital structure. It will borrow capital to the maximum extent possible often without much conscience as to its security. The ratio of net worth to total capital employed under this type of management is usually low and creditors must exercise precaution as to the security of borrowed capital. An enterprise that borrows capital to finance reasonable requirements is ordinarily sound and successful. One that conducts business on maximum borrowed capital often contains the elements of speculation and evades the full responsibility of proprietary risk. The ratio of net worth to total capital employed over a period of time is the key to the financial policy of an enterprise and an index to the responsibility of its management.

Eliminating influence of depreciation

It is always well to ascertain the ratio of cash or properties actually invested in the business to the total actual capital employed, eliminating all appreciation of book values in excess of original cost. The ratio then reveals the actual capital represented by invested capital as compared with borrowed capital. Irrespective of present appraisal value of properties, the investor and the banker are privileged to know how much the enterprise has actually at stake as compared with capital borrowed. This has an influence on the amount which the banker is willing to loan and on the investor in selecting his investments. The ratio on this basis may be supplemented by a ratio based upon the present value of properties as substantiated by acceptable appraisals. Consideration may then be given this supplemental ratio as conditions warrant. Fundamentally, the ratio on the cost basis has much the greater significance. This is particularly true when appraisals are not carefully and conservatively used.

This ratio concerns creditors in the order of their security. Unsecured creditors are concerned most, as they are the first to lose in case of liquidation. Secured creditors are primarily concerned with the margin of security pledged, but are also interested in the ratio of net worth to total capital employed from the standpoint of continuance of the enterprise as a going business. Few creditors covet foreclosures. Properties are of greatest value to a business as a going concern. The ratio of net worth to capital employed reveals to the secured creditor a measure of assurance that the enterprise will continue successfully as a going business and that borrowed capital will be repaid without encountering refinancings or foreclosures upon assets pledged. The ratio of a particular secured loan plus equal and underlying liens to total capital employed is likewise a measure of security of the particular secured loan. Junior liens and unsecured creditors would first absorb loss in event of financial difficulties.

Ratio of mortgage debt to assets pledged

The ratio of mortgage debt to assets pledged reflects a measure of the security and assurance that the borrowed capital will be repaid. The function of mortgage debt is to furnish permanent capital for a term of years. At maturity it is either paid or refunded. This is in contrast to the function of commercial loans. While current loans are primarily for the purpose of financing and facilitating movements of commodities during peak periods and should be liquidated at least once each year in off-peak periods, mortgage debt furnishes part of the permanent capital of the business over a period of years. It supplements the capital furnished by investment. In a profitable enterprise where earnings are in excess of the interest rate on funded debt, it automatically increases the return on investment.

The ratio of mortgage debt to assets pledged is usually based on present fair values of the assets mortgaged. In the case of commercial properties, the usual maximum ratio is approximately 50 percent. Public utility properties are bonded as a rule on the basis of a considerably higher ratio. The permanence and utility of properties have a bearing on the extent to which they may be mortgaged. By basing the ratio on present values, the owner of properties acquired in periods of low prices receives consideration on the same basis as one who has purchased more recently. Likewise, excessive considerations paid for properties are reduced to a safe bondable basis.

Ratios of stock equities to net worth

The ratios of common and preferred stock equities to net worth show the segregation of proprietary risk and are of particular concern in cases of preferred stock financing. This applies to any of the various classes of stock, both common and preferred, in accordance with their terms of priority. Stocks assume all proprietary risk. The particular business engaged in is their venture. Net profits or losses from the conduct of business are their reward. In case of reorganization or dissolution, they are the first to lose. The ratio of common stock to net worth and of preferred stock to net worth show the relative proportion of proprietary risk in the light of their respective provisions. The larger the common stock equity, the better the preferred stock. This is the same fundamental principle that underlies the safety of mortgage debt. The larger the junior equity, which loses first in case of loss, the sounder is the senior security.

Preferred stock financing is undertaken under varying conditions. This class of stock may be issued when it is not feasible to sell common stock, when it is not desirable to relinquish voting control, in place of mortgage issues with provisions restricting further liens on physical assets or as junior financing to mortgage issues when additional capital is required. When an enterprise is in its infancy with unproven earning power, or when the level of earnings of a business make it difficult to sell additional common stock, preferred stock financing is often re-

sorted to as being more inviting to the conservative investor.

In the normal industrial or commercial enterprise the ratio of preferred stock to net worth should not exceed the ratio of common stock to net worth. When preferred stock equity exceeds common stock equity, the preferred stock is assuming the major proprietary risk and its value is correspondingly weakened. Occasionally one sees preferred stock issued in excess of common stock equity but, in most such instances, it is protected by personal guarantees or deposits.

To realize the significant value of this ratio, it becomes necessary to analyze the net worth. This includes ascertaining how the capital stock was paid for, and a segregation of surplus into its elements of earnings retained in the business and the various forms of capital surplus.

Importance of earned surplus

For purposes of comparative analysis various ratios may be drawn from the balance sheet figures giving the relations of retained earnings to the items of contributive capital, net worth, appreciation surplus, etc. The significance of these ratios is great, when considered from the viewpoint of judging management policies.

The retaining of earnings in business is essential to survival. Competition tends to result in a fair return to the average concern under average conditions over a period of time.

This fair return, which business must normally yield in accordance with its hazards, permits adoption of the policy of distributing dividends representing normal interest return upon investment and retaining the balance of earnings in the business. Earnings retained in the business, constituting additional capital, are worthy of their hire and must earn a fair return the same as the original investment. Unless material financial reverses are encountered, these retained earnings accumulate with accelerating rapidity over a period of years upon the compound interest principle. Capital invested receives conservative dividends while, at the same time, the value of additional capital gradually increases. Of the three sources of additional capital—investments, loans and earnings—earnings are most significant. Favorable results attract the other two sources of capital; unfavorable results turn them to other channels.

When earnings are distributed through dividends, they become diffused, just as do the earnings of an individual who fails to conserve his income. A large portion of them are spent and thus lose their productiveness. Retained in the business, they are conserved as productive assets resulting in increased and cheaper production. The tendency of business today as indicated by the increasing number of mergers and consolidations, is toward larger business units. This increases competition and makes survival more and more difficult for the smaller business unit. The small business that does not conserve its earnings cannot hope to survive permanently in competition with the many financial advantages which larger business enjoys. The ratio of earnings retained in business to total earnings over a period of years is the greatest index of the general financial policy of an enterprise, as indicating a dissipating or conservative management and the sincerity with which it seeks to maintain a competitive position in the industry in the effort to insure a stable and relatively permanent existence.

Operating and turnover ratios in the financial and industrial investigation

Last of a series of articles which appeared originally in Manufacturing Industries during 1925 and 1926.

IN a former article the general use of ratios in financial analysis was shown, and some detailed discussion was given of the significance of various balance sheet ratios. But the most interesting type of analysis from a going business viewpoint is that given by a study of turnover ratios, which as a whole express the relationship between operating results and the capital employed. In other words, a comparison between profit and loss figures and balance sheet figures.

Turnover ratios as related to current assets are affected little by inflation and deflation, unless these movements are violent. Both sales and inventories are directly affected by changes in price levels and the ratio is affected but slightly in enterprises which have reasonably rapid turnover. It is only in industries which have very low turnover, where the process of manufacture extends over a period of from six months to one year or more, and when inflation and deflation occur very suddenly, that the ratio is noticeably affected by this factor. Ordinarily the relationship between purchase and sales prices remains reasonably constant.

Turnover ratios over a period of time reflect improved or less effective use of capital resulting from management and business conditions. If an enterprise has been unsuccessful, it furnishes a basis for study to determine whether capital has been inefficiently employed or whether there is insufficient general demand for the product to enable operations to be on a successful basis.

It is a self-evident condition that a capital of $1 turned twice will yield the same amount of profits as $2 turned once and the rate of return on investment will be twice as great. Under competitive conditions, $1 turned twice can do business upon one-half the margin of profit and yield the same rate of return on investment as $2 turned once. Ordinarily, operating ratios which deal with profit margins and the control of expenses are given more attention in analyzing the trend, success or failure of an enterprise. Turnover ratios are equally vital in their effect on the relationship of profits to a reasonable return on investment and in the ability to reduce profit margins in times of keen competition. Effective turnover of capital and profits are each essential factors in the determination of a reasonable return on investment. Efficient or inefficient use of capital, which is reflected in turnover ratios, has as much influence in determining the return on investment as the percentage of profits realized.

Turnover of total capital employed

The ratio of sales to total assets used in producing sales reveals the turnover of total capital employed. Total capital employed is represented by the assets of an enterprise irrespective of the source from which the capital is obtained. The portions of capital obtained through credit, short and long-term loans, and investment do not alter the amount of capital employed. The assets of an enterprise ordinarily include cash, receivables, inventory, deferred charges, plant and frequently intangibles. Receivables, inventory and plant are usually major items. Extraneous investments in securities or properties having no connection with the business should be eliminated in ascertaining turnover, as such assets yield income independently from income resulting from operations.

Normal turnover, in accordance with the characteristics of each industry, fixes the relationship between turnover ratio and operating profit margin so that a reasonable return will be realized on capital employed. Operating profits as used in this sense are net profits from the business available to pay cost of financing and yield return on net worth. An enterprise, marketing large units or higher priced products, will have a lower turnover than one selling small units or lower priced products. A lower turnover must of necessity have a higher profit margin in order to realize a fair return on the investment.

Turnover of receivables

The fundamental relationship between turnover and profit margin constitutes the basis by which operating results are to be judged. It is the starting point for determining the weaknesses or strength of an enterprise. The extent to which weaknesses in turnover have contributed to an insufficient return may be ferreted out through a process of elimination, by applying the turnover ratio to the principal assets comprising capital employed. These ordinarily are receivables, inventory and plant.

Turnover of receivables is revealed by the ratio of charge sales to trade receivables. Cash sales and receivables other than from trade should be eliminated as they are unrelated to credit extended on sales. In case of a seasonal business, the receivables must be averaged in order to obtain a more correct turnover for each of the periods under consideration. The turnover may be shown in the usual way in terms of sales times receivables as for example 5 to 1. Another form of expressing it is by showing the number of days' sales carried in receivables as, for instance, the receivables are equivalent to 45 days of charge sales. This is obtained by dividing the receivables by the average charge sales of one day's business.

The ratio of total charge sales to average trade receivables gives the composite turnover of all receivables. In a business making all sales upon uniform credit terms, and selling over limited territory, this composite ratio is often sufficient for general analysis of a business. When sales are made in many states and in different countries, and when varying credit terms are established in different territories and on different commodities or departments, the composite ratio is hardly sufficient in determining whether turnover has been favorable or unfavorable.

The ratio must then be applied to groups of receivables arising under different credit terms and in different territories.

The turnover ratio of receivables is significant in determining the effectiveness of the credit and collection department. A comparison of the rate of turnover with the usual terms of credit gives an indication in normal times of how rigidly collections are enforced in accordance with terms of credit extended. During periods of changing business conditions and periods of depression, credit departments are always confronted with increasing problems. Over such periods, the ratio is indicative of the general policy of credits and collections. The degree of caution with which credit has been extended, and the enforcing of collections, wield their influence in molding the ratio. The movement of the ratio over a period of years furnishes the key to changes in credit policies, to the ease of collections as affected by business conditions and to the efficiency of the credit and collection department in periods of depression as well as in normal times.

The benefits of a high rate of turnover, in contrast to a low one, are less collection expense, less possibility of bad debt losses, and decreased cost of financing. The longer an account is carried, and the longer collection effort is applied, the greater the collection expense. The possibility of bad debt losses is increased because customers who do not pay promptly often drift into financial difficulties. Low turnover results in increased capital invested in receivables which increases the cost of financing. All of these factors converge into the final result of an increase or decrease in return on capital employed and in return on net worth.

Turnover of inventory

Turnover of inventory may be stated on the basis of either sales or cost of sales. It is frequently shown in terms of sales as sales constitute the common basis for other turnovers, ratios of expense and margins of profit. The more correct basis, however, is cost of sales. The actual turnover is represented by the ratio of cost of sales to average inventory. The ratio on the basis of sales will usually show similar trends, but is less accurate because of the variations in profit margins. Under the retail method of accounting, the ratio of sales to inventory at sales prices gives the same turnover ratio as cost of sales to inventory at cost prices.

The composite ratio based on total inventory gives the turnover as a whole. More useful information is obtained by ascertaining turnover with respect to the various classes of inventory. The ratio of cost of sales to finished product gives the turnover of manufactured product or merchandise sold. The ratio of finished product to work in process gives the turnover of work in process. The ratio of total materials and supplies used to inventory of materials and supplies gives the turnover of raw materials and supplies. Ascertaining the ratio with respect to different kinds of products sold and principal classes of raw materials used leads to information on the movement of stocks and the balance maintained in inventory in accordance with production and sales.

The turnover ratio of inventory over a period of years is of assistance in ascertaining the rapidity of realization, the policy with respect to advantageous purchasing, and alertness of the purchasing department in buying as warranted by current business conditions. Variations reflect primarily the efficiency in use of capital. By ascertaining the ratio by departments or by various classes of merchandise, information can be obtained on the extent of excessive stocks and on slow-moving or obsolete goods. In a manufacturing enterprise, it assists in determining the degree of coordination between production and sales of the various products, and also the balance maintained in raw materials used in production. Very frequently, some materials used in manufacture are considerably overstocked while an insufficient quantity of others is carried. Surplus stock occasioned by advantageous purchasing is sometimes justified, but it has its dangers as well as advantages and can not form the basis of continuous policy. The foresight of a management is often revealed in the steadiness of turnover in periods of depression as well as in periods of advancing prices.

The advantages of rapid and efficient turnover are decreased cost in carrying inventories, less possibility of excess and obsolete stocks and minimum danger of loss from price declines.

Turnover of property investment

Turnover of property investment is reflected by the ratio of sales to plant. This relationship may be shown by the ratio of sales in dollars, or by the ratio of sales in units. The ratio of sales in dollars is more frequently used. During periods of inflation and deflation, the ratio based on sales in units supplements the ratio based on sales in dollars in that it eliminates the effect of and is uninfluenced by changes in price levels. In this respect it expresses a more accurate relationship between sales of production and plant.

The ratio of sales to property investment over a period of years is of assistance in determining the general policy of plant expansion, the wisdom of plant expansion which has been made and the favorable or unfavorable competitive position of the enterprise. A study to ascertain the causes of fluctuations in the ratio will reveal whether plant expansion has been undertaken in order to supply permanent sales demands, or whether the construction expenditures were made in the ambition to expand, relying upon ability to dispose of the added production. Expansion undertaken by the conservative management does not affect the ratio noticeably except perhaps for a very brief period during the following con-

struction. Expansion based upon uncertain volume usually results in lowering the ratio for a considerable period following construction.

A period of several profitable years in succession is exceedingly tempting to the undertaking of expansion. This was well-illustrated during the war period. The wisdom of such expansion is demonstrated in the ability to utilize subsequently the increased capacity and maintain the ratio of sales to plant investment. The ratio when compared with competitors will reveal a measure of competitive advantage or disadvantage which will have its effect in return on net worth.

Ratio of surplus net profits to net worth

The ratio of surplus net profits to net worth, when placed on an annual basis, expresses the earning power of a business from the viewpoint of stockholders. Although this, in itself, is not strictly a turnover ratio, it constitutes the basis for the relationship between turnover of net worth and surplus net profit margin. Normal turnover of total capital employed fixes its relationship with the ratio of operating profits. Total capital employed in this sense is total assets; operating profits are profits available for financing. After deducting from operating profits the cost of borrowed capital and income taxes, a comparable relationship exists between turnover of net worth and surplus net profit margin. The ratio of final net profits to sales must generally be sufficient, on the basis of normal turnover, to yield a fair return on net worth. The ratio of final profits to net worth is the final summing up of all turnover and operating ratios and reveals the success obtained through management in financing, turnover and operating.

The ratio of final net profits to net worth varies according to business conditions, competitive conditions, character of business, risks involved and management. A business well established and having stable conditions will realize a more uniform return and attract capital more readily than one that is new and easily affected by disturbances. New industries, such as the radio industry of today, are more speculative in character and must yield a higher return in order to attract investment. A succession of profitable years encourages expansion. Periods of depression bring keener competition, forcing lower returns and often eliminating the less efficient.

Ratio of gross profits to sales

The ratio of gross profits to sales represents the spread between cost of goods sold and net sales. Fundamentally, this margin in competitive industry varies within a range which will yield to the average concern under average conditions a fair return on capital over a period of time. This is essential to the survival of a business. From the standpoint of the individual enterprise, the margin is set by competition. As competition becomes keener in proportion to demand, gross profit margins narrow. Increasing demand in proportion to supply tends to increase prices and profit margins. Each enterprise endeavors to dispose of its commodities at maximum prices consistent with volume and thus realize as high a gross margin as competition will permit. From the gross profits realized, selling and general expenses and cost of financing must be paid. The balance remaining represents the return on investment.

The ratio in the case of merchandising or trading companies represents the spread between purchase cost and sales. It is the margin of the middleman as an agency in the handling of commodities from producer to consumer. Variations of the ratio in trading companies over a period of years are the result of business conditions, effectiveness of purchasing power and sales policies. Business conditions constitute undoubtedly the greatest factor in affecting demand for goods and thus influence gross profit margins continuously. Profit margins are under continuous surveillance by a management with the view of maintaining profitable turnover under existing business conditions. Purchasing power and changes in policies in purchasing and sales departments also wield an influence on the ratio of gross profits.

The ratio in the case of manufacturing companies represents the spread between manufacturing costs and sales. Cheaper production means lower competitive prices or larger profits. High production costs may mean competitive elimination.

In analyzing a manufacturing enterprise, some of the more important ratios concerning manufacturing costs are the ratio of total manufacturing cost to sales, ratios showing proportionate cost of materials, labor and factory expenses to total manufacturing cost, and the ratio of property expenses to property investment and to sales. Variations in the ratio of total manufacturing cost to sales are caused by conditions, competitive advantages or disadvantages, internal policies and disorders. The ratios showing proportionate cost of materials, labor and factory expenses often lead to information on material markets and labor conditions. The factory expense ratio should ordinarily decrease with increased volume. Assuming approximately uniform general price levels, a reasonably normal relationship exists between property expenses, property investment and sales. Property expenses include depreciation, insurance, taxes and repairs. Variations in these ratios over a period of years furnish a basis for study of the very vital issue of whether a concern can manufacture its product and market it at a reasonable profit.

Ratio of selling and general expenses to sales

The ratio of selling and general expenses to sales is significant of the control exercised over these expenses in relation to sales. Expenses constitute a first lien on gross profits and must be paid before arriving at earnings available for cost of financing and return on investment. Even in times of financial difficulties, expenses must be paid before bond interest, bond principal or stocks have any claim.

Fluctuations in the ratio over a period of years will reflect the change in relationship of expenses to sales as caused by business conditions. Sales are subject to continuous fluctuation by reason of changing demands and by the adoption of sales policies in accordance with changing conditions. Expenses, on the other hand, are reasonably fixed. When expenses are once increased in order to take care of sales expansion, they cannot be so readily contracted when sales volume diminishes. The ratio of expenses to sales should ordinarily decrease with increased volume. If the expense ratio increases with increased volume, there is usually a lack of coordination of expenses with sales and an indication of weakness in management. The increase in expense ratio to sales during and since the deflation of 1920 and 1921 is the most outstanding illustration of the effect of business conditions.

Ratio of operating profits to net sales

Operating profits constitute net profits, exclusive of income from investments and nonoperating sources, available for interest on borrowed capital and income taxes. Income from investments and nonoperating sources are extraneous to the particular business under consideration and cannot be included in the relationship of operating profits to sales. Interest on trade receivables and purchase discounts are elements of operating profits. Because of usual concern in the ratio of profits to sales before interest received and purchase discounts, operating profits are generally shown both before and after these items. Federal and state income taxes are shown as deductions with interest paid for the reason that extraneous income and interest paid are included in computing the tax and, in theory

at least, income taxes constitute a sharing of profits.

The ratio of operating profits to net sales represents the operating margin realized on sales. It is complementary to the turnover ratio of total capital employed, both borrowed and invested. The turnover of total capital employed fixes the relationship with operating profit margin so that a fair return is realized on capital employed. The higher the characteristic turnover of capital in an industry, the lower the characteristic profit margin. This ratio is not influenced by the manner of financing, except insofar as a certain ratio between borrowed capital and stockholders' equity is normal for a particular industry. The greater the average stability of earnings the greater will normally be the proportion of borrowed capital and the lower will be the average ratio of operating profits. From operating profits, the cost of borrowed capital is paid, leaving the remainder as a return on stockholders' investment.

Ratio of surplus net profits to sales

Surplus net profits represent the final net profits remaining as return on investment. Its ratio to sales shows the percentage realized as net profits and is the final result of all other operating ratios. This ratio is complementary to the turnover of net worth in relation to sales. Normal turnover of net worth to sales determines the ratio of surplus net profits to sales necessary to yield a fair return on investment which is expressed by the ratio of net profits to net worth. This relationship is fundamental to the permanence of an enterprise.

Variations in the ratio of surplus net profits to net sales over a period of years result from the same causes as influence the ratio of operating profits, namely, business conditions, competitive conditions and management. It is also influenced by the additional factor of cost of borrowed capital.

A strong financial structure can borrow money at less cost than one less favorably financed and thus increase its net profits.

It is evident that the analyses cited are just as applicable by the management in directing the course of its own business as they are by outside investigation in showing what the course of the business has been in the past.

With the movement of business cycles, an enterprise will experience normal times, periods of high earnings and periods of depression. During years of normal and high earnings, the management must conserve its resources, and keep a tight rein of control over operations and expenditures if it is to fortify itself to weather the trials of less favorable conditions. Careless financing and dissipation of earnings through dividends in successful years multiply the problems and usually result in financial difficulties in periods of depression. The managements of all sizable enterprises are constantly seeking improvements and greater efficiency which will enable marketing a better product or at less margin as compared with competitors. They cannot afford to overlook a single means of control. The enterprise that stands still and is content with itself soon finds itself in competitive disadvantages which result in eventual elimination. Survival, comparative position and success are the rewards of a definite constructive financial and operating policy, which reveals itself through intelligent analysis and the use of analytical findings to better the status of the business and the industry.

Accounting and business analysis for credit purposes

Before the Fifteenth Annual
Convention of The Association
of Reserve City Bankers,
Atlanta, April 29, 1926

Bankers and accountants can render great service to the investing public by bringing out the business facts behind the figures of the financial statements.

M̲R̲. CHAIRMAN and Gentlemen: I do not expect that from the group of men here assembled there will be any dissent or argument when I state my opinion that credit is the most vital single element in modern business and in modern life. You will probably also agree that each year sees the banks assuming a position of greater importance in distributing and controlling the flow of credit. When one talks of credit, he talks in terms of billions of dollars.

The main question is as to how these tremendous values are controlled and how loans may be given a greater element of security. To be sure, there are broad controls, such as change in the discount rate by the Federal Reserve Banks, and the maintenance in individual banks of a maximum aggregate of loans.

Such control factors are, however, of a very broad and general nature and have their biggest influence in times of stress. In normal times the chief factor of control lies in the care exercised in granting each individual loan. Thus the loans granted by small local banks carry back in total through the whole banking structure, and if they are unsound in detail will bring about a general unsoundness of the whole credit situation. It is all very well to assume that the initial credit is secured by the merchandise sold. But if the first payments are in the nature of a dollar down, or if the depreciation under use is great, or if profit margins are too low, or if the costs of repossession are high, then the initial assumption is faulty and the credit structure erected on these foundations will be tottering.

The better basis for credit extension is given by one banker as follows:

"The initial transaction should never be consummated until the seller has thoroughly satisfied himself of the buyer's

117

ability to pay. Failure to do this in every case causes the first weakening in the credit structure which follows."

Naturally, also, there can be either care or laxity at successive points in the credit chain, but the banks have it in their hands to enforce careful investigation at other points than those where they are directly concerned. Thus if the bank refuses certain paper from a finance company, that company will in turn demand a correction of conditions by the merchant or manufacturer before further paper is accepted. The merchant or manufacturer then in turn will improve the status of the original transactions necessitating credit.

Investigation for credit purposes

It is hard sometimes to realize that business conditions and business methods have changed tremendously in the past few decades, that the principles of mass production and mass distribution, of horizontal and vertical integrations of industry, of wide-spread operations and ownership, have created changes which necessitate corresponding changes in banking relationships.

In former times bank loans were smaller. They were more local in character. The banker was accustomed to knowing personally the executives of the business to whom the loan was made and to knowing by personal experience the history of that business. Because of this intimate relationship there was much less necessity of any investigation into the business of the prospective borrower and the question of moral risk became frequently the main consideration.

Today that tradition persists. The banker still insists on the importance of knowing the elements of moral risk, and may even let that factor overshadow the colder facts of business analysis. However, "hell is paved with good intentions." No amount of high moral integrity can compensate for poor business judgment in producing profits. Today, the moral risk is still important, but

other considerations must be recognized as well. If there is large doubt of integrity, the bank certainly does not want to have any relations with that business. But if integrity exists, then many other elements contribute to the final decision. Enough must be definitely known about the business, from all of its various angles, to insure insofar as possible the justification for the loan and the assurance of its repayment.

The chief dependence of the banker when making this investigation lies in a study of the submitted financial statements. Sometimes audited statements are available. Sometimes the bank requests statements from the company officials on a certain set form. In many cases only the company's own statements, per books, are available or requested.

It is important to note that there is a steady endeavor on the part of bank credit associations to improve the status of credit information. Some work has been done in standardizing the form in which data is requested from corporations and individuals. Where the set form is used, the current balance sheet, in some detail, is the most important single item. In addition to the balance sheet there is sometimes required a profit and loss statement for the current year. Sometimes also a reconciliation of surplus and an analysis of capital is required. Supplementary information relative to methods of current financing is almost always required, as well as data on directors and officers.

The function of the auditor

The banker's chief source of dependable information is the audit. In fact, it may be stated that practically all audits are made for some credit purpose, either direct or indirect. The audit results are submitted to banks, to credit agencies, to credit publications, or are used to establish the confidence of stockholders or the investing public.

118

In conducting negotiations with bankers, looking to a commercial loan, and, particularly, when a new contact is being made, most large companies rely upon certified financial statements to furnish the banker with the essential financial facts of their business. The use of auditors' certificates, therefore, is already prevalent and is steadily becoming more nearly universal in connection with transactions of this character.

In general, there are two forms of auditors' certificate: the short form and the long form. The short form may be approximately as follows:

"We have audited the books and accounts of the ———— Company for the year ended December 31, 1925, and hereby CERTIFY that, in our opinion, the attached balance sheet and statement of profit and income correctly reflect the financial condition of the company as at December 31, 1925, and the results from operations for the year ended on that date."

Such a certificate can be used only where the scope of the audit has been such, and the agreement of the company officials has been such as to permit a full representation of audit findings and the application of all audit adjustments in the financial statements.

If it has been impossible to satisfactorily verify any item (inventories, usually), or if the company officials refuse to accept the auditors' adjustments on such possible items as reserve for bad debts, amounts of depreciation, capitalization or expenses of certain items, deferred items, etc., then it becomes necessary to use a long form of certificate, in which the various qualifications as the auditor sees them are brought out and the statements certified subject to these qualifications.

Value of auditor's certificate

If the auditor has been trustworthy in the discharge of his obligation and has been granted full scope for his work, then a clearly worded short certificate has great value to the banker. It assures him that conditions are actually as portrayed in the financial statements, that assets listed as current are realizable in the current year, that any deferments are justified.

In many cases, however, the scope of the audit or the attitude of the management to the audit findings renders it impossible to give an unqualified short form certificate and the long certificate must then be resorted to. The long form certificate permits the auditor to state the essential qualifications of the balance sheet and profit and loss statement and at the same time to outline briefly the general extent of the balance sheet verification. This second advantage is frequently of great importance in furnishing the banker with satisfactory proof of the scope and thoroughness of the audit examinations.

If the auditor finds it necessary to qualify the financial statement which he issues, it is of great importance that the qualifications be stated so clearly and definitely that any reasonably well-informed person who reads the certificate will be apprised of the actual facts. If the inventories are priced at cost which is substantially in excess of current market, the auditor should state this fact in so many words. If the company has failed to make due provision for bad debt losses, the estimated approximate extent of the shortage should be stated. If the company is contingently liable in a large amount in respect to federal taxes of prior years, the fact of the liability and its estimated maximum amount should be stated in the certificate if it has not been disclosed on the balance sheet. Too frequently, audit certificates are issued to conform with the desires of the client rather than with the requirements of the banker or prospective investor. A statement so ambiguously worded as to give merely a hint of an essential qualification, which will be overlooked by nine men out of ten who read the certificate, is not in harmony with good professional standards. It is not even honest.

119

Despite the probable good intentions of both auditor and banker, there is still a gulf between the banker's conception of what an audit should be and the accountant's conception of the same. Partly this is because the banker cannot see the limitations of scope, of time, and expense, and the limitations imposed by client's relations which act upon the auditor. In part also it may be that the art of auditing from a credit viewpoint is still very young and when the credit procedures of the banks, themselves, are still undeveloped and unstandardized, it is natural that the auditors should not yet have a standardized viewpoint or procedure. It has taken many years to develop accounting technique. It will take many more years to produce refinement of analysis and special applications.

In many phases of the audit examination, the banker feels that he would like more detail than is usually given. It is always interesting to me that the banker is expected, by the client, to be content with merely a certificate, and that he has no moral or other right to have access to the detailed report.

The banker complains that only rarely does the auditor give so much as an opinion that the inventory is approximately correctly stated, and yet probably more situations are affected by inventory values than any other one item on the balance sheet. The auditor commonly is not expected to verify quantities, but is held responsible for the pricing of the inventories and for their clerical accuracy. The matters of extensions and footings are usually automatically verified for clerical accuracy. If the quantities are inaccurately determined or if certain types of items are included in this year's inventory which were omitted a year ago, the statement of the inventory values on the balance sheet and the earnings for the year may be affected very materially.

The auditors may have a perfect certificate as regards inventory value from the management, but this merely shifts responsibility, and inventory values have been known to be misstated both intentionally and unintentionally. And it must not be thought that the verification of quantities is outside the scope of the auditor's ability. In many annual audits, as well as in special audits preliminary to financing, our staff makes such verifications. We have seen inventory adjustments change so many good statements into poor ones that we hope the day will come when the scope of an auditor's responsibilities will be enlarged to cover at least a test check of inventory quantities.

In other words, the largest single item, certainly from the standpoint of the current position, is the inventory item. Generally speaking, the extent of the verification today upon the part of the certified public accountant really addresses itself to the clerical accuracy and not much of anything else.

The balance sheets that have fallen down, broadly speaking, have been those that carried with them an overvaluation of inventories, either rightly or wrongly, and if the dependence upon a balance sheet is as great as it is, it follows, it seems to me, that the largest single item in it must receive far more attention and consideration than it is receiving under present practice and procedure.

It isn't within the province of the certified public accountants to force any such verification upon industry as a whole. Rather, the primary responsibility rests with the bankers of this country. In other words, if the bankers do not require that type of verification in connection with the certification of balance sheets, it is very unlikely that the public accountants will be able to bring it about.

It is interesting to note, in this connection, that investment bankers have been and are in a position to force the verification of inventories, and I know of three specific instances within our own organization in the last three years where audits had been completed, and based upon the audit findings there seemed to be ample basis for the public financing. As a result, however, of a more detailed examination and business survey, which I will come to in a moment, it was proven clearly that the inventories were tremendously overvalued and when properly adjusted and given expression to, not only in the balance, but in the statement of profits, it finally developed, in connection with other factors, that there was no basis for public financing.

For the moment it appears that the investment banker is in a stronger position to demand a broader and more detailed examination than the commercial banker is, but I tell you, gentlemen, that you have not the protection you must have, if you are content with the limited inventory verifications of today.

We have also found, in connection with investigations for public financing, that the audit findings play but a very small part as a practical matter in the filing of a decision as to whether or not public financing should be undertaken.

After all, a balance sheet and a profit and loss account merely record history, nothing else. They deal with the past. There is nothing there, except of a general character, that would give you any indication or prophecy as to what might happen in the future. So that has led to the development, within recent years, of a type of investigation that is known as the industrial and financial investigation, which I want to discuss briefly at this point.

What I have tried to bring out in the first half of my paper are really these points:

First, a certificate upon the part of an auditor must be clearly worded, and in such language that anyone reading it can clearly understand it, and that the certificate must be read in detail by the banker in connection with his review of the balance sheet.

Second, that the inventory verification today falls considerably short of what it must be in order to afford greater protection to

the commercial banker in the making of loans.

Those are the two outstanding points I have tried to bring out in connection with the first half of my paper. The second half carries you into a field with which I gather most of you are unfamiliar—this so-called financial and industrial investigation type of report. It has been utilized so far, and fairly extensively, because such institutions as the Harris organization, the National City Bank, White Weld, Marshall Field, Montgomery Ward, and firms of that type insist almost uniformly on this type of investigation in connection with their industrial financing. It has been used for three different purposes:

First of all, for permanent financing, and it has been utilized therefore, by investment bankers.

Secondly, it has been utilized in the internal reorganization of business, when the economic conditions have changed, the managerial situation was unsatisfactory or other factors entered into it which called for the rebuilding of that particular business.

Thirdly, it has been utilized in connection with the private purchase of a going business.

So far, this type of investigation has been more or less limited to the three different classes that I have just enumerated.

Investigations other than audits

It is evident that in many cases the audit can be made more comprehensive and more useful to the banker, but there is a limit even to good audit work. Where the audit stops, business analysis begins. Such analysis makes use of audit figures and also brings out many features of product, markets, personnel, industry characteristics, etc.

Such analyses have to a considerable extent been used already by investment bankers preliminary to the issuance of securities, as revealing the probable inherent soundness of the business in the past and for the future. The commercial banker has not felt himself so vitally concerned, since he is more immediately interested in the current situation of the business and can benefit by the element of fixed asset security only in the event of shipwreck when salvage operations are undertaken.

It should be remembered, however, that the granting of a line of credit usually assumes the continuance of relations over a period of years, and that the current position in large degree depends upon the inherent soundness and earning capacity of the business. The elements of business analysis are coming more and more, therefore, to be applied to the purposes of a commercial loan. This is especially true where mercantile paper is handled by a number of bankers, so that the total amount may be in the millions, or comparable to the sums involved in investment financing.

Fundamentals of investigative analysis

The purpose of these investigations is to show whether the business is likely to be successful since, in the long run, it is axiomatic that the only good connections are those that year by year can show a balance on the right side. No banker ever lends money with the idea that eventually he may have to run the business. If he doubts the ability of the management he stays out. If he believes in the qualities of the management he may go in deeper than the mere statements warrant.

The question naturally arises as to just what may make a business a success or a failure. Under present industrial conditions the requirements of success may be broadly stated as:

Correct economic situation

Adequate and proper financing

Good management

All three factors are essential, for just as poor management will offset the favoring features of a properly financed business in a good industry, so inadequate financing or poor conditions for the industry as a whole will handicap good management to a possibly fatal extent.

In the past there have been, and occasionally still are, instances of success due to patent monopoly, secret formulas, exploitation of natural resources, or lucky chance of some sort. But now the elements of more intense competition, of high mechanical development, of broader markets, of mass production and distribution, of wider spread of business knowledge, have combined to standardize and stabilize the laws of industry and to render vital the three elements above stated.

In the analysis of the economic situation must be considered such things as the classification of product—whether necessity or luxury; whether the industry is new and experimental, or whether old and well established; whether the industry is dependent upon some other industry; whether competition is severe and of a price-cutting nature; whether the business is local or national in scope; whether the industry is on an incline or decline; whether saturation of the market is imminent; etc.

Each industry has its peculiarities. Usually it is inferred that if the product is a necessity such as food, clothing, shelter or transportation, the business will have greater permanence and be more secure than if it deals in a luxury. This is only generally true. Such luxury industries as tobacco, pianos, phonographs, moving pictures, candies, radio, etc., have successes which many of the "necessity" group do not. And things which appear to be necessities today may be replaced tomorrow by some more improved method, as carriages have been replaced by automobiles, kerosene lamps by electricity. Likewise, the luxuries of yesterday, silk stockings, for example, may be the staple necessities of today.

So not only the type of product must be analyzed, but the trend of the industry as well. In a sound and established industry, there should usually be an upward trend, due to increasing population. There may be an upward or downward trend due to increased or decreased variety of uses, or to replacement of or by another product. Thus, gypsum is replacing lime for wall plaster; concrete is replacing brick and macadam for roads; electricity is replacing ice in refrigerators; rayon is replacing silk.

In addition, the place of the particular business in the industry must be studied, whether it occupies a large or an insignificant place, whether competition is too strong, or is not annoying. The general production and price influences of the industry must be known in their effect on the business. The personnel of the company may even be analyzed as to their importance and influence on the industry.

There are many factors to be considered in connection with the industry study, some of which may be vital, or all of which may mean nothing. I know one industry today which is cutting its own throat by competitive prices. I know another in which the fundamental conditions are the same, but which is prosperous because some few men of real vision are in a dominant position in the industry. I know some businesses which are so isolated and local in character that they are almost uninfluenced by the situation in the rest of the industry. So it requires judgment to arrive at the influencing factors in the business, and to analyze their probable effect.

Analysis of the financial status must be made from both the static and the trend viewpoints. From the static analysis will be made deductions as to the adequacy of working capital, the form of net worth, the relations between sales, investment, earnings, receivables, inventories, notes payable, etc. From the trend viewpoint analysis will be made of increase or decrease in earnings, of future capital requirements, of ultimate capital structure, of dividend policies, etc.

This analysis is aided by the use of ratios, of which the most significant from a credit viewpoint are those advocated by the Robert Morris Associates.

The study of management involves two viewpoints: first, the analysis of organization and personnel in the light of present and future requirements; and, second, the study of management policies as reflected in past action and the results from operations. If a management has shown unsatisfactory operating results because of lack of foresight or because of failure to follow correct policies under given external or internal conditions there is little reason to hope that the future will be more successful than the past, even if general conditions in the industry are improved. Care must be taken to allocate past earnings which are the direct result of management control and those which have resulted from the favoring factors of patent or manufacturing monopoly, or natural growth of the industry. Care must likewise be used in determining changes in organization or personnel which may prevent comparison between the past and the future.

The complete investigation includes several viewpoints and several classes of data. The most usual is that bearing upon financial statements.

Since the ultimate purpose of every business is to produce earnings, it is natural that its financial statements are the most important and most informative of all the data which may be gathered concerning the business. These statements, however, portray only results. The causes—to be found in management, policies, economic status, etc. —which have led to these results may sometimes be inferred but must be proved by some more searching form of investigation.

If conditions in the present and future are to be identical with conditions in the past, then the financial results from operations may very well follow the same trend. But nowadays the conditions of industry are changing, and management must be alert in effecting internal changes to meet the effect of the external, if satisfactory earnings and satisfactory financial position are to be retained. Study of the financial statements over a period of years, therefore, permits the drawing of certain deductions as to the characteristics of management. For example, a study of the dividend record in relation to total earnings is most revealing.

When earnings are distributed through dividends they become diffused, just as do the earnings of an individual who fails to conserve his income. A large portion of them are spent and thus lose their productiveness. Retained in the business, they are conserved as productive assets resulting in increased and cheaper production. The tendency of business today as indicated by the increasing number of mergers and consolidations, is toward larger business units. This increases competition and makes survival more and more difficult for the smaller business unit. The small business that does not conserve its earnings cannot hope to survive permanently in competition with the many financial advantages which larger business enjoys. The ratio of earnings retained in business to total earnings over a period of years is the greatest index of the general financial policy of an enterprise, as indicating a dissipating or a conservative management and the sincerity with which it seeks to maintain a competitive position in the industry in the effort to insure a stable and relatively permanent existence.

Similar analyses give data indicative of other policies, good or bad. The ratio of receivables to sales by years will indicate either a lax or a close collection policy and may often be tied into the credit policy, especially if supplemented by data on collection losses. The size and character of the inventories, in relation to sales and cost of sales, will always be significant. The extent of accounts and notes payable, especially when analyzed by months, reveals

financial policy and control and the adequacy of working capital.

These financial analyses alone will not tell the entire story of a business, even when most competently made. Thus it may be found that the inventory is large in proportion to normal requirements, but it is rarely that the balance sheet will show whether this unbalanced condition relates to the majority of the principal classifications of the inventory or whether it is intensified through being restricted to one or two of the major classes of items.

Similarly an inspection of the factory may show the use of machinery which is antiquated in respect to the status of competitors, or building, machinery and processes which are not well adapted to the work in hand. It may disclose that the equipment arrangement has not been made with proper consideration for the normal sequence of the manufacturing processes or a lack of effective material or labor control. It may be found that the shop records are poor, leading to failure of effective follow-up on orders, or that material on hand and as ordered is not closely correlated with production requirements.

The design of the product may be found to be such as to make it unsatisfactory to the customer, or costly to manufacture. It may be found that parts are being manufactured which can be more cheaply purchased from some specialist in the line.

The findings of such an investigation may be significant, but unless they can be analyzed in connection with the financial results from operations, or in connection with the conduct of the business as a whole, they will tell only a small part of the story, since they are the effects of management rather than primary causes.

An analysis which combines both the financial and the engineering viewpoints has far greater value than could be possessed by either if made independently. Here a high cost of sales portrayed in the profit and loss statement could possibly be traced down and the underlying causes of the low margin of gross profit determined definitely. The shop investigation, made in connection with the engineering survey, would throw light on many of the elements of plant investment, inventories, patent investment, labor costs, material costs, burden distribution, etc.

Yet even this joint analysis would be faulty unless combined with a study of general business policies and external conditions. Thus any study of a rubber tire manufacturer would be worthless unless combined with a picture of the tire industry; and any forecast of possibilities would require a comprehensive study of the trends of the automobile industry. And the analysis of any industry over the past ten-year period must be set side by side with the story of business and economic conditions as a whole in the same period. In other words, the mere history and results of a business alone is not complete unless compared with the general conditions in which this history has been made. Any business which showed normal profits in the year 1921 must contain some exceptional elements, while a business which did not show profits in 1923 must be given most careful scrutiny to determine the influencing factors for that showing.

There are exceptions to general trends, and often the explanation is as simple as it is interesting. Thus one business showed higher profits and higher ratios of profit in 1921 than ever before in its history. This was solely because large orders had been secured in 1920, which were not cancelled, and which were produced under the low material and labor costs existent in 1921. This strikingly illustrated the speculative nature of the business, due to the interval between order and delivery, but also illustrated the quality of the management in not accumulating large inventories in a period of probable deflation.

Another business showed write-offs in 1920 and 1921 great enough to absorb all of the profits of the preceding seven years' operations. These losses were due to the accepting of all purchase commitments, to large actual inventory losses, and to protecting all dealers against sales price decline on goods in stock. Part of this loss may be ascribed to a sense of business ethics of the very highest type; much of the balance, however, constituted a reflection on the management in carrying large stocks and having large commitments at a time when prudence and foresight demanded a policy of the strictest retrenchment.

Analyses of this type are neither accounting nor engineering; they are more a probing into the very essence of business. In making investigations of this kind, analyses must be made of potential and possible markets, of competition, of sales and service policies, all of which mean much to the success or nonsuccess of a business, and which are the more or less intangible causes which lead to the tangible figures portrayed in financial statements.

Investigation outline

It is apparent that a considerable file of information and analysis may thus be accumulated, falling under fairly definite headings. The various points of importance may be broadly outlined as follows:

1. Financial statements complete
   (A) Balance sheets
   (B) Statement of profits and income and surplus accounts
2. Data on industry and economic situation
3. History and incorporation
4. Organization and personnel
5. Analysis of capital
6. Affiliated and subsidiary companies
7. Investments
8. Real estate and plant
9. Insurance
10. Funded debt
11. Federal taxes

125

12. Depreciation
13. Cash
14. Inventories
15. Notes receivable
16. Accounts receivable
17. Notes payable
18. Accounts payable
19. Sales
20. Purposes of loan

I realize that in this discussion I am probably considerably ahead of the times, so far as the commercial bankers are concerned. On the other hand, I take it that all of us are thoroughly dissatisfied with the present instruments of control. We recognize their inadequacy, and it is only through the closest study and the closest cooperation between all of these agencies that make for credit control that it is possible for us to bring about the changes that we will undoubtedly witness over the next ten years.

I have led you into deep water with respect to the type of investigation that I firmly believe will be common, looking ahead ten years, and I firmly believe that a large part of this type of investigation will take place within the credit departments of the banks, themselves. In other words, the credit departments of the banks will be organized on a larger and much more effective basis than they are organized today, when they are almost, if not at least largely, concerned with the assembling of financial data alone, and perhaps a little information on personnel, but they don't go much beyond that point.

Fundamentally the banker should be a better business man than the manufacturer or merchandiser himself. The banker sees many businesses, sees their good policies and their bad ones; he is in closer touch with the broad economic situation, and is in contact with many businesses in the same industry. Naturally, therefore, he should prove a competent business advisor. Yet his advice must be based upon an exact state-

ment and knowledge of the facts of the particular business. The more complete and dependable the information in the possession of the banker, the more valuable will be his service to the business.

There is another factor also that should be considered in this situation. When an investigation is made at the instigation of the banker, it frequently reveals facts which the management never knew existed. Thus the material valuable to the banker is of equal or greater value to the business management, and the company has doubly helped itself in going to the banker for merely financial assistance.

In our modern industrial development the trend is constantly toward greater size and complexity of organization. I wish I could have an hour to discuss organization, personnel and stock ownership problems. I think they go far deeper than most of us realize, and we can't begin to appreciate the fact that proper setup is going to have a very marked effect on industry of the future. But time won't permit my going into that.

The giant of yesterday is dwarfed by the consolidations of today and the latter bid fair to fall far short of the financial developments of tomorrow. The science of business analysis is still in its infancy. Daily, however, it becomes more valuable and more essential if we are to grapple successfully with the financial problems that are being forced upon us. In our relations to the great investing public, you bankers and we accountants who can combine an engineering and business viewpoint with the facts and figures of the profit and loss statement and the balance sheet, are offered today a tremendous opportunity for constructive service. It is my sincere belief, however, that your profession, like mine, can achieve its highest value to society only through a closer and more effective cooperation in laboring with these problems whose solution will mean a more sound and more stable financial structure.

The functions and duties of the office of comptroller

Before the American Petroleum Institute (as printed in their Bulletin of January, 1927)

It is in its broader aspects of interpretive and constructive work that the office of comptroller offers the greatest opportunities of service to industry.

ALL BUSINESS is divided, as was Gaul in Caesar's time, into three parts. The first part is the domain of those interested in production; the second part comprises distribution; the third part deals with finance and financial control. Yet each is only one part of the whole and all must be balanced in strength and importance. All must be carefully directed and coordinated, if the whole business is to be active and successful.

During the last quarter of a century there have been remarkable developments in the domain of production, in practically all lines of industry. The mechanical progress which has made possible the achievements of mass production has resulted in increased output per man, increased total output, and increased size of industrial units. Such mechanical progress has been forcing and driving the other two divisions of business, distribution and finance, at a rate almost beyond their capacity to maintain. Fortunately it has lent aid to these divisions in an indirect way. By mass production has come decreased unit costs, thus widening the field of distribution and decreasing sales resistance. By mechanical progress it has expanded the carrying capacity of railroads, has given the motor truck and improved roads, has provided handling devices of every sort, to permit fulfillment of sales deliveries. By quicker production and quicker delivery it has increased the rate of capital turnover, thus lessening the burden of finance.

Now in the more advanced industries further improvement in the conditions of actual production has become difficult and momentarily unnecessary. For the time being at least, further radical change appears improbable. Such progress as will come will be in the nature of refinements of processing and in the decreasing of costs. But in the divisions of distribution and financial control there can be no such breathing spell. They have fallen behind the pace set by production. They must be brought as rapidly as possible to the same parity of efficiency. Management of the business as a whole must direct the same intensity of effort to these problems which has recently been concentrated on the problems of production.

The requirements of management

Today I have been asked to give some few viewpoints on the problems of the financial and records division of business, as reflected in the duties and functions of the comptroller. He is the executive who marshals the field forces of the division, coordinating some phases of his work with the treasurer, some with the sales manager, and many with the general manager. Because his activities reach into and merge with practically all other functions of the business, the true scope and importance of his work is not always appreciated. Yet now, and increasingly in the future, the comptroller is one of the key men of business. This was not so true in the past, but the changing trends of business structure and business methods are steadily bringing him to the fore.

In earlier times, before the days of giant corporations and before the days of widely scattered operations, when the proprietor of a business was able to personally supervise his manufacturing, and when his market was largely local, it was possible to have effective management with very little aid from the records and accounts. Now, a few corporations may do a greater volume of business than did the combined industries of the country a century ago. Now production may be carried on in a dozen states and in a dozen countries. Now sales representatives may reach the farther edges of civilization and markets may be bounded by the seven seas. Management must, therefore, be omniscient and argus-eyed. Its information travels on wire and cable, steamship and steam line; over the ground, under the ground and in the air. Only by means of

this constant, current knowledge of all phases of the business can management hope to secure the foundation for judgment and action.

All information and data must be coordinated, correlated, assembled, recorded and analyzed—prepared for the use of management in definite pre-digested form. Upon the comptroller devolves the task of building and maintaining the greater part of this records structure. His judgment in appreciating significant data and in supplying management with comprehensive reports and analyses is a vital necessity. He must be alert in watching financial conditions, positions and requirements. He must be prepared to indicate the financial danger spots in contemplated policies of either production or distribution. He must be the watch-dog of the treasury. But more than all else, he is, under present-day conditions, the very eyes of the management.

The comptroller's contribution

During the past few decades the comptroller has necessarily directed his primary attention toward control over the production function of business. Hand in hand with the development of mass production and improved processing, he has provided the necessary records structure to disclose the true results of current accomplishment and to point the way toward further achievement. The comptroller's staff has been as necessary to the results attained in the production field as has the technical man and the practical operator. It is the comptroller who has made costs available and cost analyses possible, who has analyzed financial requirements and has often budgeted in advance the year's operations. It is the comptroller who has analyzed expense in plant and field, thereby stopping leaks and increasing the effectiveness of capital employed.

Now the main objective in production has been attained. Industry is organized to produce vast quantities on a basis of high productive efficiency. The pioneer work of the comptroller in this field is completed and the work still remaining is in the nature of refinement and improvement of existing accounting practices. Much may yet be done, much that will still further improve efficiency, decrease costs and improve managerial control, but the bigger problems have shifted to the fields of distribution and of financial consolidation.

In the production field it should be noted that the very drive for bulk of production has in itself led to inefficiencies which have been obscured by the lessened costs inherent to increased output, through overhead absorption and improved mechanical efficiency. Items such as excessive wage rates, excessive plant investment, raw material wastage and material spoilage still must be contended with and will be corrected over a period of time.

It is almost absurd, however, to devote time and detailed effort to reductions of 2 percent or 3 percent in manufacturing costs if the selling and general administrative costs may with the same effort be reduced 5 percent or 10 percent. For example, if an inventory can be reduced $1,000,000 without detrimental effect to sales or plant operation, a saving of $100,000, perhaps equivalent to 4 percent or 5 percent on costs, may be expected. This is a responsibility, in part, of the comptroller's office, just as would be the financial savings possible through prompt discounting of all bills. If jobbers' discounts of 45 percent are being given when the same business can be secured at a cost of 40 percent or even 35 percent, the differential saved to the company will be all net profit.

These are but a few of the general possibilities lying within the scope of real control over the financial and distribution phases of business. It is true that many elements of financial control are already effective. But it is generally recognized that costs of distribution are excessive in proportion to costs of production. Whether present bases of distribution must be revised, or whether it is possible to distribute economically under the present bases, is a fundamental question of the present day. Undoubtedly when the effort and attention of management is concentrated on the real problems of distribution, as it has been in the past on problems of production, similar progress toward economy and efficiency will be made.

In this war on distribution inefficiencies the comptroller must more than ever be ready to shoulder a substantial share of the load. The problems of control during development in the production field have been simple compared with the needs in this newer field. Production operations have ordinarily been centralized—distribution is essentially scattered; production deals primarily with material things, distribution deals largely with psychology and other intangibles; production requires the control of a single organization—distribution involves whole nations; production is the start—distribution is the finish.

In this new work to be done and in the further development of the production problems it is essential that the full field of the comptroller's work be recognized, and that the title be permitted to represent more than mere accounting functions and clerical activity. The opportunity exists in nearly every organization for the comptroller to be of tremendous value to the management. He should be the right-hand man of the general manager, the man to supply all needed financial information, the man to guard the finances, the man to forecast the future, in so far as that is possible. He should be a leader in promoting cooperation among the departments, and should have his department in such shape that he is always keeping pace in his records with all new developments in the company's activities.

Scope of the comptroller's functions

To see clearly the full scope of the functions and duties of the office of comptroller it may be well to consider them as divided into four distinct classes of work. Each of these classes is highly important and each one is entirely unlike any other, giving a range of interest to the work that is not always fully appreciated. These four classes, or functions, may be presented as follows:

1. The operating function covers the responsibility for maintaining all books of account, for proper control over all subsidiary accounting records, and for properly safeguarding the assets of the company as far as possible through adequate systems of internal check.

2. The interpretive function covers the preparation and presentation of reports of financial standing and of operations—in general and in detail—and the full interpretation of these reports for the benefit of other department heads or of the general officers of the company.

3. The constructive function includes responsibility for the development and improvement of all accounting procedures and all records procedures which are in any way related to the accounting work. This will include, of course, such internal audit procedures as may appear desirable.

4. The fourth function consists of attending to the special work which, although not definitely accounting, may nevertheless logically be assigned to the comptroller.

The operating function

Of the operating function very little need be said at this time. The duties in connection with this function are the most obvious and the most generally accepted of all those related to any of the functions, and in most discussions concerning the office of comptroller this is the one most generally emphasized and most discussed in detail.

It may be of interest, however, to pause long enough to point out that within this function there can be recognized a subsidiary division of work along three distinctly separate lines—or perhaps it might be better to say along lines that require in each case a different approach, a different mental attitude. These three lines may be denoted as:

1. General accounting

2. Subsidiary records work

3. Auditing

The general accounting, of course, includes all general ledger work, and it is intended here to include all detail work of a purely accounting nature such as payables, receivables, detail property accounts, etc.—in fact most of the detail ordinarily falling within the accounting department and all of the detail which has no direct operating tie-up.

The subsidiary records group is intended to cover the detail records work which has a direct relationship with detail operating control. These records may in some instances be kept in the accounting department, or they may be kept in some other functional division of the business. Included within this group are found costs, material control records, sales statistics and all records of this nature which have a definite accounting tie-up, but which have also a direct value in detail operating control. The important thing in connection with this group is that the comptroller be recognized as technical authority in the direction of this work regardless of whether he has the direct operating control. Proper correlations of the accounting functions with the operating requirements is often a real problem, and the question of organization is one of supreme importance not only in this connection but throughout the entire scope of the comptroller's work. It is not sufficient that he be held responsible by the management for the satisfactory performance of this work. The management should make sure that the relationship is clearly understood throughout the organization. To insure a uniform conception of personnel relationships, it is well to develop graphic charts showing all lines of authority and responsibility and to distribute functional instructions defining as far as possible the interlocking relationships among the various executives.

The third phase of the operating function, auditing, includes more of a responsibility for the comptroller than may appear at first glance, as responsibility for the operation of routine safeguards over the assets of the company falls within this field. This must not be confused with the periodical audit, conducted for verification of balance sheets and operating statements. The work referred to here includes voucher procedures on payables, the operating of internal checks on cash transactions, inventory test-checks, and all procedures which serve as a check-up in the transfer of property of all sorts, whether this transfer be between divisions of the company or to outside interests.

Summarizing the principal duties falling to the comptroller in this operating function, his responsibilities may be stated as follows:

First—He should be responsible for maintaining the necessary records and accounts to show accurately at all times the current financial condition of the company and the results of its operations in sufficient detail to permit of intelligent analysis.

Second—He should be responsible for directing all records work and records procedures which provide information either directly or indirectly that will later be incorporated in the books of account.

Third—He should be responsible for the proper functioning of all check or audit procedures designed to safeguard the company's assets against unauthorized disposition or loss.

Although the operating function obviously requires the greatest number of man-hours of the total time in the comptroller's department, nevertheless, if his work is properly organized the comptroller himself will devote less time to this than to either the interpretive or the constructive functions. The oper-

ating work is mostly routine and can well be delegated to some dependable assistant or assistants, leaving the comptroller free for the more intangible problems. This does not mean that the operating function is of minor importance. On the contrary, it is vital that this work be under proper control and accurately conducted in order that the interpretive function may yield results of any value; and likewise, if the operating function is poorly administered, very little of the potential value attending any constructive work on procedure can be realized.

The interpretive function

In many organizations, unfortunately, the accounting department is regarded as a necessary evil, an unproductive section that could be materially reduced in size were it not for certain laws and regulations, federal, state and local, that make its continuance necessary. This attitude, where existent, is frequently due to the fact that the comptroller is active in the operating function alone and is neglecting the development of the interpretive function.

It is in the interpretive function that the comptroller can appear as the most valuable aid to management; it is to this function that he should devote as much time as practically possible; it is this function that helps to pave the way for constructive action in every phase of the company's activity; and it is this function which makes the comptroller what he should be—the right-hand man of the general manager.

How to proceed in the development of this function is somewhat difficult to point out, as the conditions in each case will be radically different. The principal fact to be recognized, however, is that we all of us have varying degrees of ability in reading the story told by figures. Just as the man trained along mechanical lines and accustomed to working among machinery can watch and listen as a machine operates amiss and then quickly diagnose the trouble, whereas the man untrained mechanically must study his problem for a long time and then perhaps fail of solution; so the man trained to work with figures can read the story that figures tell more quickly, more accurately, and more completely than can the man not so trained. This then is the job of the comptroller—to read the story the figures tell, to read it accurately, to read it completely, and then to pass that story on in a clear and understandable form to the man or men most interested and most able to act upon the problems brought to light.

Sometimes the story disclosed may be one of insufficient working capital, sometimes it may be slow turnovers, sometimes it may be excessive bad debt losses, sometimes it may be excessive operating expense, or it may be failure in the distribution field. It may be almost anything or everything, and back of every story there is a mass of detail analysis to reach to the very roots of the trouble and to bring out a logical constructive suggestion for its correction. Study and analysis of this sort require time, and the comptroller must take time for this work. He must have his facts in detail. He must be able to discuss his case in detail, otherwise his comment may be discredited or distrusted and the value of his work lost.

A certain amount of this interpretive work has been more or less forced upon the comptroller in the requirement for balance sheets and condensed operating statements. The preparation of these may be included as a part of the interpretive function, but too frequently they are presented without comment, or with comment so superficial that it is practically worthless.

In connection with reports there is one very important point to be borne in mind. Delay in presentation rapidly decreases their value. A report that could be secured by the fourth of the month, if delayed until the fourteenth may very probably by that time be worth only one-tenth as much to the management as it would have been if delivered on time. Every effort should be made to speed up all reports affecting operations.

Every hour that can be saved may mean dollars, or hundreds of dollars, or thousands of dollars to the company through corrective action resulting therefrom. Short cuts should be searched out, non-essentials trimmed off and the final push given to get down to that earliest hour; always providing, however, that essential accuracy is not sacrificed to speed, that the facts as reported do essentially represent the true facts.

Of all the records, costs and sales statistics probably furnish the greatest opportunities for detailed interpretive analysis. In many organizations the opportunities are so broad in these two directions that the comptroller would do well to assign a man to each, exclusively for this work. The cost of their salaries would probably be returned many times over in the resultant savings or increased sales volume provided, of course, the men assigned had sufficient vision and intelligence to take advantage of the opportunities for constructive work that are offered.

The constructive function

The constructive function of the comptroller's office is less likely at present to be generally recognized and conceded to the comptroller than any other, that is, insofar as it extends beyond the limits of the accounting department itself, but, when one stops to consider, it is thoroughly logical that the comptroller should have a great deal to say about the development of records and procedures throughout the entire organization.

In the first place, the only common denominator by which all operations and all activities of the company may be measured and compared and judged is the dollar. Records that are not under a very tight control have a notable habit of being inaccurate. Control through the financial aspect of the records, properly tied-in with the general books, ordinarily secures the best accuracy and the most satisfactory results. This means, logically, that control over the tie-up with almost all subsidiary statistics should rest with the comptroller, and since he should control the tie-up, he has a natural interest in the procedure by which the results are attained.

In the second place, the comptroller's division is fundamentally a record-keeping department, whereas production is fundamentally mechanical or physical and sales is fundamentally psychological or economic. The comptroller has a primary interest therefore in clerical or records work, in mechanical equipment for office work and in up-to-date methods and procedures in general use. He is, therefore, better equipped to map out records procedures than is the head of any other division.

In the third place, as pointed out previously, the comptroller is to be expected to apply his interpretive function to all records that are in any way related to his books of account. Since he has this responsibility, he certainly should have the authority to direct the methods of building up this data. It would be obviously unfair to hold the comptroller responsible for the entries to his books and for the interpretation of detail data and yet not permit him to correct procedures that were leading to inaccuracies or were in their operation resulting in unnecessary expenditure of the company's money.

These three points certainly justify delegation to the comptroller of all responsibility for the development of records that in any way pertain to accounting and, since a centralized control over form changes and procedure changes is highly desirable, it is usually advisable that he be consulted with regard to records and record procedures of all sorts. In controlling the development phase of the work, the plan of having a committee to pass upon all changes in printed forms with the comptroller acting as chairman has been found to operate very satisfactorily in a number of instances.

In attacking this problem of records procedure throughout the organization, the comptroller should take care that his own house is placed in order first. There is a very human tendency in most business organizations to magnify the shortcomings of some other department and to minimize those of one's own department. First of all, the chart of accounts should be carefully studied to make sure that it is properly arranged for the necessary control with the minimum amount of work, and that it will properly absorb all desired changes that are contemplated in the various subsidiary records. After this, and only after this, is it safe to proceed with the changes affecting other divisions of the organization.

It is in the constructive function combined with the interpretive function that the comptroller can make his greatest contribution to the forthcoming development in distribution. A great deal must be done in the handling of data, in the arrangement of records procedures and in the organization of reports before the greatest value can be obtained from the interpretive work. The constructive work and the interpretive work should go hand in hand because of the interdependence between the two.

Special functions

In addition to the operating, interpretive and constructive functions of the office, the comptroller is almost always called upon to devote a large part of his time to special problems that continually arise and to certain regular duties that, although not accounting, are primarily records work and naturally associate themselves with accounting.

Among these regular duties, development and operation of a budget is probably the most important of all. In almost every business a budget in some form or other can be used to great advantage as an aid to administration and the time will soon be reached when it will be established as universally as the general ledger. True, its form will vary extensively as different conditions will demand different set-ups and different angles of approach, but the principle will be recognized and its existence in some form is assured. It is customary for general executives to claim that because their business is "different" it is not susceptible to budget control. But let me say that the more uniform the characteristics of a business, the easier it is to budget; while the more irregular its characteristics, the greater the need for placing it under budget control.

If a management has any idea of what the business is doing, or is trying in any way to direct its progress or feels that it has any future or any stability—that business can be budgeted. It is a comptroller's function to direct a budget program. It is usually, under present conditions, his duty to "sell" the management on the necessity for a budgetary control. The budget is the essence of business in all of its various phases and uses the vital part of each of the normal functions of the comptroller. It is, therefore, his best means of establishing control and of making known his real contribution toward the progress of the business.

It is probable that the great majority of the special duties are those on the border line between the office of treasurer and the office of comptroller, special problems that are continuously coming up in connection with finances of the company. Many of these duties that are assumed by the comptroller are no doubt often properly the duties of the treasurer, but it frequently happens that personnel will play a large part in the division of this work and that lines of theoretical organization cannot always be strictly drawn. The primary distinction between the office of treasurer and that of comptroller, however, should always be maintained. The treasurer has charge of the actual funds of the company; the comptroller has charge of the accounting for those funds.

It is in its broader aspects of interpretive and constructive work that the office of comptroller offers today the greatest opportunities of service to industry. The comptroller's problems are not simple and the demands upon him are heavy. He must be a competent technician and a capable executive; his judgment must be sound and his vision as broad as the problems of the industry in which he is employed. But it is an axiom of business that accomplishment and recognition are never strangers for long. Let the comptroller be big enough to measure up to the responsibilities that fall to his office and his rewards will be commensurate to the practical value of the contribution he makes to modern business.

Financial and industrial investigations

Published in *The Accounting Review*, Volume IV, 1929

The industrial and financial investigation is purely an extension of the analytical function of accounting.

I T HAS BEEN almost five years since I presented before the National Association of Cost Accountants some of my views on this subject. At that time I gave it as my belief that anyone engaged in this work was pioneering, blazing the trail in a new field of service. The lapse of five years has not led to any change in that viewpoint, despite the progress which has been made in methods of analysis and the more general usage of this form of investigation.

Because this class of work is so distinctly in its pioneering stages, there are wide differences of opinion and practice on the questions of purpose, scope and manner of conduct of such investigations, as well as in descriptive terminology. I cannot presume to settle these points. Yet, I can give our own impressions and practices, which represent more than ten years of work along these lines.

For many years there have been investigations which lay outside the field of accounting and were aimed at showing and interpreting some of the more active factors of business. Some of these were distinctly specialized, especially those along the lines of sales, and there are today many services which report on sales conditions and sales psychology, as a constructive aid to management. Other services are specialized along truly engineering lines, having in the main to do with plant facilities and processes. Some effort has been made to expand the scope of these specialized services to give analyses and reports which may be classed as industrial investigations or business surveys, but the result has been as a rule an incomplete viewpoint, mainly, I believe, because so little attention was paid to the financial factors of business.

On the other hand, accountants have been used to examining the financial results of businesses with but little thought to the factors which have combined to produce these financial results. In many cases the analysis and interpretation of financial results in their relation to the going business has been left to the management, the accountant perhaps feeling that the full scope of his responsibility was discharged when he presented the approved balance sheet and results from operations statement.

No one of these viewpoints has been complete. Business fundamentally is a complex structure, based on the three dominant elements of production, sales and finance, each of which is in itself complex. Any viewpoint which does not include all three elements, giving to each due weight in relation to the whole, is necessarily incomplete. Yet, seldom does an outside service fill the necessity for such a complete viewpoint. It is perhaps assumed that the management of the business is fully able to supply this coordination, provided each element, or all elements, have been covered in detail. A study of the statistics of business reveals the error of this thought, showing as it does that at the present time American business has a record of 23,000 failures annually, and that of a total of 452,853 companies filing corporation income tax returns last year, no fewer than 203,006 reported a deficit, a new high record. Merely on the basis of logic, if a business management requires outside service on the details of one or all factors of the business, should it not need an outside viewpoint and analysis of the business as a whole?

While, as I have stated, the principal attempts at overall analysis have been the outgrowth of engineering services and sales services, I have always had the feeling that complete analysis of a business lay more distinctly in the field of accounting than in any other. The accountant normally sees the *result* of all factors of a business, shown in the single picture of results from operations. This result is a composite picture, bearing the imprint, whether good or bad,

of management policies; management actions; operating facilities; sales conditions; market conditions; competition; financial and economic cycles; patent conditions; and other minor elements even down to the personalities of individuals both within and without the organization.

If the accountant has in his hands this composite picture of the business, why should he not be interested in the effects which have produced this result? Often the means of at least partial analysis are at his finger tips. He can often, with little effort, analyze costs, to give some more definite ideas along the lines of operations. He can analyze sales expense, to determine the more important factors, such as sales salaries, traveling, advertising, etc. He may perhaps be able to analyze sales by products and even profits by lines of products. He may be able to show the influence on sales of a certain few large accounts, or of certain geographic conditions. The accounting analysis of administrative expense may give a basis for further study of the management factors and policies.

The mere statement, in detail analyses of figures, of these factors of production, sales and expense is, however, only a beginning. Such figures are in themselves only results. The factors which have led to these detailed results are the things alive, often intangible, but which may be expected to be active in the future as they have been in the past.

There may be many who will say that I am wrong in thinking that the accountant can become a business advisor. Yet, is not that the final logical result of present trends? Is it not already expected that the accountant shall be able to render services beyond the mere examination and verification of financial transactions? What accountant today is not called upon to render services in connection with Federal taxes, with reorganizations and consolidations, with the reshaping of systems, records and procedures? Who, after seeing so many businesses in such intimate detail year after year, can

136

be expected to be blind to the many broad and composite aspects of business? Who has better bases for comparison between businesses or such a recognition of the facts that there are fundamental laws of business?

The wonder to me is not that the accountant should wish to broaden the scope of his work, but rather that the accounting profession has been so slow to recognize its fitness and opportunity for broader service to industry.

Perhaps that statement is somewhat drastic, for all sound progress is naturally a little slow, especially so during the pioneering stages. It must also be considered that there is small point to the development of any product or service unless there is a fundamental need for it. In this case, industry's need for a broader scope of accounting service has been felt only recently, primarily by reason of the development of larger industrial units and the increase in outside stock interests.

Management is no longer in its usual former position of sole stock ownership. It no longer deals with units so small that they can be effectively administered on the basis of personal knowledge and personal contacts. It no longer deals with a business influenced primarily by local conditions, but one which is subject to world markets and world conditions, and consisting of multiple operating units. Its problems are as diversified as its operations, not only geographically, but also functionally. Its problems arise not only from large operations but particularly in the processes of becoming large.

It has been stated that the most critical stage in the life of a business is when it reaches the point of being too large for a small business and too small for a large business. In the past a management passed through this stage by a period of slow growth and gradually became accustomed to new conditions and new viewpoints. Now, by reason of consolidations and combinations, management jumps suddenly from the small to the large. It must make the most use of outside assistance. It looks to the experience of bankers on the financial side. It solves some problems of production by retaining individual operating units. It calls in selling and advertising services on its problems of marketing, and in part may look to the accountant for revision of its records and systems. But the real problem is one of finding help for small experiences and small viewpoints which are suddenly thrown into the larger business world.

It is only human for individuals to feel great abilities. I may say it is splendidly human for man to plunge boldly into larger and little-known fields of endeavor. That is one of the causes of human progress. But the really important cause of progress is that each man may add to his own experience that of men who have traveled the path before him. It is strange, but it is true, that men are more apt to recognize their limitations in a physical sense than they are in the mental. No management hesitates to call in an architect when it wishes to add a new wing to the plant or erect a new plant. No management discounts the value of experienced advice in product design or in operating processes or equipment. Yet, how few managements will admit inability to cope with the necessary problems of policy which are vital to the business as a whole?

It has therefore come about that the main opportunity for accountants to develop a broader scope of analysis and service is provided by business interests which lie outside of the management. It is in many cases the banker who requests more than an audit of the figures. Preliminary to a proposed consolidation or financing, the banker is free to admit that he knows little or nothing about a given business. Nowadays the results from past operations may not reveal true future trends. In this era of change and development things move swiftly. The country storekeeper of yesterday is the chain store manager of today. Today's bus line may be the transcontinental aircraft line of tomorrow. In a more detailed sense we have rayon influencing the silk, wool and cotton industries. We see the automobile tourist influencing many things from the traffic of steam lines to the production of concrete; from development of oil fields to the rise of the crossroads community.

It has been the banker, more often than the management, who has asked that figures be interpreted into terms of management policy; of public demand; of marketing facilities; of competitive products or of patent protection. The banker's interest in such analyses cannot and does not cease after a particular financing is completed. As at least the moral representative of a large group of stockholders he is interested in the current trend of the business and becomes active in the event of declining earnings or lack of expected progress. Then the accountant must be ready to answer many questions, either in connection with the annual examination of accounts or as a special engagement.

If the banker feels the necessity for such industrial analysis, how much more should it be needed by the management, whose stockholdings are usually in the form of junior securities? Apropos of this viewpoint, I should like to pause a moment to read a brief abstract from an article recently published by Mr. B. C. Forbes, who says:

"A brilliantly successful businessman, worth many millions of dollars, was approached by a younger businessman whose enterprise was not doing very well, for advice as to what he should do. The younger man had inherited rather a large concern in an industry which was going backwards, not forwards. Therefore, although he was unusually able and extremely ambitious, he was finding it impossible to make satisfactory progress against the tide.

"Should he stay in the business under such discouraging circumstances, or should he sell out and enter another more promising field?

"Many men throughout America are confronted by like conditions. What should they do?

"The older business giant raised four questions which he asked the younger man to put to himself and answer, namely:

"First—Is the industry you are in growing?

"Second—Are you strategically situated so that you could attain domination of the industry?

"Third—How much would it cost you to dominate the industry?

"Fourth—If you should attain domination of the industry, would the profits be commensurate with the risks?

"The answer to each of the four questions in this instance was unfavorable. As a matter of fact, this particular industry had decreased for the whole country 50 percent in less than twenty years, and was still on the downgrade."

This, of course, deals only with one phase of the analysis which should lie within the scope of the modern accountant.

Of course, it is fairly easy to lay down the main points of a complete analysis of a given business, but such an outline sounds theoretical. It is difficult to see what the practical work and report may be like. Even a study of a number of survey reports is not very instructive, for in a dozen different analyses, there may be a dozen different important points involved. It is in a way hard to believe that an accountant or business analyst can spend a few weeks studying a situation and hope to find important factors which have not already been recognized and dealt with by a management which has been running with the business for years. Yet, the industrial survey is not merely a theory. It has had a practical application in hundreds of cases.

Perhaps the easiest method of explaining the scope and purpose of such surveys is by means of illustration. For example, a company was showing fair sales and fair earnings, but over a period of years had failed to show any real growth. The management believed that it was making every reasonable sales effort, and was inclined to state that no further expansion was possible without taking undue risk of loss of profits. The significant point revealed by the survey was that more than 90 percent of all sales was made in the two metropolitan areas of New York and Chicago, and that many other markets were undeveloped largely because of laziness on the part of the sales management. Following this report, the areas in Atlanta, Detroit, Cleveland, Philadelphia and several other large centers were opened up, leading not only to increased sales, but within a few years to increased plant facilities.

In 1922 a company was investigated preliminary to financing for the purpose of plant expansion. The business was the manufacture of California tops for automobiles. Study of automobile production by body types showed a rapidly increasing percentage of sedans and a corresponding decrease in touring cars. The price differential between the two types was also rapidly decreasing. The survey conclusion was that this business of California top production was a temporary one and would shortly be on the wane, due to the greater production of reasonably priced closed cars. This viewpoint was contrary to that held by the management, which pointed out that each year's operations showed huge increases over that of the year preceding. Expansion was undertaken despite the survey findings and bankruptcy ensued several years later.

Survey was made of a business using a novel idea in the chain store sales field. The report stated that the management was incompetent and should be replaced, since its talent was largely in the line of invention and not in the line of commercial operations. These findings were based on the fact that all operating expenses were high, that the record control was lax, and that profits had accrued only by reason of the novelty of the idea, which had allowed high selling prices. There were already distinct efforts at competitive stores, copying the basic novelty ideas, and these newcomers were not only more well run but were also offering the same goods at lower prices. These findings have since been supported by the actual developments.

In another case failure was predicted for a business unless it made a complete change of policy and product. This sounded queer, for it had a record of fifteen years' operations on a highly profitable basis. The warning was based, however, on the fact that the product was a remarkably patent-protected machine, which had no competition and only a limited field of users. The machine was not sold, but was leased at an unusually high rate. There was practically no selling organization. The manufacturing was inefficient and costly. The company's attitude toward its customers was arbitrary and the patent would expire within two years. It appeared highly probable that other manufacturers would then duplicate the machine at much lower costs and would sell outright to the company's customers, who would be glad to end their contact with the leasing company. Obviously past records of financial success had no bearing on the future status of this business.

These few examples serve to emphasize the point that the crucial factor in an analysis may lie within almost any function of the business. Often it is difficult to determine this critical factor until all divisions of activity have been studied, and it is dangerous to stop part way in an analysis, in the belief that the answer has been found, since there may be a number of other things which are also definitely out of line. Therefore the analysis will more or less completely cover certain basic divisions of the business activity.

Data on the inception, capitalization and financial history of the business may reveal certain management policies, especially as regards conservatism. Data along the lines of stock ownership will often have a bearing on the degree of real management interest and activity, for it is not unusual to find businesses decaying because the stock interests are held wholly or in large part by the estates or heirs of the founders, with the real management paid only a salary. Similarly, a study of the basis of pay and length of service of subexecutives is important, for full executive energy cannot be applied through dissatisfied administrative heads. The matter of age of the various executive and administrative heads must not be overlooked in its bearing upon future operations.

Another broad classification of the analysis relates to the characteristics of the product, for tied to that are the many factors of possible sales distribution by territories and by class of consumer, the possible methods of distribution, the factors of potential markets and of replacement sales; of sources of raw material and the attendant possibilities of vertical integration, which in turn have a bearing on costs and competition. In fact, the elements of product characteristics have a bearing upon almost every phase of the whole analysis, and no effort can be spared in definitely studying and classifying the nature of these influences.

The facts of manufacturing properties and equipment also are important. Inadequate facilities may cause higher costs, which may very definitely bear upon distribution, or may directly lead to lessened profits. Closely allied to this factor are the two factors of engineering design and labor, for both of the latter will also have a direct effect on costs, and may affect and be affected by the conditions of plant and equipment. For example, the fact of possession of a foundry may lead to union labor difficulties or may influence the design in an attempt to use castings where pressed steel would be more practical and ultimately more economical, thus bringing about a complex and interlocked problem, the roots of which may finally trace back into a matter of history or to some individual executive characteris-

tic. It is situations such as this which call for the most careful scrutiny and study.

In all cases a very careful study must be made of the industry within which a given business operates. The industry may be large or small; may be stable or uncertain; may be characterized largely by manufacturing effectiveness or largely by inventiveness. It may be composed of large numbers of small manufacturers or of a few large ones. It may be dominated and stabilized by the policies and operations of one large company, or by a powerful trade association of the principal companies. It may be long established or in its pioneering stages. It may be on the wane or on the increase. All of these points will have a pronounced bearing on the analysis of the individual business. Allied to these conditions is the question of the status of the particular company in the industry, whether it be dominant or dominated, widespread or obscure, known for quality and service, or successful by reason of lower prices.

These and many other considerations must be weighed in the course of the complete analysis, to result in a summarization of points which are important either as facts or as positive or negative conclusions. It must be understood that all of this work is designed to be analytical rather than corrective, though naturally a corrective result is partially attained. By this I mean that criticism merely as criticism is largely valueless, and that if certain factors of a business are found to be faulty, there must be the constructive sequel of suggestion for improvement. Acceptance of suggestions and their adoption into the course of the business lies within the province of the management, and that, as Kipling says, is another story. A doctor is expected to prescribe, but not to forcibly inject his medicine.

This discussion of the analytical function of the accountant might lead to the idea that the making of industrial surveys is a distinct profession in itself, or at least a very distinct division of the accounting service.

As a matter of fact it possibly could be practiced that way, but as such would be limited and would not generally benefit the accounting profession. So much of the necessary analysis is based upon an examination of the accounts, and the conclusions arrived at may be so greatly dependent upon the accuracy of the accounting data used, that in most cases an audit of the business over a period of years is an essential part of the whole work. In the final report no one can definitely say where each begins and ends, independent of the other, for they are fundamentally one thing, and therefore it has been customary to use a rather cumbersome designation, "Financial and Industrial Investigation."

Because the work is still so largely in a pioneering stage it is probable that undue emphasis has been laid upon the more unusual phases of the analysis, and so to regard the survey as a new and distinct development, rather than as what it is—purely an extension of the analytical function of accounting. I cannot emphasize that point too strongly. But, as time goes on and the work is more generally used and accepted, and as its standards become better established, this viewpoint will be so natural that present distinctions will have been forgotten. The outcome of our present elements of analysis will be broader visioned accountants and accounting work which naturally considers all phases of a business—the true function of accounting as distinguished from auditing.

There is no doubt that the schools of commerce have a large part to play in the future development of the investigating function of accounting, pioneering as they have in the past, but in broader fields. Since business is made up of the various elements of engineering, selling, producing, and financing, must not preparation for service to business give a more full consideration to all of these elements? Training men to qualify merely as auditors, and trusting that experience will provide analytical viewpoints and ability will be insufficient, and instruction, it seems to me, must go step in step with industrial progress and new conditions, but always a step ahead.

N.A.C.A. EDITORIAL DEPARTMENT
NOTE

Among the many effects brought about by the stock market crash of October, 1929, was the temporary eclipse cast over the mergers that were pending at the time. It is unfortunate that this eclipse also tended to stifle thought and discussion concerning the fundamentals underlying the merger movement. So many mergers had been put together during the bull market solely because it was easy to sell their securities to the public that the real fundamentals which are supposed to underlie mergers had, in many instances, been temporarily forgotten.

We believe that it is particularly fitting at this time, when the pace of business has slowed down somewhat, to examine these fundamentals and place before our members the thoughts on this question from a man who has had wide experience in this field. Mr. Arthur Andersen is a Charter Member of the N.A.C.A., and is the head of one of the well-known public accounting firms in this country. He is a native of the State of Illinois and has long been a resident in the Chicago area. He received his Bachelor of Business Administration Degree from the Northwestern University School of Commerce, and was for a number of years a member of the faculty of that institution, serving as the head of its Accounting Department for some time. He was one of the authors of the text material used in that University and his writings have appeared frequently in various journals of an accounting and business nature over the past few years. He is a C.P.A., of the State of Illinois, and a member of a number of professional and business associations. His paper was delivered before the Kansas City Chapter by one of his associates, Mr. W. Penn Lukens.

The possibilities and the dangers inherent in mergers, consolidations and acquisitions

Before the National Association
of Cost Accountants, Kansas City
Chapter and Published in the
N.A.C.A. Bulletin of May 15, 1930

A broad test of possible mergers is that advantages of mass production and mass merchandising best apply where the elements of personal supervision and personal service are least necessary.

IN THE PAST few years increasing attention has been given to the matter of mergers, consolidations and acquisitions, not because such combinations are any new thing in business, but because circumstances have made them more feasible and more readily accomplished. The general attitude toward mergers has been so favorable that it is often assumed that any merger is desirable and advantageous, just because it results in larger operating and distributing units. Such an assumption is dangerous. In any proposed consolidation there are factors both favorable and unfavorable, and no analysis on the basis of general theory alone will answer the question of whether probable advantage outweighs possible disadvantage.

When any consolidation is proposed, it is customary to prepare fairly complete statements of results of operations and financial position of the constituent companies and to set up pro forma combined statements, picturing the results which have been attained in operations and which will obtain in the way of assets, liabilities and capital structure. Important as such a picture is, it cannot be accepted unquestionably as an indication of what will take place when the actual new business unit is functioning as a single entity. The factors of management, markets, methods and men all will have changed and the history of the future will not be directly comparable with the history of the past.

The belief that mergers are inevitably beneficial is perhaps the result of many obvious examples but also may be due to the psychology of this country in admiring anything huge. Yet a large organization has much the same susceptibility to defective operation as has the small business and, in addition, has potential weaknesses peculiarly its own. Of course it has strengths just as much its own, which may offset some weakness but which do not eliminate the chance of weakness. In fact, pursuance of a merger policy may in itself be a great weakness unless the greatest care and intelligence are used, in that there is temptation toward too rapid a rate of expansion. Properties may be added one after another too quickly to allow for proper control and coordination, resulting in an industrial indigestion which is highly uncomfortable and may possibly be fatal. A study of the history of some of our postwar mergers will illustrate this point.

When several different businesses are merged, a major operation is performed. If it is well performed, the intent and result is attained of eliminating all of the various individual weaknesses and retaining all of the numerous individual strengths, plus the added advantages possible only because of increased size. It is rare for this perfect result to be secured, for many recent mergers have been based on financial considerations rather than on careful economic and industrial analyses, and even at best there are human faults and human errors to deal with, which modify theory and lead to practical compromises of action. Nevertheless, the period of consolidations which has just been experienced has a tremendous value, not only by reason of the impetus given to this trend, but also because the results attained will serve as examples for further study, analysis, and test.

It has been stated that there are certain basic advantages inherent in mergers and consolidations. The first thought naturally is that of the "mass" principle of operation. Sheer size is, of course, possible through growth from within, as is demonstrated by the Ford Motor Company, by Sears, Roebuck & Company, by many of the larger banks, and numerous other manufacturing and merchandising institutions. It is more easily and rapidly attained, however, by consolidation, and this principle has been fairly actively applied over the past fifty years. The idea of mass operation usually applies to the savings possible through large volume

purchasing and large volume production. The latter implies the spreading of fixed charges in factory and administrative expense over a greater number of units of product; and it is the reason for the economies possible in volume purchasing, since it in turn passes back mass production to the vendor. It also usually passes back a further element of assured demand, which can result in savings through uniformity of operation during the year and through elimination of selling expense. As a matter of fact, it may be doubted whether "mass production" advantage is an outstanding factor in these huge consolidations due to the tendency to diminishing return. That is, limitations of size of the manufacturing plant forced by limitations of supervisory control, labor supply, and other factors give the huge corporation little advantage over the merely large business. There may be some advantages in mass purchasing, however, though geographical separation of operating units limits this to some extent.

Mergers are consummated usually for some one primary purpose, as in the case of "vertical" integrations which look toward control of raw material and "horizontal" integrations, which as a rule are aimed at improvement in either distribution or production. The "vertical" type of structure in its highest development would aim at ownership and operation of basic raw materials, perhaps in the form of coal and ore supplies, cocoanut groves, linseed mills, oil wells, or timber tracts, etc. It might perhaps regulate the movement of such materials over its own railroads or steamship lines. It might operate processing or refining plants, blast or open-hearth furnaces, sawmills, flour mills, and so on. The purpose of such control is usually twofold: first, to insure continuity of supply without the possibility of exorbitant costs and, second, uniformity of quality of raw materials used. As a corporation becomes large it occupies an advantageous position as a purchaser of material, although as it becomes still larger it may be at some disadvantage since its proportionate use of raw material is so great and since its need of uniformity of operation renders it vulnerable to any interference with its material supply. If the large corporation controls its raw material operations, it may institute economies not possible to any one of the number of material suppliers, applying a merger advantage to a preliminary stage of its processing and hence further reducing the ultimate product cost.

The true "vertical" merger, of course, goes beyond the point of control over raw materials and intermediate and final processing, for it also aims at control over the final distribution of product. Perhaps the best illustrations of this form of consolidation are the well-known ones of Standard Oil, U. S. Steel, and Ford. Other types of organization effected through mergers are the "horizontal" and the "circular" consolidation. The former involves the grouping together of various businesses making practically the same product, and was the original form of General Motors. The latter is the grouping of businesses making allied or supplementary products, usually having the same distribution outlets, and well illustrated by the General Foods and Standard Brands consolidations. The present General Motors' policy which results in products such as "Frigidaire" and radios, and an interest in aircraft, also follows this "circular" principle.

One operating advantage which is confined largely to consolidations is that of having one plant devoted entirely to one product. In the ordinary business, manufacturing complexity, and therefore inefficiency, is introduced by the production of several distinct products in one plant or by producing a wide variety of sizes and styles of a given product which is occasioned by the desire for diversification or the necessity for variety. Where a number of businesses in the same industry are merged, it is often possible to rearrange operations so that one product comes from one plant, another product from a separate plant, and so on. It may even be possible, where there is only a basic single product to segregate either sizes, styles, or models by plants, or to segregate operations by plants. For example, where each plant would have the departments of stamping, machine shop and assembly a combination of plants not too widely separated might permit one plant to be devoted entirely to sheet metal work, another to machine operations and products, and another to final assembly and shipping.

It is obvious that the large corporation has a positive advantage in its ability to support research and development work on a much broader scale than can be afforded by the small concern, a familiar example being the "Proving Grounds" of General Motors. Not only can more money be allowed for these purposes but the actual scope and trend of research can be such as to lead to revolutionary developments. The apparently theoretical science and almost detached experimental attitude of such men as Langmuir, Coolidge, even Steinmetz and Jewett, would not be possible in a small situation where the demand would be for immediate, provable results. It is not entirely a matter of permissible expense but also one of permissible time. The small business does not have a long life expectancy while the big corporation believes in, expects, and practically works toward the achievement of a long-continued existence. Moreover, it is often possible in the large business to make practical tests impossible to a small one. For example, the General Electric Company could afford to have a considerable number of electrical refrigerators in the hands of the public for three or four years as a field test before it began actively and commercially to produce and sell them. The A. & P. stores can try out new merchandise or merchandising ideas or arrangements in several units over a period of months or years, keeping test records of results, with no disturbance of general plans, where the small business might not even survive such a test of new methods.

A further reason for consolidation lies in the elements of patent and process control. In general, this is not the primary or sole reason, but may be a contributing influence where other advantages exist, though there are some consolidations, such as the Radio Corporation of America, where this constitutes the main purpose. A patent has been defined as a license to litigation and its usual strength lies in the unwillingness of any other company to invite the exercise of this license. In most cases, compromises are effected where there is actual contention or patent interference, such compromise being in the form of cross licensing, patent pooling, royalty agreements, etc. In some few cases, acquisition of the infringing business has been brought about either after adjudication of a license suit or during the process of the suit. Aside from patent situations as a basis for merger, a strong patent position may make a business very desirable of acquisition by some other company from the viewpoint of product diversification. The same condition applies to a business having a well-guarded or a well-developed manufacturing process. In any merger proposal, it is essential that the facts regarding patents be clearly known for there are occasional situations in which this will have a bearing on acquisition price or on economic desirability.

It may be said that all of the preceding advantages have a bearing on manufacturing or production. Another distinct field for consideration is that involving sales. To this apply the factors affecting prices, selling expense, distribution methods and facilities, and exploitation of trade name. Since the most trying of present industrial problems lie in the field of distribution, it can be assumed that many of the present day consolidations are promoted with a view to the corrections and advantages possible through the merging of businesses in the same competitive line.

In a recent article by Mr. Harry A. Toulmin*, the following comment is made on

* "Merger Makers Must Meet These Tests"— Forbes, February, 1930.

price trends in merger situations: "In the sixty lines of manufacturing examined, twenty-six were those including mergers and twenty-one were without mergers. In the merger group, prices rose from 19 percent to 28.8 percent as against 110.6 percent during the same period for the non-merger group. Where limited mergers were present in a third group, average prices rose 70.7 percent for the same period".

Analyses of the figures of many of the large corporations reveal that there is decided evidence of a trend toward a lower ratio of profit to sales—in other words, lower prices have passed on to the public the financial benefits of consolidation and even more. Whether this is deliberately an attempt to induce greater economic consumption by reason of lower prices and broader market, or whether it is the result of more closely determined costs and more carefully calculated fair return on capital invested, or only the result of competition between giants, is a matter of speculation. Certain theories may be developed, such as assuming that the larger businesses must have good records and information, therefore are likely to be well posted as to costs, and that hence the whole trend of business is toward a smoothing out of price irregularities, toward more uniform percentages of profit, and toward price lowering rather than price cutting.

One effect of consolidations on prices normally is that the creation of a huge and fairly dominant company in an industry, operating with certain definite economies and having a fair knowledge of costs, tends to stabilize the industry practices, to eliminate the weaker concerns, to prevent extremes of prices, and to minimize destructive price cutting.

Perhaps the one result of merging several companies which is given the most attention and which is the main factor in promoting consolidations, is that of reduction in selling expense. The general theory is that the administrative sales office can supervise the sales effort of a greater number of men and can spread a fixed expense over a greater volume of sales. A secondary theory is that one salesman can handle several related sales products with very little more effort and time than he can handle one, provided the sales outlets are identical. A third point is the elimination of duplicate—perhaps triplicate or quadruplicate—sales personnel in identical territories. Naturally, these theories do not work out one hundred percent, but they are basically sound enough to show a benefit in most instances. It should be calculated normally, however, that the immediate effect of consolidation from such a sales viewpoint is a decline in the sum total of sales of the businesses joined. This is due to the cross-transfer of customer grievances, to some disinclination on the buyers' part to be solely dependent upon one source of supply, perhaps to less intensive sales effort, and similar factors.

The condition may be encountered by the combined management that the unsatisfactory reaction of salesmen prevents full realization of theoretical advantage. For example, a salesman on commission may have been earning $6,000-$7,000 annually. Given a more complete line of products and with some competition eliminated, he might, on the same commission basis, be able to make $12,000-$15,000. Yet often the effect is that he slows down in sales effort, decreases his time on the road and is content to sell only enough goods to earn $7,000-$8,000. The remedy of decreased commission rate is dangerous, and the remedy of decreased territory removes much of the sales benefit sought. The point to be observed is that it is unwise to calculate too optimistically the possible advantages which appear inherent.

The elements of reduced selling price and reduced selling expense are involved in another objective of large enterprises, that of *control* over distribution. In the past the jobber or independent agent had a real place in our economic structure and the question of his status is still sufficiently unsettled to be the subject of open discussion. In the past, few manufacturers were able to afford the attendant expense of selling either to the retailer or ultimate consumer. The details of seeking a thinly scattered market, of handling a multitude of small transactions, of carrying large stocks and of giving adequate immediate service over large territories could only be economically cared for by the grouping of numerous items which went to the same ultimate sales points. This distribution function will always remain, but the change lies in the placing of this function. Development of chain stores has resulted in a concentration of multitudes of small purchases into fewer groups and larger purchases so that the chain system central purchasing department and warehouses supply the jobbing function. Logically then, the chain system insists on buying directly from the manufacturer. On the other hand the consolidation of manufacturers often is aimed at creating a wide diversity of product and great volume of sales and the corporation, through branch offices and branch warehouses, is fully justified in claiming the jobbing function. Here, therefore, is a conflict of consolidations and of basic policies. Both are actuated by the same motive of economy of total operation but the manufacturer has the additional motive of securing control over selling effort. If he is content to let the chain merchandiser assume the jobbing function, he may soon find himself in a badly dependent condition. Considerable percentages of his output will go to a few principal customers; prices may be dictated by the chain; even the quality, type, design, and nature of his product may be specified by the outside selling organization.

Partly from the viewpoint of assuming this distribution function, but also for reasons of quick service, accessibility of material, flexibility of labor market, etc., some consolidations are guided by the acquisition of geographically diverse businesses. Factories in the east, middle west, and on the west coast are coming to be expected of a concern doing a national business, and plants in

Europe, Africa, and China are not unusual to international organizations. This imposes difficulties in administration, but these may be far offset by advantages in distribution and service.

The element of diversification of product through consolidation has been mentioned in reference to the distribution problem. This sometimes works out in the sense of producing a broader line of a given product —increased number of sizes, styles, models, or qualities—or in several products which are allied from the viewpoint of sales outlet. Thus the General Foods Corporation and Standard Brands produce a varied line of food products all of which are sold to the retail grocery stores, delicatessens, and food shops. General Motors and Chrysler have a wide variety of what is basically one product. Then there are companies having a list of products which are associated either because use is made of the same basic raw material or because manufacturing processes are similar. This factor explains why General Motors can make "Frigidaire" and radio sets and why Glidden produces paint, type metal, battery plates, and margarine.

There is a merchandising advantage, related to the matter of diversification of product, in the acquirement of a minor company by one with a well-established trade name. Then the lesser known product may be sold under the well-known brand, profiting from its prestige, perhaps to secure a higher selling price or else a greater volume of sales. The only requirement is that similar quality be maintained in the newly-acquired product to that of the old.

In addition to the selling and manufacturing advantages, it is probable that the greatest reason for diversification is broadly financial. As corporations become financially large with high public participation in capital, the elements of continuity of earnings and security enter in more strongly. If operations are confined to only one industry, it is possible and even probable that earnings will show considerable variation between years. If two or more distinct industries are served, these cyclic fluctuations tend to be minimized and the business is more nearly subject to broad economic and industrial influences.

Financially, also, the point must be considered that as the result of size comes considerable ability to secure capital for further expansion. Size permits listing on the stock exchanges, creating a more or less permanent market for securities as warranted by increased earnings or as necessary for further acquisitions.

Certain other advantages inherently possible as the result of consolidations are more general in nature and are fairly well recognized. The first is, of course, the reduction in administrative overheads; salaries of officials (while actually greater) are spread over such an increased sales volume that their ratio as an expense item is considerably reduced; the functions of purchasing, accounting, traffic, credit, etc., may be combined for the several entities and their cost ratio for personnel thereby reduced; and office space and similar expenditures may be reduced. The second point is the general improvement in management which may be secured through the higher quality of personnel. A process of retaining the best abilities of various units in important administrative positions or of seeking outside for more capable executives permits an increased effectiveness of all functions not possible to a smaller organization. A third general advantage is more intangible but may be equally important and that is the improvement in goodwill. It may be created in part by the larger advertising and sales programs which are possible, by reduced prices which result from passing on a portion of savings to the public and by a definite, businesslike policy of giving service.

Mergers are profitable if they invest in public service. Public confidence and goodwill are essential and this fact is generally recognized by most of our larger corporations at the present time. The old fear and suspicion of the public for huge enterprise was based primarily on the distrust of monopoly, and the memory of "trust busting" days is still recent enough to give pause to any adoption of policies which would tend to arouse any thought of the old practices which were once prevalent.

Considering only the foregoing factors, it would seem that consolidation is a natural cure for most business ills. The trouble, of course, is that consolidation merely creates the possibility of improved conditions and that management must formulate the policies and execute the moves to take advantage of these possibilities.

Blocking or hindering the achievement of desired ends is the ever existent human error and human weakness. As a result, consolidation may give rise to positive disadvantages. The most common of these is the obverse of one of the most generally recognized advantages—that after consolidation, general overhead may be created which is added to the unmodified overheads of all of the former individual businesses, handicapping the combined structure with an unanticipated expense burden. This may be brought about in several ways. Thus, perhaps, none of the administrative personnel is dropped and many salaries are raised because the feeling is general that the larger business should bear larger remunerations. Because of some desire for centralized control, additional records, accounts and systems are introduced. The whole thought is toward being a big business rather than an economical business. Often it takes one or two full years of operations staggering under excessive expense before sound viewpoints are restored. In similar fashion there is often the desire to set up very elaborate and expensive central sales and administrative offices. One instance is recalled of a force of 200 draftsmen working in office space which was rented at a cost of $3.00 per square foot per year, these men for the most part having been brought in from plant offices where the square foot cost approxi-

mated $0.40 per year. The establishing of central offices in some city such as New York or Chicago as against former plant offices in Peoria, Kalamazoo, Utica, or Springfield means increased rates of pay for everyone from comptroller to office boy, and the expense difference must be closely weighed against the economies of centralized work and the advantages of accessible and respect-commanding location.

A much less obvious danger, but one no less powerful, is that in the process of organization revision there may be an almost complete loss of the individual initiative which has been responsible for the success of the predecessor companies. Naturally, this may come about through the actual fact of consolidation when former owners sell out completely to the new corporation and retire from business, but it is also possible when most of the former personnel is retained. If the old managements remain, but do not hold stock in the corporation, management interest is lost. The remedy of creating profit-sharing contracts is feasible but dangerous. They may drain the expected earnings of the new business or they may be set too low in view of the general financial results attained.

Moreover, even if all financial interests are properly cared for, an attempt to centralize the management and control may remove from the operating units the elements of close personal supervision that have been the custom for years. With the various principal executives grouped in offices remote from the plants, various plant inefficiencies may develop, operating difficulties arise, and employment discontent occur, which proceed unchecked.

The same conditions of single control instead of former multiple controls and the consequent enforced contact of men previously more used to working alone leads to almost unpredictable results. There is very often an almost political jockeying for power. The qualities of strength and dominance in some one man which may have brought about the merger and which may have seemed admirable during the process of merging may be interpreted as arrogance, stubbornness, or selfishness after the deal is completed. Where the organization may have been preplanned to control adequately the various factors of management, dissatisfaction may lead to withdrawals which wreck the proposed plan. There may be disruption due to clashes of personal temperament or there may be trouble due to the desire of each former executive to regard his unit as the most important with the best personnel and the most effective policies and systems. The desire to elevate former employees to higher positions often causes as much trouble as any desire for personal prestige.

Even where there are few elements of discord, the human factor may be operative to cause trouble. That is, the new company is larger than any former single unit; its problems are greater and its policies are different. Perhaps no one in the predecessor companies is adequately equipped in experience and viewpoint to be fully capable in his new duties. It has often been said that the most critical point in a company's history is when it is too big for a small business and too small for a big business. But at least the management is given a period of time to grow in experience to meet the complexities of a growing business. Under the method of consolidation, there is no time, experience, or preparation given for individual growth. The executive of a small business one day is part of a national organization the next, and this is true of all who have any general administrative function.

Not only must the business contend with inexperience of personnel but, as has been indicated, with the sudden inflations of personal importance. Too often men do not apply fully their given abilities to a new situation, partly because individual equity is diluted, partly because individual responsi-

bility is narrowed in scope, but partly because they feel too important to work hard.

Another limiting factor of human initiative sometimes applies where the former executives have made considerable money in the market through enhancement of stock values by reason of the merger. To many it may have been a new experience in the field of easy money. Their attention becomes diverted from the operations of producing and selling goods to the operation of buying, selling, and manipulating stock. Eventually the business suffers from lack of attention and, of course, stock profits pass out of the range of manipulation.

It is evident that some few of these potential personnel weaknesses are inherent only in consolidations, but the majority are possible also where large size is attained independently of consolidations. In other words, very often huge size in a corporation leads to personnel weaknesses. This is contrary to the vague general belief that mere size is a guarantee of strength. In a naturally growing organization it is well now and then to take inventory of the personnel situation in relation to the increased scope and responsibilities of the various executive and administrative heads, and perhaps to make shifts in organization plan and replacements or additions of personnel in line with the growing needs of the business.

In cases where largely increased size will result from mergers or acquisitions, it is vital that the questions of personnel fitness, adaptability, temperament, etc., be given the most careful scrutiny. In fact, it might well be the rule that no final merger steps be taken until an analysis of personnel and organization, present and proposed, has been made and the results either approved as satisfactory or else completely sound revisions developed to take care of the potential weaknesses revealed thereby.

All of this may sound pessimistic, but fortunately all of the potential dangers rarely occur in any one given situation and most of them are correctible if recognized. Usually, too, elements of outside viewpoint and outside control have been introduced in conjunction with the financing of the consolidation which are reasonably alert for evidence of personnel and organization weaknesses. The point which may be noted is that the potential advantages inherent in consolidations are mainly in different fields from the possible disadvantages and that neither tend to modify or affect the other. An economically sound consolidation may be thoroughly wrecked by weaknesses of personnel and it is not sufficient to consider only the plus or only the minus side of the question when any merger is contemplated. Nor is a careful presurvey alone sufficient in safeguarding against disaster since either unsuspected strengths or weaknesses may come to light after consummation of the deal.

The factors of advantage and disadvantage which have been pointed out perhaps may seem theoretical in nature, yet practically all have been observed in operation in one situation or another. Whether any given proposal is advantageous may be fairly well determined if time is allowed for a careful analysis of the situation. Each company involved may be studied as to individual characteristics, the industry factors may be determined and a fair picture may be drawn of the probable results to be secured by the process of consolidation. Inherent advantages are seldom obscure and many of the possible weaknesses may be anticipated and guarded against.

Some much broader viewpoints must be taken, however, in considering the general feasibility of mergers or in attempting to indicate the types of industry or the types of situation in which mergers will be desirable. For example, in an article by Mr. A. A. Hadden* it is stated that in 79 percent of 850 companies questioned, price cutting is listed as a major problem of the industry. Ten industries are listed in the order of the intensity of this factor as follows:

1. Chemicals
2. Textiles
3. Lumber and wood products, brass and bronze products
4. Stone, clay and glass products
5. Printing
6. Food products
7. Paper
8. Iron and steel products
9. Leather
10. Machinery

Since consolidation has in general an effect of price stabilization, it might be expected that consolidations would be beneficial in these industries in the order of their listing.

Another broad test that is worth thinking about is that advantages of mass production and mass merchandising best apply where the elements of personal supervision and personal service are least necessary. Thus industries in which production may be highly automatically mechanized, such as the automobile business, steel production, soap production, oil refining, textile working and some phases of food preparation are most susceptible to successful consolidation. Where merchandising is largely a matter of price, as in the Kresge, Woolworth, Grant, etc., stores, large scale merchandising is feasible. Where service also must be considered to some extent as in the A & P, Penney, Kroger, etc., stores, some provision usually must be made to secure it through local management interest, the real merger advantage lying in large scale purchasing. In large department stores handling quality merchandise, in specialty shops, etc., where personal service and contact is predominant, large scale and widely spread operations are rarely feasible and hence merger advantages are at the minimum.

*Does Competition Fix Prices—Bulletin of the Society of Industrial Engineers—January, 1930.

151

In seeking logical merger opportunities, the first thought is of an industry in which there is a large, continuous demand for the product, where great mechanical equipment is essential, or where an exact standardization of procedure is possible under all conditions. On the other hand, some industries already may be consolidated to the point where further merging is difficult. The result of a rather broad analysis, considering most of the factors involved, indicates that the best present merger possibilities lie within the following industries:

1. Drugs, medicines, and cosmetics
2. Office and business equipment
3. Food products
4. Automobile parts and accessories
5. Chemicals
6. Electrical equipment
7. Machinery and equipment
8. Railroads

In many of these industries the necessities for consolidation are found in consideration of the problems of merchandising which are becoming especially critical as regards the drug and food lines.

It is unlikely that the change in status of the stock market will create any great change in the status of mergers. It is true that many pending mergers were temporarily or permanently abandoned as the result of the market break of which Sears-Penney, Ward-Hartman, and National City-Corn Exchange may be noted as typical. But many are only delayed and many new combinations will be proposed. There is just as much reason and perhaps even more reason for carrying out mergers in difficult times as in prosperous times and the main difference will lie in the financial means adopted. In the past year or so it has not been possible to finance publicly and many acquisitions have been for cash. In the future there will, of course, be many sound security offerings to cover economically worthy consolidations and many will be effected also on an exchange-of-stock basis.

One fact which may tend to promote a large number of smaller acquisitions in the current year is the exceedingly strong liquid capital position of many of the larger businesses, resulting from the sizable earnings of the past few years and in many cases from the correction of capital structure made possible by the easy financing conditions of the recent bull market. Many corporations appear even to be overfinanced and may acquire smaller businesses just as a means of securing adequate return on available capital and of diversification of product. The stock market deflation has largely increased the possibility of such small acquisitions on a favorable basis.

While many industrial situations have been improved as the result of mergers already accomplished, it would seem that many of the corrections have been palliative rather than permanent or basic. The great problems of distribution have barely been recognized. It would seem that the ultimate logical trend is that toward a distribution of product directly from producer to consumer and various moves have been made, perhaps unconsciously, toward this end. For example, Drug, Inc., has 10,000 Rexall stores, 524 Liggett stores and 800 Booth stores and is constantly adding to these distribution outlets; but it also controls factories producing rubber goods, candy, food products, stationery, and a long line of medicinals. It has factories in a dozen cities and retail stores which reach 25 percent of the population of the United States. The Walgreen chain is continuously adding to its retail drug stores and just as continuously acquiring its own producing sources. Montgomery Ward and Sears Roebuck have for a long time been controlling much of their own production and are intensively cultivating direct retail store distribution. Many of the chain food stores are seeking control over production which will carry their own brand names.

These moves are most noticeable in the attempt of retail outlets to acquire control over production. At the same time the pressure applied to various manufacturers by the growing strength of the distributing chains is pointing to a necessity for protection of these producing interests. This may be shown particularly in considering the food chains since their development is greatest. A given producer at present may find that as much as 25 percent of his output is being taken by the chains at prices which barely absorb overhead. Pressure to secure a price increase is probably ineffective and may even result in loss of an account. The producers look forward to two possibilities —either that the percentage of sales to chain stores will increase to a point where absolute dictation of destructively low prices is possible, or that the chains will develop or acquire their own sources of production. The situation of the producers who are dependent upon sales to chains is none too bright.

The apparent present method of combating this situation lies in consolidation of producing units for the purpose of regaining dominance over the distributing units. If a chain wishes to discontinue handling a given brand of canned vegetables, for example, it can find half a dozen other nationally advertised brands which, in general, will be equally acceptable to the consuming public, or it may introduce its own brand, trusting that this exception will not attract any particular attention and will be carried along by the chain store prestige. But if the producer of a given brand of canned vegetables also controls a brand of canned fruits, of condensed milk, of pickles and condiments, of cheese, of cocoa, etc., then enough pressure can be applied to prevent the store dropping the brand of canned vegetables.

Whether this is only a theory is hard to say, but when Standard Brands are considered, producing yeast, baking powder, coffee, etc., or General Foods, with a line of Postum, cereals, coffee, tea, cocoa, cocoanut, syrups, gelatine, tapioca, mayonnaise, cake flour, condiments, etc., it would appear that the principle is at work. These consolidation moves are tentative as yet and there is room for several tremendously large food product mergers. Along with the true food products may be considered those lines which use in part the same food store outlet—such as soaps, toilet paper, matches, ginger ale and other soft drinks. The list of companies which may in the near future be considered for food group consolidations is long and most of the companies are nationally known.

The possibility of such huge food group mergers is perhaps only a sort of defensive or intermediate step in line with the ultimate direct-to-consumer trend. Size and dominance of the producing units opposed to size and dominance of distribution chains would lead to a deadlock with retrogressive economic tendencies. Admission of the real trend, on the other hand, would lead to full consideration of the thought of consolidating huge producer with huge distributor. It is not too farfetched even now to visualize the thought of consolidation between, say, Kroger and General Foods, yet both groups are small in size now as compared to what they will attain ten years from now.

The situation as regards food products perhaps has been emphasized as though it were the only line in which such trends exist, but this emphasis is given only because there the trends are already being translated into action and conditions are more nearly ripe for the ultimate move.

It is evident that the trends in consolidation will carry far beyond the present stage and that the moves which may be made will write new pages in the records of business, economic and perhaps political theory and history. Some of the possible changes are almost staggering in their immensity and one wonders if human ability is capable of understanding and directing the forces which must be created, used, modified and experimented with. The encouraging thought is that what man has done, man can do, and that all past progress has been built upon previous progress. Certainly, the coming three decades promise to be as interesting a period of business achievement as have the past three in breeding and nurturing our new race of industrial giants.

The major problem created by the machine age

Before the National Association
of Cost Accountants, Detroit,
February 26, 1931

*It is time that our much
vaunted industrial system paid
as much attention to the
unemployment of labor as it does
to the unemployment of capital.*

ON THE SEVERAL occasions in which I have appeared before the National Association of Cost Accountants, I have always felt the urge to speak freely and perhaps a bit philosophically on certain important phases of business. This is largely for the reason that I believe there is in this organization a real breadth of viewpoint and a depth of understanding in respect to the fundamental conditions upon which all business rests.

That wonderful film, "Power in the Making," which has just been witnessed, brings home the tremendous mechanical development that has taken place in this country in perhaps the last decade or two, with greater emphasis on the last decade. Many of us are inclined to accept this growth as a natural thing, and we fail to realize that for an industrial civilization to continue to exist, it must continue to serve mankind in the broadest possible sense, which is the purpose of all civilization. We fail to take into account the dangers which may be inherent in the rapidity with which these machine changes are brought about. Therefore, I think I can say that business statesmen should be far more concerned today with the broad meaning of the unemployment situation that exists than with merely the immediate means of relieving the effects of this unemployment. The depression itself, of course, was not solely and wholly attributable to the unemployment situation any more than unemployment results solely from the depression. There are many other collateral things which have entered into it, one of which is undoubtedly the drop in the value of silver. But as against all the factors that have been brought before us as accounting for the extreme condition of unemployment, I think we can lay our finger on the one single outstanding condition, namely, the intensive development of mass production.

It has been said that all things carry within themselves the seed of their own destruction, and in the past year I have been wondering if this is true also of our present industrial system. I speak not as an economist, a statistician or as a radical, but rather as an interested eye-witness of events that cannot help but have profound meanings. For over a year the air has been thick with subjects of discussion. Bankers have dealt with matters of national and international credits, trade balances, gold movements and so on. Economists have pondered over the means of interpreting and correcting cyclic movements. Manufacturers have had their problems of excess capacity, keen competition, declining commodity prices and revision of costs. But all men have had one subject of discussion in common, namely, unemployment.

If there is a germ of destruction within our present industrial system, it is that of the growing element of unemployment. It has been said that the most beautiful thing in the world is youth, and a pity it has to be wasted on children! But in my opinion nothing is more beautiful than a steady job, and that usually becomes more valuable as the age of its possessor increases. It is increasingly difficult for men who have crossed the 40-year line in age to find jobs, or make new connections. Unemployment itself is a simply defined thing. It consists merely in a lack of work for one who desires to work. The complex factors enter in when one seeks the causes of unemployment and the results of unemployment. Basically there are four types of unemployment which may be defined in terms of fundamental cause as (1) residual, (2) cyclic, (3) social, and (4) technological, which is a word of more recent coinage. The last named is the type which seems to me to be the most dangerous, for it is truly created by the present machine age and if not checked by intelligent action will continue to grow in volume and in evil effects.

Residual unemployment is that which has been always with us and probably always will be. It is produced by restlessness and unfitness. It is that due to an interval between jobs. Normally, it is of small percentage, is not particularly harmful, and is not susceptible to any present practical control.

Cyclic unemployment is that which appears in times of industrial recession and is the type which is most evident. It comes about because of a diminished production, which is usually the aftermath of overproduction. I have little patience with the view that in a country like this we must have our depressions in order to continue to go forward. In other words, if these depressions are a necessary consequence of prosperity, then are we not paying much more for prosperity than prosperity itself is worth? These industrial cycles have occurred very definitely in the past hundred years, with elements of almost uncanny regularity. They have been the subject of voluminous study and analysis and everything about them is clearly known, except how to prevent their recurrence. Such unemployment is regarded as almost inevitable but is, on the long scale, temporary. It is to relieve cyclic unemployment that thought is given to unemployment insurance, to workingmen's doles, and so forth. I believe the American workingman does not want paternalism, yet always it seems that more thought is given to lessening the ill effects of cyclic unemployment than to preventing it.

Social unemployment is the name I have given to the lack of work caused by the increased efficiency of workers when they are massed together for productive purposes. For example, ten men might be engaged in making shoes entirely with hand tools and hand labor and their average output may be one pair per day per man, when each worker performs every operation on one shoe. If the ten men are grouped together, each performing certain operations on all shoes, the increased dexterity of operation may result in a total output of fifteen pairs of shoes per day. Obviously, in this case the potential employment of five more men is lost, which may be classed as social unemployment for that five. A more practical present-day application of this is seen in the operation of packing plants, where there is a tremendous percentage of hand labor with simple tools, but where high efficiency is attained by the subdivision of operation, the careful planning of the work and the large volume of material consecutively handled without lost time.

Closely allied to the factor of social unemployment is that of technological unemployment. It is caused by the increased efficiency of workers when they are provided with proper machine tools. It may be very simply illustrated by the fact that one man with a steam shovel replaces 100 men with shovels. It is very intricately illustrated in any one of our modern factories, where, by the use of standard and special tools, of conveyors, of automatic machinery, of subdivision of operations, of carefully planned routine, the per man output per day may be as great as the per man output per year might be otherwise. It is extremely difficult to evaluate all of the factors of technological unemployment, for there are tremendous compensating elements. Thus, under the machine system, it is possible to make things which could not possibly be made under the hand labor system and so employment in huge amounts is created.

Social unemployment and technological unemployment thus go hand in hand. Machine methods of production could not very well be effective without the social grouping of workers, and social unemployment would have little consequence were it not for the reenforcing effect of technological unemployment. Thus, it is possible to consider social unemployment as an integral part of the former. Similarly, it is difficult to disassociate this from a pronounced effect on the other two types of unemployment. Tremendous machine development permits tremendous output, and the overgearing of production thus possible permits accumulation of stocks and may result in cyclic unemployment. In times of activity the demand for increasing output requires that there be effective machine operators but, as demand falls off, there is sterner competition, costs become important, personnel requirements are tightened, and the general tendency of American industry of the better managed companies is to make closer and more careful study of personnel requirements, and translated in terms of individual function, they not only study present capabilities but they go back into heredity to determine all the factors. In other words, the demands that are to be made upon the coming generation with respect to measuring up to higher standards of everything will be far beyond what you have witnessed in our generation and, of course, ours is correspondingly higher than that required of the preceding generation. Personnel requirements are tightened and only the most efficient, younger and more physically fit of the workers are desired. Dexterity is demanded rather than skill. Therefore, larger numbers of the semi-unfit are rejected and residual unemployment increases. Truly, technological unemployment is the major problem created by the machine age!

It may be questioned just how real this bogey is. For an answer one needs only to turn to data compiled by the Federal Reserve Board, recently published, showing the volume of manufacturing production and the corresponding number of employees for the past 30 years. If the output per employee is taken as being unity in 1899, then the output per employee was approximately 1.63 in 1929, and despite decreased output and the effort to maintain employment was still 1.42 in 1930. In other words, two men today can produce the output of three men in 1899. Unfortunately, this comparison does not begin to tell the whole story, for practically this entire change has taken place in the last ten years. It is interesting to note the years taken to bring about the development in the generation of power, as illustrated in the movie that we saw tonight. Despite our tremendous volume of manufacturing in 1929, there were less actual employees in that year than there were in 1917, 1918, 1919, 1920 or in 1923.

It is, of course, easy to say that as men are released from one class of industry by improved effectiveness of equipment, they are absorbed by some newly developed industry. This has been the "luck" upon which we have rested so far. The old "machine fear" has been held by labor for more than the past hundred years and in specific instances has led to riots, strikes and destruction of equipment, and more passively to restricted output and "soldiering," but thus far there has been no drastic culmination of the replacement of men by machines. This is because the machine factor has, to a considerable extent, always carried with it a twin factor which tended to nullify the possible evil effects of machine production. The human ingenuity which has made machines possible has also succeeded in devising new things for machines to produce. In the last century one new industry has followed another in a procession of miracles, so endlessly that one ceased to expect an end. Now, we must give thought to the possibility of a continued ingenuity in the development of machine processes, with a slackening in the devising of new products.

Perhaps there are devices for human use far beyond the realm of present imagining, yet the rate of increase in new devices cannot be maintained. The necessities of the human race are fairly simple in their broad classification and, in the past, luxuries have been converted industrially into necessities. In the order of their importance and of their development, our necessities are food, shelter, clothing, transportation and amusement. The basic elements of the first three have long been developed and are now subject only to refinements. The factor of transportation really has only been developed industrially in the past hundred years, and our

railroads, steamship and automobile industries are partial indices of its importance. They also are partially by-products of the necessity for amusement, while the phonograph, radio and moving picture industries indicate how seriously we take our amusements. Thus two of our five necessities are only recently of large development. Communication is a part of transportation and a part of amusement, so to the industries already noted may be added our telephone and telegraph systems and a good part of the printing industry. It would appear that practically the major part of our present industrial activity is devoted to our two recently acquired necessities. Can anyone suggest where we may find two or three new necessities to take up the slack in employment created by a more perfected mechanization of those we now have?

While these basic facts of technological unemployment have been evident for the past several years, their importance has been obscured by a decade of industrial prosperity where employment has been created by the artificial stimulus of credit and nothing more and nothing less. Now, when the pinch has come, they reveal their influence. Recently a prominent economist stated, "The development of a new industry to absorb large numbers of workers, as did the automobile business ten years ago, is unlikely in the near future. . . . The long term trend of factory employment, especially in the industries where the machine predominates, is downward." Similarly, the editorial comment on a recently published book significantly states, "It emphasizes the increasingly important problem of unemployment in prosperous times rather than during business depression." These and similar comments indicate the truth of the idea that man does much constructive thinking in times of adversity.

This trend of comment indicates that thought is being given to an analysis of the factor of unemployment in relation to the whole scheme of industry. But, in addition, there are various stray literary sparks which indicate that thought is being given to the constructive answer to some unemployment problems. Thus, from a publication of the United States Chamber of Commerce comes the comment, "The acceptance of the theory that prosperity is contingent upon the continuous employment of virtually the entire working population places a large share of the responsibility for stabilizing employment squarely upon the management of industrial enterprises." If there is any criticism of American business, it lies in this direction, as I see it, namely, there has been an inability to recognize this rather important and serious trend which in itself would inevitably create problems that would call for the greatest brains that this country can produce in the way of business statesmanship. From another source we hear, "It is time that our much vaunted industrial supremacy took account of its own shortcomings and paid as much attention to the unemployment of labor as it does to the unemployment of capital." That sounds like a socialistic statement. It is not anything of the kind. It means merely that the capitalistic principle, which probably is the only satisfactory method of working out the problems of all of the peoples of the world, must be modified in order to meet changing conditions, in order to discharge its responsibility, not only to the capitalists, to whom it must look for leadership, but also to the large majority of workers that make up in part the capitalistic system.

Another editor believes that: "Work should be shared among many employees during depression periods rather than dismiss a portion of the working force." Less technical, and therefore less obscure, is the comment, "Every worker, almost without exception, when he starts discussing unemployment, declares emphatically, even vehemently, that the remedy is the shortening of the work week, also the day."

The present critical aspects of the problem of unemployment have been largely conditions have been changed in the past ten years. This speed was in part caused by the intense stimulus to production brought about by the war (both war and postwar). In other words, many of us failed to realize that the condition which led to the prosperity of 1929 was really an accumulation of necessities which could not be met during the war and that as soon as the war was over we started out to fulfill these requirements. What were they? Buildings, concrete roads, automobiles, and many other things. That was the basis to start with of the intensive manufacturing demand which existed following 1920 and 1921 and made up in a large measure the period of prosperity that then followed. Perhaps also the depression of 1921 caused a lot of constructive thinking and planning on the part of our masters of industry. Another factor, of course, has been the injection of a huge volume of credit in this period to permit radical change in manufacturing equipment and methods. A subfactor in the problem has been the injection into industry of an increasing number of women workers.

This latter phenomenon has been variously interpreted. Some lay it to the necessity for women workers when man power was depleted by the formation of huge armies. Some class it as a psychological trend. "The new freedom of women,"—women desiring recognition of economic parity with men. Both of these forces have probably had a share, but the real factor is that of our old enemy, technological unemployment. That is, woman's original work in caring for the home has been tremendously decreased by the benefits of the machine age, and women thrown out of employment in home care have sought employment in other fields. Machine assistance to home care must not be interpreted merely in terms of washing machines, vacuum cleaners, electric irons and other direct aids, but must include the indirect effect of our huge textile industries, the clothing industry, baking industry, canning and meat packing industries, and so forth. It must also include the effect of electric light and power, of automobiles, of improved home building and heating, and of the effect of apartment and hotel life. The old adage that woman's work is never done can now almost be translated to mean that nowadays it is never done by the woman herself. Of course, the usual compensating factors have appeared in that the textile and clothing industries provide employment for hundreds of thousands of women, that innumerable women clerks are required in distribution, that use of automobiles by women in their spare time has led to larger growth in that industry and perhaps even that there is greatly increased production in bridge tables and playing cards. The sum total, however, is an increase in technological unemployment.

On the other side, factors have been at work which have tended to minimize the growth of unemployment. Our improved standards of living and other elements have led to legal regulation of child labor, thus eliminating some workers. They have led to compulsory education, thus providing for a greater number of educational workers and to employment in the construction of school buildings. Voluntary education, made possible by greater per capita wealth, leads to the existence of 800,000 students in our colleges and universities who are consumers but not producers. There has also been a trend toward shorter working hours per week, not from recognition of any distinct economic law, but largely for physical, social or psychological reasons.

Unemployment in any form is a problem created purely by our social structure. If we may think back to prehistoric times when man existed as an individual, when necessities were the simple stark matters of food and shelter, it is evident that there was no unemployment. If man was hungry, he sought food. If this employment did not net a sufficient return, he died. Only the capable workers survived. The first social order of mankind probably had to do with the matter of protection, which is one element of shelter, and is man's second necessity. It is probable that industrial cooperation was an almost immediate sequence as men found that food and shelter could more readily be procured by group effort than by effort of a lone individual. Still there was probably no unemployment, but the ground for unemployment was laid since where there are group resources there are always possibilities of charity.

In these first social groupings and, in fact, wherever the social grouping is small, it is difficult for unemployment to exist. In the days of early settlement in this country, mankind had advanced far in mentality, in civilization and in equipment, yet primitive conditions of necessity existed. In those days the old law was asserted by Captain John Smith when he stated, "Those who won't work shan't eat." There is an individual consciousness as distinct from a state consciousness, since the burden imposed by any unemployment was instantly felt and directly translated into increased effort of other individuals.

Now, however, the burden is more intangible. By reason of our present social structure, the individual always carries a large indirect burden. As a nation or a state, we support the insane, the feeble, the criminal, and hundreds of thousands of industrially unfit. That is merely one penalty of civilization. It is a by-product of civilization. A different form of burden is imposed by the necessity for protection, for legislation, for administration, for education, for streets, roads, libraries and what not. How many people are thus indirectly employed to the benefit of the state as a whole in this country I do not know. Our friend Benito Mussolini has, however, taken an exact census of the number in Italy and gives the figure at 527,769. This country has three times the population of Italy so, if the ratio holds, we have around one and one-half millions of state servants. I am inclined to think there are more than that number. Certainly, we have more than that ratio in the city of Chicago.

In Italy there are now 533,000 unemployed, so if these are added to the state employees it is found that each group of 20 workers, or perhaps less, must support at least one man who is not productively engaged. In the United States our figures on unemployment are much greater. There are between six million and seven million idle. If state employees and our industrially unfit are added, I believe that right now, each group of five workers is supporting one person not productively employed, in addition to women, children and the aged, who constitute a family rather than a state responsibility.

I have no intention of lumping the industrially unemployed with the million or so who are state employed or the other million or so who are industrially unfit. The above combination of figures is merely a cold presentation of the fact that it is possible, by reason of our social organization and our industrial efficiency, for five workers to replace fairly adequately the productiveness of six. In other words, we are as a nation, and perhaps as a world, too effective.

The factor of productivity is made up of the two elements of effort and time. Now, if effort is too productive, the element of time must be decreased. If five men, working 54 hours a week, can meet the constructive requirements that should be spread among six men, the simple mathematics of the problem is that six men could work only 45 hours a week.

There is not the slightest doubt that the above statement is so elementary that every statistician, economist, sociologist, or even every thinker in the country will be able to rise up with loud and provable objections to the idea. Many will claim that there cannot be too much production since man is a creature of limitless desires and, if given the opportunity, will accumulate and use an inexhaustible volume of material goods, which, of course, he cannot do. Thousands of us know that we can eat about so much or we can drink about so much. We can wear about so much and our physical needs are not nearly so great as we are sometimes led to believe. If there is any releasing of time as the result of the further development of the machine age, it should be largely used in a cultural application of leisure time which certainly does not address itself solely and wholly to consuming more material goods. Of course, mankind as a whole can consume more than it now does if the opportunity exists, but unless mankind becomes 100 per cent socialized, with all human efforts merged for the common good and equitably redistributed, there can be no approach to a general realization of desires. The nearest approach that is possible under our present economic system is to give each individual the opportunity to earn in proportion to his ability. At the present moment there are millions of people in this generally prosperous country who do not have the chance to work. There is nothing for them to make which will have a proportionate value in a country which, according to economists, is suffering because there is too much of everything.

Theories for the cure of this situation are many and varied. One idea is that if everyone should be gainfully employed, receiving good wages, the resultant earning power would mean resultant spending power which in turn would support the increased productivity created by the increased employment. This may be called the "wheel within the wheel" theory and almost approaches the principle of perpetual motion. The difficulty seems to lie in the fact that the people and the activities of the United States cannot be sufficiently insulated from the rest of the world to permit an ideally frictionless rotation of this sort. As the tempo of the wheel increases, credit and money tend to flow out of the country and so does production. We are geared up not only to meet internal consumption but also a part of world consumption. If world ability to pay for its share of consumption is then restricted, the wheel is slowed, so overproduction occurs before the spinning can be slowed to the newly balanced rate. A similar effect can be produced if for any reason there occurs a recession from the standard rate of demand for any one product. Thus, if production is geared in accordance with the fact that an automobile needs replacement each five years, then production of cars of an improved type, which will last for seven years, will lead to a two-year slowing up of production. But if any one element of production slows up, the entire wheel must slow up.

Such irregularities prevent control of the industrial wheel. For example, all industry has been used to the fact that iron and steel eventually disintegrate into rust and must necessarily be replaced by newly produced metal. Now, if the use of a rustless steel becomes universal, which need never be replaced by new metal production, can anyone calculate the actual effect on industry?

Such an effect is obtained also from an entirely different cause. If in our industrial wheel the speed has been set by the fact that 100 men are required to give a certain volume of production, consider the result when improvement of machine processes permits 70 men to give the same unit production. Either production must increase, for which there is no corresponding consumption, or consumption must be stimulated or else 30 men stand idle and must be supported in idleness by the remaining workers. It is very evident that too many factors are continually busy influencing industry to permit of any real nicety of its regulation.

Added to what may be called the normal fluctuations of industry are those which are highly artificial but none the less profound in their effect. The most disturbing of these are the ones caused by manipula-

tion of credit. Basically, all that any man can contribute to this world of life is labor. His labor may take any one of an infinite variety of forms and may have a widely varying value. Moreover, its value may be gauged on two different bases—that which it appears to have at the time it is expended in the eyes of his associates and that which it has on the long time scale to humanity which, of course, is the sustaining value. A poet may die of starvation while succeeding generations loudly proclaim the beauty of his works. An emperor may live in splendor and be cursed down the ages for the destruction he wrought. Industrially speaking, we are concerned with the value of labor in terms of current exchange. For labor is traded for labor; money is a medium to facilitate this exchange; and credit is the anticipation of labor not yet performed.

Thus labor can be stored, both before and after its creation. When a man borrows a thousand dollars, he anticipates his ability to make it produce a profit for him. In effect, he uses the stored labor of others to augment his own, securing a mass advantage. The difficulty lies in telling whether credit represents stored labor or anticipated labor. If it is undeniably stored labor, we claim that it is sound credit. If it verges into the field of anticipated labor, we call it inflation. It is because credit may thus depart from the field of actualities that it complicates the economic situation.

In the past ten years credit has had a tremendous influence because it has been used in such tremendous quantities. When the United States loaned money abroad, or extended credit, it, in effect, transferred a lot of labor hours which immediately started to work making goods in competition with our own production. It has seemed in many cases that this country loaned money to other countries in order that they might be able to buy goods from us. By use of these goods they increased their own productivity. This productivity may eventually enable them to repay the loans but in the meantime our own outlet will become more and more restricted and our idle plant capacity will impose heavy fixed charges, while our workers will be idle. For instance, what are we going to do in the shoe industry where we have a plant capacity permitting the production of nine hundred million pairs of shoes a year, when the consumption in the United States is only three hundred million?

Of course, it is dangerous for me to depart from my topic of unemployment into the field of economic and financial theory, but dollars and labor hours are in my eyes one and the same thing. If we make the dollars work hard in the form of improved equipment, the labor hours need be fewer. And if certain economic conditions cause the dollars to be idle, they should also cause workers to be idle.

At the present moment there need not be so much concern because dollars are lying idle, for they cannot starve. But when workers are idle, they must be supported in some fashion. Perhaps too much attention has been paid to making the dollars earn a profit and too little to the profit of the workers. That sounds socialistic, doesn't it? To me it is just business sense, and the readjustment of this problem in its final analysis is going to call for the best business ingenuity that can be found upon the part of leading business men. Now, after all, success in business can only be true success if it is translated into terms of success to the whole social order. None of us can isolate ourselves, single ourselves out and call ourselves independent, act independently of the rest of the world. After all, we are only small cogs in this whole scheme of mechanism that goes on endlessly and endlessly. It is but a short journey that we have on this earth in which we must do the best we can for those about us and those who come after us.

If it be conceded that there is not enough work to give all workers a good eight- or nine-hour day but that there may be enough to give all workers a six- or seven-hour day, is it not more desirable to follow the latter course of keeping the greatest number employed, regardless of some increase in the cost of production or some individual discomfort? Such a procedure would be an expedient and an experiment, but the result of such a policy would rapidly become evident. If the necessary volume of production increased, perhaps a half-hour or an hour could be added to the working day in preference to the seeking of increased production by reason of increased mechanical efficiency. Such a proposal may sound retrogressive, but is it any worse than the present spectacle of enforced idleness, charity and suffering?

We have many proverbs bearing upon the desirable effects of adversity and necessity, based upon the idea that increased pressure promotes increased thinking. That is the benefit which will come out of the present situation. Let us hope that the policies resulting from such constructive thinking will take the form of long-term correction rather than of temporary remedies and I have every confidence that such will be the result.

If there can be any summarization of these random thoughts on a most vital subject, it may be expressed in the idea that two factors for reducing unemployment are readily applicable and must be used carefully and deliberately. First, every effort must be applied to the development of new products, especially of those which will fall into the classification of necessities and will displace least our present products. Second, there is inevitably a shortening of the number of working hours per week, with less than a corresponding reduction in wages. Of these two factors, the former has already played its greatest part and cannot be relied upon for any decisive future effect. The latter has been used only to a minor extent in the past, but will be the real effective agent of the future.

The accountant and his clientele

A William A. Vawter Foundation
on Business Ethics Lecture,
Northwestern University School
of Commerce, 1932

*The accountant has an impartial
viewpoint and a broad experience
with business concerns. He is able,
therefore, to make a worthwhile
contribution to the enterprises
which he serves.*

IN THIS PERIOD of rapidly changing economic and industrial conditions, the accountant, like other business and professional men, may well pause to consider the changes which have come in recent years. He needs to analyze the developments affecting his profession, to estimate his present place in the business world in terms of the services which he is able to render to his clients and through them to the public, and to decide what further developments in the scope of his activities and his relations with his clients and the public may be expected, or may be desirable in the future.

Generally speaking, in the early days of accountancy practice, the outside accountant was considered by the client merely as a checker of accounts and a detector of defalcations, who compiled financial statements for the use of those intimately connected with the business. It was not unusual for the client to judge the success of an accountant's work almost solely by the extent to which errors or irregularities were discovered. He was employed by and reported to the management, which in those days was in most cases identical with the ownership or at least the controlling interest in the business. The accountant was regarded primarily as a technician, a handmaiden of business, entirely subject to the control of the client, and his claims to professional status and dignity were not generally recognized.

Change in status of accountant

Economic and business developments, particularly of the last fifteen years, have had an important influence upon accountancy practice, and have given the accountant a new and more prominent place in business affairs. This change in status has naturally brought with it corresponding changes in the relations between the accountant and his clientele, and it will, therefore, be of interest first to consider briefly how the scope of accountant's services has widened in recent years.

Perhaps the first major factor in point of time resulting in increased emphasis on accountancy has been the federal and state tax laws which provide for taxes measured by income, invested capital, or other bases involving accounting determinations. Federal income taxes, particularly during the period of the excess profits taxes, opened up a large field for constructive service by accountants. Additional impetus to the forward movement of accountancy was given by the accelerated growth of large-scale corporate business, and the trend toward mergers and consolidations, together with the accompanying widespread distribution of corporation securities, in connection with which accounting statements of operating results and financial position are obviously of particular importance.

Broadening of accounting service

As accountancy assumed a larger part in the scheme of business there followed not only a notable increase in the demands for accountants' services, but also a substantial broadening of services which they were called upon to render. They have been called upon to assist in preparing budgets, to act in arbitration matters, to advise on contract provisions involving accounting questions and on financial and dividend policies. The work of the accountant in recent years along the lines of fact-finding investigations has been a noteworthy extension of his field of activity.

A factor which aided the accounting profession in meeting its increasing responsibilities has been the improvement in the personnel of public accounting organizations, which has resulted from the recruiting of staff additions from the graduates of the numerous university and college schools of commerce. These schools have developed courses of study which give the students a broad academic background and a general appreciation of the economic laws operating in the business world.

Increase of responsibilities

The opportunities for greater service by accountants to the business world naturally brought them additional responsibilities. The accountant became something more than a checker of accounts and compiler of financial statements for the use of those intimately connected with the business. His consultative and advisory services have become increasingly important and his interpretations of the facts developed by his investigations have been given weight in the analysis of business problems. Today his reports are given wide circulation and he can no longer feel that his responsibilities end with his client; they extend to all who read and rely on his reports. His relations with his client have thus become more complicated and are now on a more professional basis.

The period of change has been a trying one. It has been difficult for the clients to adjust themselves to a recognition of the accountants' responsibilities to outsiders (such as bankers and holders of securities) who have an interest in their affairs. It has been difficult for the accountants to adjust themselves to the rapid movement toward the enlargement of services and responsibilities. It even became a moot question in the accounting profession as to whether this enlargement of the accountant's sphere was proper. Some regarded the movement as wholly unsound, the opening of a territory into which the accountant could not venture except at great risk of loss of professional standing. Others saw in the movement an opportunity for greater and more constructive service to business. The determination of the extent of the responsibilities of the accountant to others than his clients has been a difficult problem, a problem which promises to grow more important as greater attention is given by the public to the duties and obligations of corporate managements to their shareholders.

Two important movements in accountancy

A consideration of all of the various aspects of the relationship between the accountant and his clientele would be beyond the limitations of this paper, and I propose to discuss two movements in the accountancy field to which I have referred and which I consider to be of vital importance.

1. The development of broader and more constructive service by accountants in the way of fact-finding investigations, budgetary installations, and the variety of services which may be called advisory.

2. The broadening of the accountant's responsibilities to the vast group of shareholders, investors, bankers, and others having an interest in business enterprises but not a part in the active management of their operations.

Fact-finding investigations

An important extension of the scope of the accountant's work in recent years has been in the field of fact-finding investigations which he has been called upon to make in connection with mergers, purchases of businesses, underwriting of securities, etc. It is interesting to note that this extension of the accountant's field was to some extent forced, not by business managements desiring an independent check on their policies, but by outside interests who, in the consideration of some proposed transaction, were not satisfied with cold certified figures and wanted more information regarding the business. They wanted to know why the enterprise under consideration was able to make the showing revealed by the certified financial statements, and whether it was reasonable to expect that the factors con-

tributing to such a showing would continue in the future. They wanted to know what elements of strength and weakness lay behind the financial statements.

It was unsatisfactory to attempt to secure the desired information from the management of the business; very often the information requested was incomplete and there was sometimes a question as to its authenticity. A good part of the required data was of like character to that normally obtained in connection with the audit work and could be secured with the expenditure of a minimum of additional time. The accountant by training and experience was well qualified to present the data in an orderly, concise manner. It was natural, therefore, that the accountant should be asked to expand the audit work to include an investigation of important phases of the business.

Business survey by accountant

Such investigation work is basically fact-finding, but it was logical that the accountant's opinion should be asked regarding the interpretation of the facts after they had been obtained. The accountant has an impartial, detached viewpoint, and by reason of the variety of his contacts with business concerns, he has a broad background for his business judgments. He has been able, therefore, to make a worthwhile contribution in the weighing and correlating of the facts and in judging their significance as affecting the future of a business enterprise. It is obvious that an investigation of such purpose and scope represents a relatively new development in the field of accountancy and places the accountant in an entirely new position in the business world; it will be worthwhile, therefore, to pause and examine briefly some of the features of a business which are considered in that connection.

The history of any business is strongly influenced by external conditions beyond the control of its management. Thus periods of general prosperity and depression which have a vital influence on all industries are more pronounced in their effect on particular ones. The action of competition as regards intensive advertising, selling efforts, price changes, or the development of new products exerts a powerful influence over sales and profits. The factors of public whim and change in methods of living may have a temporary or permanent influence on the history of any particular business or industry.

An investigation of these external aspects would answer, among others, the following questions: What economic need does the industry and product fill—does the industry manufacture basic commodities or luxuries, and is the product for the consuming public or for use in production? What is the character of the demand for the product with respect to seasonal influences and periods of prosperity and depression? Is the industry growing, stabilized, or declining, and is the company itself of growing, stabilized, or declining importance in such industry? Is competition keen as manifested by competitive advertising campaigns and price wars in the past? Is demand capable of periodical stimulation through advertising and other forms of sales effort? What is the mortality rate of the industry, that is, what is the record of the successes and failures of the various companies in the industry? Has the company a competitive advantage due to its location as regards raw materials, market, or labor cost, and what is the relative importance of raw materials, fixed investment, and labor in the manufacturing process of the specific industry?

Quality of management

In the investigation of the internal aspects of a business, a study of the quality of the management is perhaps the most important feature. To be sure, it is of an intangible nature and it may be difficult to convince an investor that it is good collateral for a bond issue, but still it is as necessary and as fundamental as the brick, mortar, and steel that are embodied in the physical plant. The technique of modern management is fast becoming standardized and because of this tendency it is becoming more subject to analytical study.

The managerial talent of the present-day successful enterprise should be a homogeneous group with a definite plan of coordinated effort. In analyzing a particular situation to determine how nearly the ideal is reached, data regarding age, experience, length of service, and salary of all the permanent personnel of importance are helpful. Whether capable understudies for those in important positions are available or are being trained, the extent to which inherited stock interests or family ties are responsible for the filling of key positions, the extent to which executives are financially interested through stock ownership, bonus plans, etc., are all important questions bearing on the quality of the management of an enterprise.

A study and report on the corporate history and organization also gives an excellent insight into the quality of the management. The conservatism of the management, its success in guiding the company through past financial storms, and the soundness and foresight of its past financial program may be developed by an analysis and study of the surplus, capital stock, and funded debt accounts and a general view of the major financial transactions disclosed by the minutes and other records.

Source and trend of earnings

Another important feature of the internal investigation is the determination of the source and trend of earnings. The study of the results of operations should cover a period of at least five years and preferably ten years. If a shorter period is used, transitory variations may be mistaken for trends. The summary statement of profit and loss accounts and supporting detail statements should be carefully analyzed to determine any abnormal factors that should be taken into consideration.

Some of the factors which should be reviewed are: relation of officers' salaries to shareholdings and dividend payments; effect of market fluctuations of raw material prices on profits; the effect of controllable expenses such as maintenance, advertising, promotional salaries, etc., on the income account; the basis and consistency of depreciation provisions; the amount and nature of abnormal profit and loss items; and the effect of the discontinuance or addition of various departments and products.

After the general analysis of the profit and loss account has been made, detailed consideration should be given to the more important items. Usually sales are an important item, and in many cases it will be advisable to analyze the total by products, by classes of customers, and by geographical distribution. Such an analysis may reveal unprofitable products, or too great concentration of sales to single customers, industries, or locations.

This brief summary of a few of the important points that are covered in a business survey will serve to illustrate the type of data that is obtained and to indicate the significance of such data in any study of a business enterprise.

In recent years, particularly during this period of business troubles, the managements of many businesses have recognized the help that the accountant may render in the consideration of problems in the way of fact-finding surveys covering part or all of their business. Such surveys are obviously of just as much importance to the management as more general surveys are to outside interests, and may be used as a guide in the fixing of financial and operating policies, in internal reorganizations, or as a check on the management's judgment on such problems.

Budget control

Another of the important developments in accountancy in the last few years in which the professional accountant has made a substantial contribution has been the use of budgets as a means of control of the operations of a business. This form of accountancy concerns itself with future transactions rather than completed transactions. Many business men have not understood the function of budgetary control and have regarded it as an extremely complicated and technical device. Reduced to its fundamentals, it is the mapping and subsequent carrying out of the financial program according to a definite well-ordered plan. In accomplishing this specific end, however, there are many useful purposes served.

It provides a basis for administrative control and aids in coordinating the activities of the various departments. It can be used as an aid in controlling and planning production to cover seasonal variation with a minimum disturbance of operation and employment. It assists in the control of inventories to the end that excesses are avoided. It provides a basis for controlling and reducing expenses. In fact, the development and operation of a budget will bring to light certain expenses which no department will be responsible for and which otherwise would have passed over unnoticed. Of course, a budget, however well-designed, is not a general panacea. It is not a substitute for good management but is a useful tool of good management.

Miscellaneous services of accountancy

There is also a wide variety of miscellaneous services of a constructive nature which accountants are being called upon to undertake to an increasing extent. Arbitration work, consultation on contract provisions, financing and dividend policies, and advice on current accounting problems are a few of the many miscellaneous services now being performed by accountants. There have been a few cases where professional accountants have been appointed as receivers, or as members of reorganization committees, and the time may come when in this country, as in England at present, it is the rule rather than the exception to appoint accountants as trustees of estates or in bankruptcy, as receivers or liquidators, etc.

As a result of the constructive services which have been briefly indicated, the accountant today is coming to be regarded as a business adviser, whose counsel is sought not only at the time of the periodic examination of accounts, but continuously during the year. In fact, it is not too much to say that the accountant of today who is most successful, in the broadest sense, is the one whose clients rely on him for advice on accounting and business problems just as an attorney is looked to for advice on current legal questions which arise. It may not be inappropriate in this connection to refer to the statement of Professor J. H. Jones, the well-known English economist. When asked why his articles on current economic problems regularly appeared in *The Accountant,* Professor Jones replied that he used this publication since he felt that accountants furnished the best medium through which to get his thoughts and ideas over to the leaders of business.

Change in relation of accountant to his client

From the above brief survey of the development of accountancy practice it is obvious that the relations of the accountant to his client have undergone considerable modification since the days when the practice consisted largely of detail auditing, to the present, when the accountant has attained a definite place in the structure of business, and has been afforded an opportunity to become an important factor in business affairs. It is also obvious that the ethical problems involved in the present-day relationship of the accountant to his client are greatly different from those of the earlier days, when the relationship and hence the ethical problems were evidently more nearly those of an employee and an employer.

This development of a broader conception of the functions of the accountant is closely related to the second important development in accounting practice which has had a significant influence upon the relations between the accountant and his clientele—the widening of the responsibilities of the accountant to the vast number of investors in corporation securities, investment bankers, and others having a legitimate interest in the affairs of his clients.

Obligation of accountant to safeguard investors

The striking corporate development of business enterprises in the last decade and the current trend toward combinations and mergers is causing grave misgivings in the minds of many thoughtful people who see in the growing power and influence of business corporations a serious social problem. One phase of this social problem is the safeguarding of the interests of the millions of individuals who have invested their funds in corporation securities. Impressive pictures are drawn of the wide diffusion of ownership of corporations and the centralization of the management and control in the hands of the "insiders" who have little difficulty in maintaining their position under the existing corporate procedure; the rank and file of shareholders grant proxies perfunctorily at the request of the management, and the shareholders' meetings are only formal affairs. Publicists of the crusader type decry the shortcomings of corporate managements in their relations with their shareholders and their failure to recognize the trust imposed in them. The question of the protection of the public from the giants of corporate business, which was popular a few years ago in the "trust-busting" era, seems to be giving way to the more modern question of the protection of the investor. On every side are heard pleas for greater publicity of corporate statements, increased candor toward shareholders, and a higher order of industrial statesmanship.

It is clear that the separation of the management and ownership of corporate business places the management in a trustee relationship with the shareholders, and that this relationship involves definite responsibilities and obligations on the part of the management to a large group of persons outside of the managerial group. It is equally clear that the trustee status of the management imposes upon the accountant an essential responsibility to the investors. They properly should look upon the accountant as an impartial investigator in whom full reliance may be placed for the fairness of the certified financial statements, and for the disclosure of all information relative to the accounts to which they are rightfully entitled, whether such information be favorable or unfavorable to the interests of the management. The accountant is sometimes engaged by the board of directors but more often by an important official of the corporation. It may be seen that his position is somewhat anomalous—auditor of the trustees, yet subject to the trustees' instructions as to scope of audit and continuity of employment.

Ethical problems of anomalous position

There may arise in this connection ethical problems of the utmost nicety to be solved by the accountant. Suppose, for example, that the principal managing officers of a corporation are not heavy shareholders but derive their principal compensation from a bonus arrangement based on earnings. The immediate apparent interests of the management may emphasize to them the importance of near-term operating results, while the ultimate interests of the shareholders may not best be served by such policies. Insofar as the management in such cases attempts to improve the current earnings situation by application of overliberal accounting policies, the accountant must strictly guard the shareholders' interest.

A problem frequently met is the extent to which the accountant must insist on the inclusion, in his report, of facts of which he believes the shareholders should have knowledge, but which, in the opinion of the management, would unduly disclose to competitors information to the ultimate detriment of the corporation. In such cases the accountant must very carefully consider what effect any action of his will have on the interests of all legitimately interested parties.

Another point which may be mentioned is the tendency on the part of some executive heads of corporations to refer to their controllers all questions relating to the accounts and their presentation. The accountant may feel that it is his duty in regard to certain matters to be sure that they come to the attention of the president or chairman of the company, and that it is desirable that he personally discuss them with these officials. Although the enlarged scope of the present-day accountant's duties makes such contact easier than in the old days, there still arise situations when the utmost tact is required on the part of the accountant to bring a problem to the personal attention of the president, when he feels that such procedure is essential.

Method of engaging accountants

The question of the method of engaging accountants is receiving considerable attention at the present time, as is indicated by the fact that last November the New York Chamber of Commerce authorized the appointment of a special committee to investigate the accounting practices of corporations with particular attention to methods of engaging independent accountants. It is said that the committee will consider the possible desirability of recommending that accountants in the United States be elected by shareholders, as is the case in England.

In England, auditors are elected annually by the shareholders and may be present and permitted to speak at any general meeting of the company where the financial statements are presented. After being once elected, the auditor cannot be removed at a shareholders' meeting without previous notice to the shareholders. In Germany, a recent presidential decree provides that the accounts of corporations must be examined by independent auditors who are elected by the shareholders.

Regardless of the method of engaging accountants, it is obvious that their widened responsibilities demand an exceptionally high standard of professional conduct. The indispensable element in accountants' reports is integrity. If the confidence of the public in the integrity of accountants' reports is shaken, their value is gone. To preserve the integrity of his reports, the accountant must insist upon absolute independence of judgment and action. The necessity of preserving this position of independence indicates certain standards of conduct; he should not have a financial interest in the business of any client of sufficient importance to him to influence his independent position and he should not accept business or social favors that might create an obligation which would make the maintenance of an impartial attitude difficult. The accountant's dealings with his client must be fair and open and he should insist upon a reasonable fee for his services, a fee that will permit him to conduct an adequate examination into the affairs of his client.

Attitude of bankers and the public

In connection with the consideration of the professional obligations of the accountant, I wish to refer briefly to certain aspects of the attitude of bankers and the public in general toward accountants. There is a regrettable lack of support of accountants in their efforts to obtain sounder financial statements and adequate disclosures of information having an important bearing on the accounts. Little or no concern is given to the reason behind a change in the company's accountants. If the accountant is

compelled to surrender an engagement by reason of his refusal to meet demands of a client which he considers improper, it is discouraging to see the work assigned to a less scrupulous accountant with no questions being raised by the outsiders, particularly shareholders and bankers. I hope that the day will come when every change in accountants will be a matter of real concern to the outside interests, and that if the explanations of the management are unsatisfactory, the accountants will be given an opportunity of presenting their position.

Closely related to this indifference of the public to the need for the support of accountants in questions involving the integrity of accounts, is the tendency on the part of the public and even of business men and bankers to classify all accountants in one group. No one questions that there are wide differences in the competence and reliability of legal and engineering firms, physicians, and other professional men. There are equally wide differences in the relative standing of accountants. The primary consideration in the selection of accountants should be their reputation for competence and integrity. The amount of the accountant's fee should be a consideration but it should be no more controlling in the selection of accountants than in the selection of other professional men. If the accounting profession is to render the maximum service to the business world and to the public, there should be developed a more discriminating consideration of accountants and accountants' services.

Public lacks understanding of financial statements

It is probable that one reason for some of the criticism leveled at corporate financial statements, even when these have been prepared in the best of faith and with a desire to disclose in a reasonable manner those facts relating to the enterprise to which the investor and public are entitled, is that there is a lack of understanding of such statements, particularly their limitations, and the nature of the work performed by the accountant whose certificate accompanies the accounts.

Many otherwise well-informed persons regard financial statements as exact pictures based on well-defined rules applied with mathematical exactness, and appear to assume that the accountant's certificate is based on a detailed check of the client's records for the purpose of verifying that these rules and regulations have been correctly applied. To such persons there is no room for questions of judgment to enter into the preparation of financial statements. If this were the real situation it is obvious that the accountant could never have progressed from the original idea of his function, already referred to in this paper, of being largely a detector, by means of detail checking of accounting records, of irregularities and defalcations.

All who have had intimately to do with the preparation and interpretation of accounting statements recognize, however, that financial statements include many items, the money value of which is based on estimates, and that the relative importance of such items is so great that financial statements may be regarded more correctly as estimates than as exact fact statements. How can provisions for depreciation, reserves for bad debts, amortization of intangible assets, reserves for shrinkage in the values of investments having no quoted market values, and similar items be measured exactly? They are matters of judgment, not only on the part of those who initially prepare such statements, but also on the part of the accountant whose duty it is to approve or disapprove the essential soundness of such judgment. Judgment of the management of an enterprise as applied to its accounting matters will naturally be colored by the general policies of the management; whether they are, for example, ultra-conservative, or based on a desire to make the best showing possible. The accountant will insist that the accounting policies be within the field of generally accepted practices, but this field is broad.

There are many accounting problems in regard to which equally competent accountants may honestly differ, and it is not surprising, therefore, that there are many cases where a difference of opinion exists between the accountant and the client as to some phase of the client's accounting policies. If there are any doubts in the accountant's mind as to the correctness of his judgment, he cannot ignore the judgment of his client and insist upon the presentation of the accounts on a certain basis. The certificate covering the accounts is the accountant's, however, and the client must concede the right of the accountant to include in it any disclosures regarding the basis of stating the accounts that the accountant feels are necessary. It is quite apparent, therefore, that the accountant's certificate should be read carefully, and that most careful consideration should be given to any qualifications and comments included in it.

Accountant's obligation to include qualifying comment

It is possible, of course, that in an extreme case the manner of treatment or presentation insisted upon by the client may be, in the accountant's opinion, so at variance with established practice and principles that the most carefully prepared certificate would not adequately put the reader on notice as to the facts and their significance. Under such circumstances, if he cannot persuade the client to his point of view, the accountant has no choice but to withdraw from the engagement.

It may be of interest to review briefly some of the situations where the accountant finds it necessary to include in his certificate important qualifying comments and explanations. Such occasions arise in general when the accounts as presented by the client are not satisfactory to the accountant, and if the accountant is unable to persuade the client to his point of view, disclosure of the situation becomes necessary in the certificate.

Depreciation a typical problem

One of the best illustrations of this type of problem is that of depreciation. This question often has two aspects: first, the adequacy of the provision for depreciation for the current period, and second, the continuity of the company's depreciation policy over a period of years. In the first case, the accountant bases his opinion of the provision for depreciation as made by the client, and of the adequacy of the reserve, on his broad experience with the problem in industry as a whole, and in the particular business with which he has to deal, and on his broad range of experience with the general problem. The client, however, often feels that his opinion, buttressed by his intimate knowledge of his particular business, is the sounder of the two.

Let us suppose a situation where the accountant feels convinced that the provision as made by the client, which has, let us say, been approved by the board of directors, is entirely inadequate. He can and should, of course, endeavor to convince the management that his view is the correct one and induce them to make the appropriate changes in their accounts. If he is unable to do so, however, can he entirely disregard the company's position as reflected in the accounts and as approved by the board of directors, and insist on certifying the accounts on his basis? Obviously he is in no position to handle the matter in this way and, therefore, his only recourse is to state the accounts on the basis as approved by the management, but to disclose the facts in his certificate so that the reader may form his own conclusions.

It is also found on occasion that clients appear to use the depreciation provision as an equalizer of profits between years; during prosperous years generous provisions are made against lean periods when the depreciation is reduced. It is quite obvious that modifications of depreciation policies between years should be disclosed in the accountant's certificate if the client refuses to make appropriate reference thereto in the accounts themselves.

Research and development costs

An illustration of a different type of case where the very nature of the problem may require full disclosure by the accountant in his certificate is that of the accounting treatment of research and development costs.

In recent years there has been an increasing tendency for large corporations to spend considerable sums of money for research and development work. The rules for accounting for these expenditures are by no means so well crystallized as are those for other matters, and there is therefore room for the exercise of good judgment as to the proper treatment of such expenditures in any individual case, depending on all of the facts which can be ascertained. In actual practice it is found that some companies charge expenditures for research and development currently to profit and loss; others have adopted the policy of accumulating the charges and amortizing them over a period of years. Suppose that a company has capitalized all of its research and development costs, and its rate of amortization is, in the opinion of the accountant, quite inadequate. The accountant has no claim to infinite knowledge and, in fact, emphasizes his own disability as a prophet. How can he then insist on a change in the company's accounts, against the judgment of the client? On the other hand, it is plainly his duty to point out in his certificate the facts relating to the accounting treatment of research and development expenses when in his opinion reasonably conservative methods have not been followed.

Disclosure of "cold storage earnings"

As an illustration of the practices in which some managements indulge with a view to equalizing profits between years, and the problems of disclosure on the part of the accountant with respect to them, we have what has been termed as "cold storage earnings." That is, profits which have been realized in past years are frozen, so to speak, in the form of excessive or secret reserves which are melted down in time of fancied need to flow into and swell the current profit and loss account. Equities in prior years' earnings of subsidiaries not consolidated which are taken up in the form of dividends in the later years in which paid; contingency reserves and secret reserves which have been created in prosperous years and are used to absorb ordinary profit and loss charges in lean years; excess reserves created for accounts receivable, loss on inventories, investments and other assets, which are reduced in subsequent years by credits to profit and loss accounts, are examples of what I have in mind. A somewhat similar class of items are those income items of non-recurring or special nature, such as profits from sale of capital assets or investments. If such items are not stated by the client in the accounts in such a manner that their nature and importance are fully set forth, it is apparent that full disclosure is required by the accountant in his certificate.

In this connection it may be mentioned that many people appear to think that the more conservative the accounting policies of a company, the more praiseworthy they are. Excessive provisions for depreciation, creation of secret reserves, scaling down of assets to nominal book values, etc., are by some considered the hallmark of good accounting. When the business was largely managed by its few shareholders, who were fully aware of the situation, these practices may have had some merit. In these times, with management largely divorced from ownership, this point of view is no longer valid. The proper aim is to be neither over-conservative nor unduly optimistic but to state the accounts year by year on the most accurate and consistent basis possible.

Educational work of the professional societies

Considerable progress has been made by the profession itself through its societies, such as the State Societies of Certified Public Accountants, The American Society of Certified Public Accountants, and the American Institute of Accountants, along the lines of bringing to the attention of the interested public generally a fuller appreciation of the problems which have to be met in the preparation of financial statements. The American Institute of Accountants has had presented, by its officers, talks on various pertinent subjects to bankers, lawyers, business men, students, etc. It has promoted joint meetings of accountants, bankers, and members of stock exchanges regarding published statements of all types of companies. Permanent committees on cooperation with stock exchanges, bankers, etc., are functioning. Other committees are cooperating with interested groups on such problems as accounting terminology, bankruptcy reform, international double taxation, the natural business year, etc. Similar work is carried on by the other professional societies mentioned. Recently, a more active interest in accounting statements has been manifested by the New York Stock Exchange, which has issued important rulings for the guidance of companies whose securities are listed on that Exchange.

Changing standards of business practice

It must be admitted that, on the whole, the accounting and reporting policies of many companies during recent years are subject to considerable criticism when viewed in retrospect. The conditions inherent in the business situation at the time were such that undue emphasis was almost inevitably laid on current earnings and the short-term viewpoint. There was, for example, a greatly increased interest in current financial statements on the part of the public in appraising the values of securities, and a desire for maximum profit showing by corporations which were considering mergers or consolidations or the issuance of securities. In cases where the managements have sponsored large expansion programs or acquisition, they may have felt that their judgments needed to be quickly vindicated; shareholders are inclined to wait impatiently to see promised benefits actually materialize.

These tendencies caused many business men to question the conservative canons of accountancy. Managements which admitted that conservative policies might be best from a long-term viewpoint argued that current considerations forced them to more liberal policies.

These conditions cannot be regarded as indicative of dishonest managements; they simply reflected the optimism that prevailed everywhere during the boom period, and the belief that a new order of business procedure was needed to meet the changed conditions. In these days of disillusionment and greater realism in our thinking, the public is prone to forget that corporate managements were not alone in this belief; ideas which are now well exploded were held and sponsored by eminent writers and economists, and it could hardly be contended that accountants as a whole were uninfluenced by conditions of the period of inflation. Arguments for more conservative methods were challenged on the grounds that such methods were old-fashioned and were not applicable to the new order of business. It was only natural that in some instances the viewpoint of the accountants became colored and they yielded, reluctantly I hope, to the persuasive arguments of the new business philosophy.

It is natural that with the passage of time and resulting changes in business conditions, particularly in the relationship of business to the social order as a whole, the ethics of business will change. Notwithstanding the criticisms which have been leveled at the moral and ethical standards of corporate management, especially during this period of depression when weaknesses in the existing order of business are popular subjects, there is no question but that there has been a real improvement in business standards. The words of the distinguished Norwegian philosopher and humanitarian, Frit Yof Nansen, may well be applied to the world of business when he says—"Moral rules cannot be expected to be any more absolute or everlasting than any other ideas of man. What is considered to be moral will naturally change with time and circumstances. Many moral commands still proclaimed today are flagrantly out-of-date and even harmful."

New methods a matter of slow growth

New methods and practices which are demanded by new conditions are not developed overnight; rather, they are a matter of slow growth. It is difficult to uproot the traditional attitude of secrecy and idea of unrestricted control of corporate affairs which prevailed during the days when the owners were the managers and they had no obligations to outside investors. Many of the large and forward-looking corporations, however, have recognized that the increasing public ownership of corporate business demands new standards of corporate practice. They see that the confidence of the public in corporate business has been weakened, and they recognize that an essential element in their future growth and prosperity unhampered by restrictive legislation is the development of public confidence based upon a full appreciation of the fiduciary aspects of the obligations and responsibilities of the management. Such corporate managements are setting new standards of accounting and reporting policies, and as these higher standards become more generally accepted, the movement toward sounder and more informative financial statements will be greatly accelerated. I venture to predict that accountancy will assume a much more prominent place in the world of business in the future than it has in the past, and that the relationship between the accountant and his clientele will undergo considerable further modifications.

I believe that accountants are rapidly coming to a fuller appreciation of their opportunity to lead in the establishment of increasingly higher ethical standards within the field of their business contacts, and that with the support which is being given to their efforts by collateral agencies, a definite contribution will be made by the profession as a whole to improved standards of accounting and reporting practices of American business.

An NRA enigma: what constitutes "selling below cost"?

Before the American
Trade Association
Executives, Chicago,
September 13, 1933

*Now we are close to the truth
that business exists as a service to
mankind and cannot prove
superior to humanity.*

IN the majority of industrial codes which have been formulated to date, under the National Industrial Recovery Act, it has been defined as an unfair competitive practice for any member of an industry to "sell below cost." In most of these codes the term "cost" is indicated or assumed to be the total or overall cost to make, sell and deliver the individual products to a consumer. It seems that industry has suddenly seized upon the idea that selling prices can be standardized and regulated according to the overall costs of individual products, in individual businesses. Actually this is not feasible under a capitalistic system, where some elements of competition and of reward for individual initiative and ingenuity must be retained; nor is it possible to accurately determine the overall cost of a product. In writing into its codes many of the provisions relative to not selling below cost, I believe industry is for the most part only making use of a currently popular phrase with small conception of the principles or problems which are involved.

What is "cost"?

The term "cost" unless carefully defined is ambiguous to an extreme degree. Economists in general use the terms "cost" and "cost of production" in a different sense from the accountant. To an accountant, cost generally means the cost to manufacture, and does not include the additional expenses incident to distribution of the product, general administration of the business or items relative to the financing of operations. As used in most codes, therefore, costs—these overall costs—are something entirely different, in fact something almost new when related to individual items of production; for in the past there have been relatively few instances where the allocation of the general expenses of a business

179

to the individual items made and sold could be made to reflect the true situation. The distinction between overall cost and the better known unit production cost should be clearly recognized.

The determination of unit overall costs represents in general a field of cost accounting as yet undeveloped, and one in which accuracy of results would be an unreasonable expectation. In fact such cost must necessarily be mere approximations, subject to question from many angles.

For example, every business man knows that some products require only a minimum of selling effort, either because of low price, or because of long-established public acceptance. Other products are constantly pushed by intensive advertising. Some perhaps are highly competitive and some are unique because of design or patent-protected construction. What sound basis then can possibly be set for the allocation of selling and advertising expense to all products, when the only common factor is their dollar cost or dollar sales value? Or what can be done in allocating an intensive advertising campaign over sales for the next several years? Should "institutional advertising" be spread equally over all sales, thus loading a standard low-price line as heavily as a "specialty" high profit margin line? Similarly there will be problems in the allocation of administrative and financial expense to products.

It is evident that if the prohibition against "selling below cost" is to be used in industry codes, it must first be carefully defined as to whether it means "cost to manufacture" in the accounting sense, or "overall cost" in the economic sense. If it means the latter, then, in my opinion, industry is writing into its codes a mandate which is impractical of application and is contrary to all of our present concepts of business.

A fallacious viewpoint

The misconception concerning the meaning of the phrase "not to sell below cost" appears to be based on two things—first, a lack of knowledge as to what constitutes cost and cost finding, and second, the feeling that therein lies a possible utopia which will permit a price regulation which will perhaps enable all businesses to operate at a profit. There is a failure to grasp the fact that the origination of the phrase was purely an attempt to guard against vicious price-cutting practices, and to promote among all businesses a better operating control through the use of cost analysis. If it is used at all in a code, it should be clearly understood as meaning production cost — that is, cost which includes only the elements of material, labor and proper allocations of manufacturing overhead. An attempt to make it include all of the costs of doing business would have the effect of making it illegal for a business to operate at a loss. One has only to look back over the past few years to realize that a prohibition against selling any product at less than the approximately calculated overall cost would be an absurdity. It is impossible to positively wed selling prices to total cost. Every business man knows that there are times when the life of the company depends upon going ahead in spite of a temporary loss. If prices should be set according to total cost, even if such costs could be determined, they might at times be so high as to prevent sales. They might be far out of line with competition in the industry and out of line with competition from substitute products.

While it is true that we are changing some of our conceptions of business practice, and especially of competitive practices, I do not think it safe to assume that we have achieved perpetual prosperity, and thus will never again need to undergo a period of selling at a loss. Even under normal conditions most businesses make some sales at a loss, as when heavy selling and advertising expense is necessary in the introduction of a new product; or when some work is taken on a "burden absorbing basis" in order to improve the status of operations as a whole;

or when some products are handled at a loss in order to complete a "customers' line" of products; or when certain "loss leaders" are offered. This last condition is already the subject of some violent argument under the new codes. Perhaps some of these conditions, under certain circumstances, are those which are considered "unfair trade practices" and are supposed to be eliminated by the code provisions. But I do not believe they can all be broadly ruled out. The real questions, however, concern the calculation of cost which may be used as a standard in testing selling prices and the colossal job of "policing" under such a code provision. For example, are the "costs" which are supposed to regulate selling prices those which may be calculated from the operations of the preceding year, or from the preceding six months, or must they be currently calculated costs which may be constantly changing? Another consideration is whether the selling prices of every business should be checked against its costs, or whether the comparison should be made only in the event of accusation. To anyone who has seen the time and effort involved in investigation of an unfair trade practice case under the Federal Trade Commission, involving the matter of costs, any serious thought of a broad application to all industry of a rule that no sales shall be made below cost seems almost an incredibility.

The fallacious idea that an industry code can be formulated which makes it illegal for a business to sell any product at less than its overall cost should be definitely dismissed. Instead, industry will do well to adhere to the idea that code provisions may be included which are designed to prevent vicious price cutting and to promote the establishment of uniform industry accounting and uniform methods of calculating production cost. If this is done, then the NRA codes will be the means of accomplishing a great forward stride in industry practice and control. The point to guard against is the assumption that this is an easy

matter and that only a short time will be required for its attainment. The facts are that relatively little has been accomplished in the development of uniform industry accounting; that every business is in some respects different from every other; that the systems used must fit the business rather than that business should be forced to fit a system; and that patience, time and technical skill and experience of a high degree are necessary in working out the problem for a given industry.

The Act does not authorize cost basis

The prevalence of this use in industrial codes of an injunction against selling below cost would lead to the belief that it is in some way mandatory under the National Industrial Recovery Act. This is not borne out by a study of the facts.

If we examine the Act itself (H. R. 5755) we find the following phrase as a clue to the origination of the idea: "Whenever the President shall find that destructive wage or *price cutting* or other activities contrary to the policy of this title are being practiced in any trade or industry . . . etc." This also ties in with the stated policy of the Act—"to eliminate unfair competitive practices"—but neither phrase bears definitely on the subject of costs, unless there is the further assumption that "destructive—price cutting" means cutting prices to less than cost.

The first official discussion of the Act was contained in the President's Bulletin No. 1, issued on June 16, 1933, the same day the Act was approved. In it there is the explanation that—"We are relaxing some of the safeguards of the anti-trust laws. The public must be protected against the abuses that led to their enactment, and to this end we are putting in place of *old principles of unchecked competition* some new Government controls." There is also a somewhat contradictory injunction that—"if we now inflate prices as fast and as far as we increase wages, the whole project will be set at naught. We cannot hope for the full effect of this plan unless, in these first critical months, and even at the expense of full initial profits, we defer price increases as long as possible."

Evidently it would be difficult to read into these phrases any prohibition against selling below overall cost. In fact, the opposite is true, if the last quotation alone is considered, for if a business had been operating at a loss, as so many did in the first six months of 1933, and then it raised wages and increased the number of employees, yet "deferred price increases as long as possible," it would inevitably be selling products at less than their total cost.

In NRA Bulletin No. 2 the only possible reference to price regulation is in the statement that industry codes should contain —"such means as each industry may find necessary to protect its constructive and cooperating majority from the wasteful and unfair competition of minorities or recalcitrants." In NRA Bulletin No. 3, which deals entirely with the President's Reemployment Agreement, there is no reference to either prices or costs. Officially then, there is very little which may be construed as necessitating any code interpretation that selling below overall cost is to be prohibited.

Origin of "not to sell below cost"

Before the Act was signed, the National Association of Manufacturers issued a "Model Code for Self-Governing Industries" in which will be found the following suggestions:

"Each of the above divisions, and any others which may subsequently be formed, shall proceed at once to provide for standard methods of costing which shall be used by all manufacturers within that division for the purpose of this section of the code.

"It shall be an unfair method of competition for any such manufacturer to sell below reasonable cost. What is statistically known as the 'mode' may be used as a reasonable cost, but must be so approved. (Note: It might instead be provided that no producer shall sell below his own cost of production.)"

Attention is called to the fact that the cost herein discussed is the cost of production, which to an accountant means the cost to manufacture (namely, material, plus labor, plus manufacturing expenses) and not the overall cost.

Probably most code makers have studied this "Model Code", and it may be accepted as containing the inception of the idea that selling below cost constitutes an unfair trade practice. In it the idea was fairly reasonably proposed. The industry control body was supposed to establish some basis whereby it could determine whether any member of the industry was selling below a *reasonable cost of production,* because such vicious price-cutting could not help being unfair competition. It apparently did not propose that industry should be legally restrained from operating at a loss as would be the case if "cost" was made to include all of the expenditures of a business. It did not attempt to set up a device whereby a legally permissible regulation could be transmuted into a price regulatory provision. But it did indicate that the use of some standard methods of costing would be a desirable feature for industry.

A modified conception

Some weeks after the publication of the "Model Code", there appeared in a bulletin of the Chamber of Commerce of the United States the following query and answer, as information to code makers:

Q. May an industry agree not to sell below cost?

A. Industries may not only agree not to sell below cost (individual cost) but such agreements are desired by the administration. Any rule on this subject should set forth the various factors which must be considered in determining cost and be based upon the uniform cost system approved by members of the industry.

This interpretation varies from that in the "Model Code" in more positively specifying the use of the agreement, in stating that the cost used shall be that of the individual business, and in failing to give any definition of what constitutes cost.

At intervals, from the fore part of June to the middle of July, various "Code Services" also mentioned this feature, suggesting that agreements not to sell below cost might be almost compulsory, but also indicating that there was no government formula for cost and that industry in general had not arrived at a definition of "cost."

Our own interest in the matter led to consultation with several NRA officials about the middle of July, only to show that the matter of definition of cost was still a problem. One official believed that an *exact* definition of cost would be excluded from the codes, but that they might contain some definition of general principles applicable to the term "cost." Another official gave as his belief that the solution would lie in the working out of agreeable arrangements within each industry, which arrangements very probably would also include uniform cost accounting for the industry. The general impression gained from this preliminary discussion was that no one had decided what constituted cost, either from the viewpoint of a single business or for an industry as a whole.

Nevertheless, the use of code phrasing bearing on this subject was becoming general. Among fourteen of the codes which had been approved prior to September first, ten specifically defined selling below cost as unfair competitive practice. In codes submitted but not yet approved, it also appears to be the rule that "selling below cost" is prohibited. There might be some point to all this if the term "cost" were defined as that cost which included only material, labor and manufacturing overhead—sometimes called "cost of production" and sometimes known as "manufacturing cost." This, however, is not the case. In some codes there is no definition of cost. In others it is made to mean total or overall cost. In still others it is made to include a conglomeration of charges which fall into a variety of accounting classifications. Unfortunately the code makers for the various industries appear to have grasped at a phrase and generally to have misinterpreted the intent, or else to have used a phrase without any attempt to interpret or define its meaning.

Present code phrasing

A few quotations, chosen at random from various submitted codes, will serve to illustrate the different interpretations and expressions which have resulted. Thus the code of the shipbuilding and ship repair industry stated:

> "To accomplish the purpose contemplated by this Act, the members signatory to this code agree that it shall be an unfair method of competition to sell below a reasonable cost arrived at by a system of formulae established by the associations."

and thereby left a lot to the imagination or to further development.

A different expression is found in the code of the National Boot and Shoe Manufacturers, which recites:

> "The practice of selling below cost is detrimental to the industry; and each manufacturer shall submit upon request a statement from a certified public accountant recognized by the co-operative body for the industry as qualified, to the effect that such manufacturer has a proper cost accounting system; which statement, however, may not be accepted as final by the co-operative, either as to cost accounting or as to selling below cost."

The electrical manufacturing industry was very much more explicit, providing that

"every employer shall use an accounting system which conforms to the principles of and is at least as detailed and complete as the uniform and standard method of accounting set forth in the Sixth Edition of the Manual of Accounting, prepared and published by the National Electrical Manufacturers Association, and a costing system which conforms to the principles of and is at least as detailed and complete as the standard and uniform method of costing to be formulated or approved by the Board of Governors or Executive Committee of National Electrical Manufacturers Association, with such variations therefrom as may be required by the individual conditions affecting any employer or group employers and as may be approved by the Board of Governors or Executive Committee of National Electrical Manufacturers Association, etc."

Adding also the prohibition that

"No employer shall sell or exchange any product of his manufacture at a price or upon such terms or conditions that will result in the customer paying for the goods received less than the cost to the seller, determined in accordance with the uniform and standard method of costing hereinabove prescribed. . . ."

This association appears to have understood the intent of the Act, to have followed somewhat the principles set forth in the "Model Code" and to have provided a basis for industry control, but the code phrasing leaves one much in doubt as to the meaning of the "cost" specified.

This code provision may be compared with the following quotation from a code draft, which may have missed the intent of the Act, but which missed very little in the line of business expenditures, classifying practically everything as a part of cost:

Selling below cost—

It shall constitute unfair competition for any manufacturer to sell his product below cost, except on close-outs. Cost as used herein is defined to include the actual cost of raw materials and supplies; fair wages for employees; power, light, heat, water and other miscellaneous operating expenses; repair and maintenance of buildings and equipment; executive, supervisory, sales and office salaries and expenses; advertising and promotional expense; distribution and delivery expense; rent for show rooms and warehouses; legal and collection expenses; bad debt losses; depreciation and obsolescence of buildings and equipment at the rates provided under the Federal Income Tax Law; interest on indebtedness; insurance; taxes; and other expenses necessary and incidental to the manufacture and sale of the product. After a uniform cost accounting system shall have been adopted for the industry, such system shall be used by all manufacturers who are members of the industry in allocating the above items of cost on specific products.

Impracticality of present interpretations

One might go on interminably quoting provisions from code after code, bearing upon the prohibition of selling below cost and the definitions of cost computation, but the only effect would be to confirm the following conclusions:

1. That there is nothing inherent in the interpretations or requirements of the NRA to change the basic factors of cost determination which have heretofore been acceptable from a sound accounting viewpoint.

2. That any code prohibition against selling below cost is meaningless unless the term "cost" is carefully defined and unless some provision is made as to the methods and principles of computing costs.

3. That there appears to be too little knowledge on the part of industry as to what constitutes proper cost determination, and too vague a conception of the detail and complexity of proper cost-finding systems.

4. That industry is rather lightly writing into its codes provisions on cost and accounting which will be extremely difficult and expensive of fulfillment, and which may in some instances be unwarranted.

5. That many code provisions as now formulated will be impossible of attainment and will not accomplish either the intent of the act or the desires of the industry.

This last conclusion is particularly true in view of the attempt to so greatly extend unit cost determination to include selling, general and financial expense, in an effort to build a cost which will be directly comparable with the selling price. Industry would do well to realize that cost finding has a far greater value than that of providing some basis for the determination of selling prices. The use and the results of an effective cost system provide management with a dependable means for securing more effective operation, for eliminating wasteful and uneconomic procedures, for promoting high individual efficiency, for better meeting competition, for currently securing information on plant operations and, generally, for maintaining control and for developing sound business policies. It is true, of course, that as management is provided with more dependable knowledge through improved cost and accounting procedures, this knowledge will be reflected in prices, and may go far in eliminating vicious price practices which have prevailed in the past.

Desirable cost provisions

It becomes evident therefore that the code which is to really benefit an industry should clearly differentiate between two elements which have heretofore been intermingled. The first is some desirable regulation of prices, and the second is the establishment of satisfactory (perhaps in many cases uniform) accounting, cost and operating records, under some centralized, supervisory control. The former eventually may come to have a relationship to the latter, but at the present moment prices and costs may not safely be too closely allied.

Therefore it would be well in most codes to merely provide that the code authority be given the power to study the problem of improved accounting and cost finding for the industry, and to take such steps as may be found desirable in the establishment of uniform cost and accounting procedures. The matter of price regulation should be covered in another section, in a different and more practical manner.

The determination of manufacturing costs has its greatest value in matters of operating control, and to be fully dependable and effective should result from a currently effective system of cost finding, controlled by the books of account and including all items of manufacturing expenditure, distributed to products on some satisfactory and uniform basis. From an accounting viewpoint, the components of cost are as follows: direct labor plus direct material equals prime cost; prime cost plus manufacturing overhead equals cost of production; cost of production plus selling and delivery expense (including advertising and promotion), plus administrative expense, plus financial expense, equals operating cost; operating cost plus operating profit or minus operating loss, equals selling price. (This, of course, ignores non-operating adjustments.) In sound accounting practice "cost" is taken to mean the "cost of production" as herein defined, and no other interpretation is advisable in a code which specifies the development of a system for uniform cost finding in an industry.

The procedures which may be followed in regard to details will be influenced by the type of cost system, which is determined to be applicable to a given situation. Thus there are "Production Order Cost Systems," "Operation Cost Systems," "Process Cost Systems," "Standard Cost Systems," and numerous others more specialized or less well defined. There are peculiar "allocated" cost systems usable in certain industries, and there are combinations of two or more of the above systems necessary to meet certain circumstances. All of these have been studied, worked upon and applied at some place or some time, and each requires a specialized knowledge of its particular application if its installation and use is to be successful. The type which should be used is dependent upon the particular product and method of processing of the given business, and perhaps upon the necessity for making the best use of existent records and customs in the business. Among the plants in a given industry, it might not be unusual to find several different types of cost systems already in use. In applying cost finding to an industry, a system of uniform accounting is an essential prerequisite to a system of uniform cost finding. Unless the charts of accounts are in all essentials identical, with the make-up of each account well defined, the costs of each plant will be dissimilar. Sometimes too, considerable improvement in the industry may be accomplished through uniform accounting alone, leaving the cost problem to a later date.

Possible price control provisions

The code provisions which prescribe the use of uniform industry accounting and uniform cost-finding systems thus will be of immense value to business as they are made effective, but required selling prices should not, at the present moment, be too closely allied to the costs which might thus be determined. I believe that a more practical method is required to fit the immediate need for some degree of price regulation, and to bridge the interval before dependably calculated costs are attainable.

It is true that price fixing of a type to result in monopolistic practices is undesirable and illegal under the N. I. R. A., even though Federally regulated price fixing is a method employed under the Agricultural Adjustment Act. Price control, however, is something else. Price control means that prices must not go so low as to destroy industry nor so high as to destroy trade. It should provide some competitive range in the price scale, and allow of the superior profits which may accrue to a superior quality of management.

A method of control is developed in the lumber code which, though perhaps too closely tied to costs, seems to have the proper trend. At least it escapes the pitfall of individual plant costs. It specifies the power of the code authority to set minimum selling prices which shall serve as a cost protection, these prices being for the present based upon such cost information as is available, but eventually being related to the costs secured through use of uniform industry cost methods. Since the code authority includes several government representatives, there is some assurance that the minimum selling prices determined will be such as to protect the interests of the consumer public. This is a rather practical method of preventing vicious price cutting, and recognizing the fact that it may be some time before the industry cost-finding systems provide complete or dependable figures for control purposes. I look for an increasing use of this form, rather than acceptance of what has heretofore been the usual phrase "not to sell below cost."

The steel code also offers a practical method, in providing open price quotations on basing points, with a penalty for selling below the quoted prices. Use of the idea of clearing all price lists through the code authority may be found in some few codes, and seems quite practical, even though it may not be as stringent a form of control as may be necessary in some industries. I do not feel that the necessities for price control are being approached frankly, either by in-

186

dustry or by the government, and I believe that one of the main stumbling blocks in the path of proper code development has been the governmental fear of anything that sounded like price fixing. Despite the waiving of the anti-trust laws during the life of a code; despite the strong control exercised by having government representatives on the various Code Authorities; and despite the announced fact of a new conception of control over industry, the old bug-a-boo of monopolistic price fixing still casts its shadow of fear.

It would seem desirable that frank recognition be given to the fact that cost recovery or cost protection is the desired aim. But in avoiding code phrasing which might *sound* at all like price fixing, sanction has been given to code provisions prohibiting "selling below cost" which, if they could be made effective, would lead to a more positive and less controllable price fixing than anything heretofore known. The incoherence and inconsistency of many of the submitted codes is less the fault of the industry code committees than it is of the inhibition against a frankly clear recognition of principles.

Some aspects of the "New Deal"

I do not want you to feel that I am being overly critical in this discussion of certain phases of the industry codes which have been and are being formulated. American business has had suddenly thrust upon it the necessity for accomplishing in a few months a task which, in a process of normal evolution, might not have been brought to completion in the next twenty or thirty years. It is faced with a new era, in which some of the old principles of individualism and self-interest must give way to principles of cooperation and public interest. We are a young nation and have much to learn. The changes in industrial structure, which are being brought about by what we believe to be the pressure of an internal emergency, may shortly be highly beneficial in enabling the nation to meet the pressure of international industrial competition. It is difficult for this country to know or understand the changes which war and postwar conditions effected in the international coordination of the great European industries.

Briefly, my point is this: that an era of industrial change is upon us, in which many of our previous concepts must be modified, not only as a national matter, but also as an international necessity. The first step is cooperation among businesses in an industry. The second step is cooperation among industries from a national viewpoint, wherein the public interest takes precedence over individual self-interest. Accompanying these changes in viewpoint and action must come the improvements in operating effectiveness which are partly the by-product of release from destructive competitive practices, and partly the result of improved records of operations.

Many businessmen feel that they have been caught up by a tidal wave which completely alters all of the former trends of industry, but my belief is that there has been no radical change in trend. Rather, the pressure of necessity has resulted merely in a surge or intensification of the trend which has existed for the past several decades, and which has been manifested in the growing use and importance of trade associations; which was misapplied in the nineties in our use of trusts; which permitted the strong recent trend toward consolidation and combination in business; but which has not been really understood or properly developed in any of these manifestations. Now we are close to the truth that business exists as a service to mankind and cannot prove superior to humanity.

The Act may not accomplish 100 percent of all that its sponsors intend, but it fosters the step forward, both socially and economically. The natural trend of business in this country has been steadily toward better wages and shorter working hours, and the Act merely serves to accelerate the tempo of this trend. Similarly it aids the existent trend toward industrial cooperation and control. Man progresses by experimentation and out of our first crude efforts comes the eventual practical result. I have confidence in the capitalistic system which has made this the greatest nation in the world. I have confidence in the courage and ability of our people, in whom the energetic, pioneering strain is still strong, and I firmly believe that out of the seemingly drastic readjustments of the present will come an acceptance of permanent principles which will lastingly benefit our nation and eventually the entire world.

Duties and responsibilities of the comptroller

Before the Controllers'
Institute of America,
Chicago Control,
November 27, 1934

Under a sound organization plan the comptroller reports results and operating conditions to the directors, without fear or favor, and this freedom from prejudice is of great importance.

DURING the past five years most business men have had reason to doubt the theories and principles of business conduct which previously served them as dependable guides, and many concepts have perforce been changed, or at least modified, by the experience of these years. But now this period of doubt appears to be nearing an end, and today there is stronger evidence than ever before that certain principles of management and of personnel organization are sound. There is increasing evidence that where these principles are observed the chances for successful operation are materially better than where they are ignored. This presumes, of course, equality in other factors that may affect such a comparison.

The fundamental requirement in any business is *men*. There is no substitute for the leadership that can be given by men with the knowledge, intelligence, courage, energy, enthusiasm and resourcefulness which most executive positions require; so let us not forget that the *man* is the most important factor in every position in every organization.

In the days when individual business enterprises were small and one man could supervise personally all activities of a given business, the requirement as to personnel organization was almost exclusively for men having the required qualification for the work. With the growth of large organizations, however, a new need was encountered. There came to be many men engaged in directional and administrative work within a single business. Specialization was developed to a high degree. Each man was charged with responsibility for some particular phase of activity. And with this distribution of responsibility it has become increasingly important to define the field of activity for each and to clarify the functional relationships among all. As this specialization has been carried along, certain logical and practical classifications of duties have been developed through experience under which a smoothness of operation can be attained, and under which the best interests of the company can be satisfactorily guarded. So, in business enterprises of the present day, it is more than ever important to have competent men for the principal positions, and in addition, it has become necessary to provide a plan of organization under which these men may work without the conflict and interference that usually occur when positions are not defined and ambition spurs each one to encompass as much ground as his individual judgment dictates.

The coordinated effort of a properly balanced organization creates a force much greater than that which could be produced by a corresponding group of equally qualified individuals working without a previously established plan as to the division of their duties and responsibilities.

To attain this coordinated effort of a properly balanced organization, three things are necessary. First, each major position must be filled by a man who will discharge satisfactorily the specific duties of his position. Second, a spirit of cooperation must prevail which is dependent, in large part, upon general acceptance of the thought that the interests of the individual are closely allied with the interests of the organization as a whole. Finally, the entire group of major executives must work in accordance with a previously established plan of action in which each man plays his proper part and in which each part is an integral portion of the plan as a whole.

It is to this final requirement that particular attention should be given. One of the most common obstacles to effective coordination in business organizations is a tendency to stress unduly the importance of some one position or individual, and correspondingly to place restrictions upon other individuals which are entirely out of keeping with their purported functional positions. Due to individual ability or force of personality, it frequently happens that the head of some one function of a business is permitted, or even encouraged, to dominate policy formulation and conduct of the business in general. The prerogatives of other department heads are usurped, they are prevented from functioning in their normal capacities, and a general condition of unbalance is created. This occurs even though the other positions are competently filled, and it represents a basic distortion of functional lines rather than a justified compensation for weaknesses in personnel.

Of the generally recognized and more usual functional positions in modern business organizations, that of comptroller has probably suffered most from this tendency to encroach. This is understandable, as the comptroller's function is a comparatively recent development, made necessary by the large size of modern business organizations, and it has come into existence so unobtrusively that many people fail to comprehend the fundamental change which has taken place. There is a tendency still to think of the comptroller in terms of bookkeeping, and to regard the position as a necessary evil which in large part has been forced on business by the quantity and complexity of our tax laws and various governmental regulations. The comptroller's function today is unquestionably one of the major functions of business administration, and the importance of the position should be fully recognized.

One of the principal reasons that the correct degree of importance has not generally been attached to the comptroller's position lies in failure on the part of comptrollers themselves to visualize their true function, or in a lack of ability to do the job that is theirs by the right of sound organization. In creating a more widespread knowledge of the comptroller's duties and responsibilities, the "Controllers Institute of America" is performing a great service to its members, to accountants, to comptrollers in general and to industry as a whole. No doubt there are differing opinions as to the proper placement for many of the duties which one might assign to the comptroller, but close study of the problem over a period of years has made possible the preparation of an outline of duties and responsibilities of this office which shortly will be presented for your consideration.

This outline is submitted as a theoretical assignment of duties, and accordingly a word of caution may be advisable. As previously stated, the fundamental requirement of any business is men. Since no two human beings are identical and seldom, if ever, will two men be found with identical qualifications for any position, it often is advisable to permit some modification of the theoretical plan in order to take advantage of individual abilities and qualities. There are, accordingly, two conflicting forces at work—the need for molding the plan to suit the individual, and the need for establishing and preserving correct functional organization. A satisfactory balance between these two must be maintained. It is unwise to distort a sound organization plan for the sake of an individual; conversely, the best results can not be obtained if a plan of organization is insisted upon, into which the individuals will not fit. When this problem is very pronounced the answer is probably some change in personnel.

The duties of the comptroller require that he perform work relating to every function of the business, and accordingly organization relationships with every other functional head must be worked out. The relationship which appears to present the greatest problem and to cause the greatest confusion, however, is that with the treasurer. This is undoubtedly due in part to the fact that record keeping and finance are closely allied, and in part to misconception of the treasurer's true function. For years it has been customary for by-laws to provide for the office of treasurer, and to have the treasurer subject to appointment by the board of directors. This has given the office of treasurer a certain prestige that the comptroller, usually an appointee of the president or general manager, has not enjoyed. Due primarily to this condition, a tendency has existed to regard the treasurer as senior to the comptroller and, in many cases, as at least the functional director of the comptroller's activities. By-laws in general have not kept pace with the changes in business needs and business custom which have led to creation of the function of comptroller as an office of major importance. There are exceptions, however, and there appears to be at present a marked tendency in larger corporations to recognize officially the importance of the comptroller's position.

During recent years, numerous papers have been written on the duties and responsibilities of the comptroller. Most of these have dealt with the question broadly and have presented rather general definitions of the comptroller's function, although in some instances these general definitions have been supplemented with detailed illustrations of ways in which a comptroller could function properly. But in these papers it is most unusual to find, in definitely crystallized form, concise yet comprehensive statements defining the comptroller's function in the more detailed manner required for practical application. It would appear that enough generalization has been indulged in, and that enough illustrations have been given. Accordingly, in this address, a departure is to be made from the more usual and perhaps more interesting type of presentation in favor of the somewhat drier, but probably more useful, detailed outline.

In view of the great amount of confusion that still exists as to the proper dividing line between the true function of the comptroller and the true function of the treasurer, it may be well to present outlines for both; and perhaps the office of the comptroller will be the more clearly understood if the office of treasurer is defined first. In these outlines it is assumed that there is no higher ranking financial officer in the organization than the treasurer. Obviously, if the organization includes a financial vice president, the duties of both the treasurer and the comptroller will be changed. More will be said on that subject later.

The treasurer, speaking broadly, should be responsible to the board of directors for the receipt, custody and disbursement of all funds of the corporation, in the form both of cash and securities. He should be accountable to the president for the administration of these duties in conformity with policies established by the latter, by the executive committee, or by the board itself, and he should accept any other responsibilities, either special or routine, that may be assigned to him by the president.

More specifically, the duties and responsibilities of the treasurer may be stated as follows:

1. *Policy formulation*

As the officer primarily responsible for the financial function of the business, the treasurer should develop recommendations with respect to financial policy, to be submitted to the executive committee or board of directors for their approval. To the extent of his authority, he should see that the company has a financial program adequate to meet future requirements over a period of years, and he should negotiate loans, either short or long term, if and when required.

2. *Bank relations*

He should be responsible for the fostering and maintenance of desirable relations with those banks and banking interests which are of most value to the company for both present and possible future advantage in the conduct of the business.

3. *Investments*

Subject to approval by the executive committee or board of directors, he should formulate an investment policy and should invest the available funds of the company in accordance therewith, giving proper consideration to such factors as safety of principal, dates of maturity, marketability, yield, etc.

4. *Deposit of cash receipts*

He should be responsible for seeing that all cash received by the company is deposited intact with depositaries approved by the board of directors.

5. *Custody of cash and investment securities*

He should be recognized as the responsible custodian of all cash and investment securities owned by or in possession of the company, whether as their own property or in trust, and he should take all steps necessary to assure the safety of such items. However, with regard to securities, it is customary to have these placed under dual control as an added safeguard. Some of the duties included in this responsibility are—

(a) Study of the financial condition of depositaries employed.

(b) Bonding of those officers and employees of the company who are in positions of trust with respect to the company's cash or securities.

(c) Arrangements for hold-up and burglary insurance and similar risk coverage that conditions may make advisable.

(d) Arrangements for the protection of cash and securities, and employees handling these items, by the employment of guards, money transfer agencies, etc., where such provisions may be desirable.

6. *Disbursements*

The disbursement of funds and the releases of securities should take place only in accordance with his order or instructions issued by him, and he should take the necessary steps to guard against any deviation from this practice. (This applies only, however, to the actual release of cash or securities, and should not be confused with the approval of vouchers for payment, which properly is a function of the comptroller.)

7. *Time of payment*

In accordance with and subject to the

financial policy of the company, he should direct the dates at which vouched bills are to be prepared for payment, and in this connection he should indicate whether bills are to be anticipated, discounted, paid net when due, or deferred. In such regulation of payments, the interests of other functions of the business should be considered and the plan adopted should be one for the general good of the company.

8. *Distribution of funds*

He should direct and control the distribution of cash among the company's several depositaries. He likewise should control the number, location, and amounts of the working funds required throughout the company.

9. *Credits*

He should guide and direct the extension of credit to customers, and pass upon credit problems involved in payments to vendors and all other credits allowed by the company, in conformity with general policies established by the executive committee or by the board. This does not include responsibility for the approval of advances or loans made to officers and employees. Such advances, other than routine advances for traveling and similar purposes, should be subject to approval by the board of directors.

10. *Collections*

He should be responsible for the collection of all moneys due the company from debtors of all classes, and he should see that no arrangements entailing credits to debtors' accounts for other than cash are made without proper authorization. In routine cases, of course, he may delegate authority to subordinates.

11. *Nonoperating property*

He should be responsible for the management of properties held as investments and for the maintenance, lease and disposition of properties which have ceased to be used in the conduct of the company's regular business. Certain of these functions may be delegated to other department heads for practical reasons, but it should remain the responsibility of the treasurer to safeguard such investments and to maintain nonoperating income.

12. *Insurance*

He should be responsible, through the placing of insurance, for providing the company with adequate safeguards against loss arising from accident or natural hazards, subject, however, to any specific instructions which the board of directors may issue. His responsibility in such matters should include the selection of underwriters, determination of the coverage required, renewal of expiring policies and, in general, all matters pertaining to all classes of insurance. Insurance policies may be turned over to the secretary for safekeeping, if desired, excepting corporate life policies with a cash surrender value, which should be deposited with securities in the company's safe-deposit vault.

13. *Official signatures*

He should validate all corporate instruments requiring the signature of the fiscal officer and should receive and execute garnishments and other processes of law directed to the corporation involving the payment of funds.

14. *Reports*

He should present reports at regular intervals to the executive committee and to the board of directors, giving an account of his stewardship of the company's funds and other important points in the fiscal affairs of the company.

That concludes the outline of suggested duties and responsibilities for the treasurer. Upon comparison of this outline with that for the comptroller, which follows, it will be noted that dividing lines are quite clearly drawn and that but little opportunity remains for confusion between the functions of these two officers.

The comptroller, speaking broadly, should be responsible to the president for the maintenance of adequate records to permit the preparation therefrom of statements showing the financial position of the company and the results of operations, by accounting periods. He should prepare regular reports, based on the records, for presentation to the board and to the several officers and department heads of the company and should submit such special reports as may be called for. He should be charged with the maintenance of audit control over operations of the company and with responsibility for the accounting system generally. He should accept any other responsibilities, special or routine, that may be assigned to him by the president.

In more detail his functions are as follows:

1. *Books of account*

As the principal accounting officer, he should be responsible for the administrative direction of all work relative to maintaining the company's books of account in such a manner that the records will show accurately the financial condition of the company at the close of each accounting period and the results of its operations. In this connection, he should have full responsibility subject to the board of directors, for the accounting policies followed. In those instances where subsidiary records relating to the books of account are placed under the administrative supervision of an individual not directly subject to the comptroller's authority, the comptroller should exercise a functional direction over all such work and be responsible for these records in their effect upon his accounts to the same extent that he would be responsible were such records maintained within his own department. This should apply to the accounting records of subsidiary companies as well as to the subsidiary records of the parent company.

2. *Internal check*

He should be responsible for the proper functioning of adequate internal check or auditing procedures designed to safeguard the company's assets against unauthorized disposition or loss arising from negligence or dishonesty on the part of employees. Where practicable, he should provide automatic cross-checks whereby the acts of individuals entrusted with cash, securities, merchandise, or the authority to receive, hold or issue any of these, shall be checked by or against the work of different individuals, preferably in other departments or sections of the organization. These automatic checks should be supplemented where necessary by actual audit work for assurance that no loss to the company will result from clerical errors, neglect of clerical duties, or intentional dishonesty on the part of any employee or officer of the company.

3. *Access to securities*

Although responsibility for the safekeeping of all marketable securities and similar items held in the company's safe-deposit boxes or vaults rests primarily with the treasurer, it should be the responsibility of the comptroller to so fix the requirements for access to such boxes or vaults that an adequate cross-check is maintained. The presence of two responsible individuals should be required in every instance, one of whom should be the treasurer or an authorized representative, the other the comptroller or an authorized representative. The purpose and results of each visit should be made a matter of definite record, supported by the signatures of those present.

4. *Reports for management purposes*

He should prepare or cause to be prepared statements reflecting the financial condition of the company and the results of its operations for presentation to the board of directors and to the several officers of the company, regularly at intervals conforming with the company's accounting periods. He should likewise prepare statements regularly for the several department heads and sub-department heads providing them with all pertinent data on operations or other details of the business which may be of value to them in the effective performance of their respective tasks.

5. *Analysis and interpretation*

The financial reports for the board of directors, and other reports where desirable, should be supplemented by his written comment calling attention to important points for consideration, including significant trends or ratios. It is his responsibility, in general, to provide interpretations of the figures assembled for report purposes and to assist the entire organization through his analyses of financial and operating statements.

6. *Reports to stockholders and releases to the press*

The comptroller should review carefully all reports having financial significance that the board of directors or officers of the company may submit to stockholders, to security exchanges or to the press. It is extremely important, under the present Securities Act and Securities Exchange Act, that all data so released shall permit of complete substantiation and that no opportunity shall be afforded, within reasonable limits, for erroneous assumptions to be drawn by possible readers. Although responsibility for the release of such statements ordinarily rests with the board of directors or the president, and the comptroller usually is not in a position of final authority with respect thereto, the comptroller should guard against the possibility that those directly responsible may act on the basis of faulty or incomplete information.

7. *Forecasts or budgets*

As as aid to effective planning for future operations and as a means of measuring the accomplishment represented in actual performance, the comptroller should supervise and direct the development of operating and financial forecasts or budgets covering in each case that future period which appears best suited to the opportunity and the need for such calculation. The heads of the several departments within the organization should be required to prepare their own individual estimates of income and expense covering their respective operations, but it should be the duty of the comptroller to consult with each department head and to effect a reconciliation of the various departmental figures to arrive at a consolidated forecast (or budget) based on balanced activity. Where the figures finally submitted by department heads are, in the opinion of the comptroller, either contrary to the best interests of the company or impossible of attainment, he should review such figures with the president and/or the general manager.

8. *Revision of system*

He should be responsible for all methods and procedures employed in the accounting and clerical work of his department, and should be expected to make changes from time to time in the interest of better safeguarding the company's assets, more accurate or more suitable data, promptness in the presentation of reports, and greater economy of operation. With respect to methods and procedures in clerical work in other than his own department, he should have the privilege of investigation and recommendation for change, and he should supervise such change upon approval of the department head affected.

9. *Mechanical office equipment and forms for accounting and clerical use*

The purchase of all major items of mechanical office equipment should be subject to his approval, and no new forms should be adopted for use until approved by him or by an individual whom he has designated to act in such matters.

10. *Costs and cost estimates*

He should be responsible for the determination of unit product costs, with that degree of accuracy and in that form best fitted to meet the requirements of the sales and manufacturing functions of the business as well as accounting. He should likewise direct the preparation of all estimates of future costs for assurance that all elements of cost are properly observed, but this work need not be done under his administrative control if it appears expedient to have it placed elsewhere in the organization.

11. *Sales prices*

Responsibility for sales prices rests primarily with the chief sales executive, but the comptroller should collaborate in the establishment of price schedules whenever the sales prices are dependent upon or are closely related to costs. He also should be familiar with all provisions as to price, terms, etc., that appear in the industry's code of fair competition, and he should call attention to any instance where proposed prices or terms appear to be in violation thereof.

12. *Receivables*

He should be responsible for seeing that all transactions where the company assumes or extends a position as creditor are properly recorded in a special group of accounting records provided for this purpose, and he should cooperate fully with the treasurer in matters pertaining to the collection of these notes or accounts by preparing special analyses and reports of the condition of such accounts, both individually and collectively, as required.

13. *Inventories*

He should be responsible jointly with the executive in charge of plant operations for the overall accuracy of physical inventories that are to be taken up on the books. He should prepare or approve the instructions under which inventories are to be taken and should provide for the necessary audit or check of the counts, description and pricing, to provide assurance of the fundamental truth of the inventories reported. He should have full responsibility for all extension, classification and other clerical work incidental to the final determination of values.

14. *Insurance*

He should be responsible for the preparation and submission to the treasurer of periodic statements of the insurable value of buildings, equipment, inventories and other insurable assets, if any, to provide the treasurer with the proper valuation basis for the placing of insurance. Similarly, he should provide the treasurer with payroll summaries for use in connection with employers' liability insurance.

15. *Taxes*

He should be responsible for the preparation of all income-tax returns required by Federal or state governments, and he should provide assistance in connection with the preparation of personal property, franchise or other tax returns upon request by the secretary or the treasurer.

16. *Disbursements*

He should enforce procedures which will provide that no disbursement of funds may take place without proper audit and approval by duly authorized persons.

17. *General*

The comptroller should participate in the consideration given to all major projects broadly affecting the future course of the company. He, more than any other except the general officers of the company, must have a comprehensive knowledge of the present operations and future plans pertaining to all functions of the business.

That concludes the detailed outline of the comptroller's duties and responsibilities. An attempt has been made to include therein an indication of the nature of his duties in sufficient detail that his position will be properly defined, and yet in a form sufficiently broad to cover numerous details not specifically mentioned.

For a complete understanding of the comptroller's position, however — for an understanding of the opportunity that is his to serve an organization to the full extent that his position offers—some further comment may be helpful. It is not enough merely to go through the routine of performing the duties outlined. The truly big man in this truly big position will contribute something beside that; but unfortunately most comptrollers need to tear down certain barriers in thought that restrict their point of view and accordingly limit their opportunities.

The accountant's mind is trained to fine mathematical accuracy, to the treatment of details, to rigid departmentalization. His point of view is normally, and quite naturally, from the side of accounting and finance. The comptroller's greatest function in business and his greatest opportunity for service lie in his ability to see, or to sense, the operating problems, and to make his accounting statements serve the *operating* personnel. Most comptrollers can prepare statements that meet a company's needs from the financial point of view. How many can prepare statements that truly cover the operating requirements? True, some comptrollers will give the operating people what they ask for, and that helps, but the real need is for the comptroller who can go beyond that point, who can combine a knowledge of figures and accounting with a sense for the use of figures for operating purposes, and who accordingly can prepare operating reports that are better than the operating people themselves can specify. The company that has such a comptroller is fortunate, and the comptroller that fills such a position is a big man.

A discussion of the duties and responsibilities of the comptroller would not be complete without giving some attention to the relationship that should exist between this officer and the general executives of the company, and with the board of directors.

In view of the responsibilities that are now placed squarely upon the directors, responsibilities which have been morally theirs for years and many of which have been made legally binding by recently enacted laws, it is of considerable importance to them that they obtain complete and unbiased reports as to the company's financial position, results from operations and miscellaneous accounting and statistical information. The one individual in the company's organization who, above all others, should be best able to present this information is the comptroller. He is in more or less direct contact with the detail accounting records; he must be acquainted with the activities of all functions of the business; he should know better than any other man how to analyze and interpret the accounting and statistical data which are available. To justify his position as a major executive of the company he must have mature judgment and a good sense of relative values. Under normal conditions, the comptroller can offer a better combination of analytical ability, knowledge of accounting in general and knowledge of the company's accounts in particular, than anyone else in the organization.

The comptroller is in the most detached and impartial position of all the major executives. He has no responsibility for policy or administration of sales, production, finance or general management. Under a sound organization plan, he can report results and operating conditions to the directors without fear or favor, and this freedom from prejudice is of much importance when reports on company activities are involved. If the directors receive an accounting report prepared under the direction of some other officer, there is always the possibility that either intentionally or unintentionally the information presented will be shaded in a way to either minimize or emphasize certain points where personal interest enters the picture; or, it is quite possible that certain errors or failures may be completely obscured. Figures are as clay in the hands of the sculptor. Too often have we seen the disastrous result of relying upon financial statements issued by overoptimistic, insincere or biased persons, even though they may be what the world calls "honest."

It is this importance of a detached and unbiased viewpoint which offers the crowning argument against combining the functions of treasurer and comptroller in one man. Costly errors in judgment, or in the interpretation of policies, can be made by the financial officer as well as by other officers, and it is highly desirable that the accounting reports to the chief administrative officer and to the board disclose such errors if made. If the reports were presented by the financial officer there would be a quite natural tendency to so arrange the figures that errors of this type would not be readily seen. The comptroller, if independent of the financial officer, is in a position to report on a purely unbiased basis the results of *all* operations, and the financial condition resulting from *all* operations, including transactions which technically are nonoperating in their nature. The only subject matter of the comptroller's report in which he has a personal interest, if responsibilities are properly functionalized, is the operating expense of his own department.

As implied previously, there are other reasons why it is advisable to have both a comptroller and a treasurer, each independent of the other. Until recently internal check was the only argument generally advanced to support this division of responsibilities. More recently, however, there appears to have developed a recognition of the fact that the experience and capabilities required for one function are different from the requirements for the other. With this it has come to be realized, in the case of the larger companies at least, that the position of comptroller calls for administrative and technical abilities that can not be exercised satisfactorily if the individual must give a considerable part of his time to the company's finances and special matters extraneous to the duties of a comptroller. Conversely, the treasurer may have pressing financial problems of the utmost importance which will not receive the needed amount of attention if he must devote a large part of his time to administrative matters.

And now, what of the comptroller's relationship with the company's chief executive and with the board of directors?

As indicated previously, it is most desirable that the board shall obtain its financial statements exactly as prepared by the comptroller, and it would appear upon first thought, perhaps, that the comptroller should be responsible only to the board. But the board meets usually with intervals of at least a month between meetings, and in the meantime the chief executive of the company is responsible for conducting the business in accordance with policies and plans laid down or approved by the board. The most efficient operation is normally obtained when all activities are coordinated under a single head, and it would appear logical, therefore, that the comptroller's function be included with the rest, subject to direction by the chief executive.

The conflicts in lines of authority which may appear to result from this arrangement are more imaginary than real. Under this arrangement the comptroller is made subject to the administrative control of the chief executive to the same extent that other officers are correspondingly placed. A difference exists only in the fact that the comptroller shall have direct contact with the board through his reports, a privilege which may be denied other officers.

Presentation of the reports may be arranged in at least three ways, as follows:

1. The most satisfactory arrangement from many angles is to have the comptroller as a member of the board.

2. Next in preference is the practice of having the comptroller meet with the board during a sufficient part of each of their sessions to present his report in person.

3. Still satisfactory is an arrangement whereby the comptroller's signed report would be presented to the board through another officer, in most cases the president. In such instances the officer presenting the report could be permitted to add a supplementary report of his own relating to the substance of the comptroller's report, but in no case should he be allowed to substitute his report for that of the comptroller.

Under any of these arrangements there is danger that the comptroller may be dominated by the chief executive and may not voice his true beliefs or opinions. The comptroller is, of course, in an uncomfortable position in the event serious differences exist, and he will no doubt think twice before taking a position adversely critical of the management, but certainly the board's chance for a true picture is vastly better than when this channel for true information is obstructed by barriers imposed through the form of organization. Then too, there is more encouragement offered the comptroller to speak frankly if he can be made to feel that his report will receive as fair consideration by the board as that of some other officer.

Naturally under such an arrangement it is imperative that the board not only appoint the comptroller but that it also retain the authority to regulate his salary. It is only natural for a man to be influenced by the location of control over his income.

Now let us consider for a minute the question as to how the existence of a financial vice president will affect the status of the comptroller and, also, whether the office of financial vice president is logical or desirable.

In answering that question it must first of all be recalled that the man is the most important factor in every position in every organization. Given satisfactory men to fill the offices of comptroller and treasurer, the office of financial vice president would be superfluous and a hindrance to sound organization, as it would interpose an organization step between the comptroller and both the chief executive and the board. In making that statement it is assumed that the financial vice president would act as a senior officer over both the treasurer and the comptroller. If he should have jurisdiction over the treasurer alone, there would then be even less justification for the office,

as in that event he would in reality *be* treasurer and should have that title.

Unfortunately, however, it is not always possible or feasible to provide an organization with two satisfactorily competent men for the positions of treasurer and comptroller respectively, and in those cases where a man of unusual ability is already in the organization, or is available from the outside, it is sometimes more satisfactory to give such a man responsibility for both functions of the business. This is not a desirable solution, however, and should always be regarded as an expedient rather than as sound permanent organization.

When such a situation does exist, a rather difficult problem is presented in the reallocation of duties and responsibilities. Below the financial vice president the line of demarcation between the two functions should be preserved. The system of internal check will be weakened inherently, to some extent, by the unification of control over the two functions, and any further merging should be carefully avoided, particularly where internal check is involved. The treasurer probably should retain more of his functional duties than the comptroller, as many of the more important functions of the latter would pass to the vice president. Responsibility for reports to the board of directors nominally would then rest with the vice president rather than with the comptroller, although the comptroller probably would still do the major part of the work in preparing the analyses and comments. More detailed recommendations as to the distribution of duties would require too much time for presentation here, and, furthermore, in most cases a standard set-up can hardly be applied. As the position of financial vice president is most frequently created to meet some unusual situation, it is hardly likely that any standard can be set which will offer much chance of fitting individual cases.

In conclusion, a brief bit of advice is offered to all men who occupy positions as comptrollers. Remember that accounting, records work and all the related duties represent only one function of the business. The comptroller is responsible for that function and should do all in his power to gain and to justify recognition as an important functional head and officer, but he should not attempt to usurp the prerogatives of the president or general manager. The comptroller provides the data for intelligent direction and control, and he should counsel with department heads and the general executives; but, most emphatically, he does not *control* the business. When the comptroller begins to dictate rather than advise, when he tries to convert lines of functional control into lines of direct control, he then is riding either toward a general managership or toward a severe fall, and in a very great majority of such cases it will be the latter.

Be reasonable, be fair and if possible be wise.

The future of our economic system

Delivered at Northwestern
University, The Contemporary
Thought Series, December 5, 1934

*Our future economic system
will have many of the
characteristics of the past,
particularly an adherence to
individual initiative along
with social coordination and
cooperation.*

*The greatest economic rewards
of the future will go to those
who honestly accept the task
of making this world a better
place for all people.*

IN THE past few years there have been written many books and many more articles dealing with the problems of economics. One hesitates to add to this abundance of words and thoughts, but some justification may be found in the size and complexity of the subject and in the present lack of uniformity of conclusions. The people of the United States are of an eager, inquisitive and aggressive nature. When things happen which they do not at once readily understand, they seek for reasons, analyses and explanations. So under the stress of the depression which for four years has borne heavily upon the nation, destroying the efforts and the plans of many lives, the people have wished to know why and how it all has happened, in the hopes thereby to prevent or lessen the chances of future disaster, and also, on the basis of sound analysis, to devise the correct methods of recovery from this catastrophe.

I believe that very few men are in accord as to the cause of the depression, and I know that few are in agreement as to any detailed plans for recovery and prevention. My own conclusions are by no means clear, and it is with great reluctance that I venture to comment upon a subject which has already been ably discussed by expert economists. My expressions are not those of a theorist but should be accepted as the comments of the man on the street—of the business man who is trying to understand; who hopes that he may be able to keep his people at work; and who trusts that not all of the principles and efforts of a lifetime have been in vain.

My early knowledge of this world was of a place in which effort and initiative were necessary for success, and in which the material and spiritual rewards corresponded to the energy and talent expended. That early conception I have retained as a guiding principle, and to the present moment have found no reason for mistrusting its soundness. I have always been able to accept seriously that quotation from the third chapter of Genesis in which the Lord decreed to Adam and the sons of Adam—"In the sweat of thy face shalt thou eat bread, till thou return unto the ground; for out of it wast thou taken; for dust thou art and unto dust shalt thou return."

Considering the vast number of individuals, no two alike, in millions of different environments, of different races and heredity, it is difficult for me to think in terms of regimentation of effort or of common aims. Yet there must always be certain general principles of working and living which apply to all mankind, and which can be classified and studied under the broad designation of the science of economics.

The main difficulty in any discussion of economics is that so few people have more than a vague idea of what is meant by that word. It has been called a science — the science that treats of the development of material resources, or of the production, preservation and distribution of wealth, and of the means and methods of living well for the state, the family and the individual.

In earlier times economics was regarded simply as the science of material wealth. Now it is coming to be looked upon as the science of man's temporal well-being in the widest sense. If this is the true definition, then for purposes of study it may be divided into three great branches: first, pure economics, or the science of value or exchange, which concerns itself only with general principles and has often been restricted to purely material considerations; second, social economics, or that which applies the principles of pure economics to the problems connected with the growth and well-being of organized society; third, national economics, which studies these problems and principles from the viewpoint of the statesman, and treats of such questions as the tariff, taxation, currency, public education, national sufficiency, international relations, etc.

Even if this more careful definition is accepted, there is still some error in classifying economics as a science. Since it deals so largely with the human factor, and since human nature is so changeable and subject to so many outside influences, economics can never partake of the nature of the exact sciences. It cannot be a careful sequence of permanent and detailed principles, but becomes mainly the observed result of massed conditions, changeable and in part unpredictable. The study of economics, therefore, in my opinion, must consider first, the precise and orderly principles which could be developed if human nature could be subdued and regimented into perfect accord with sound theory; and second, the practical modification or perhaps total disregard of such principles in view of the fact that the human race never can be completely logical and selfless.

It is this persistence of individual thoughts, motives and ambitions, which so disturbs the plans of all who have tried to apply a single, pure and uniform theory to any considerable mass of humanity, whether along lines of economics or even of religion or warfare. This is especially true in these United States and has, as a trait, long been recognized. The nation was in fact founded upon the principles of individual freedom, and these principles have been encouraged by the rich areas of natural resources, which have provided great material rewards for those who have had the courage and the energy to make use of this birthright.

The application of pure economic theory to the affairs of mankind has long been the Utopia of dreamers. If we go back 2300 years to the days of ancient Greece, we find, in Plato's "Republic" the expression of the perfect state. This first great student of political science imagined a community in which every human effort was perfectly coordinated for the benefit of all people. The state should be ruled by a selected group of "Guardians," carefully selected and trained in the science of government.

Their power was to be supported by an armed force, the "Auxiliaries," these being necessary against outside attack rather than as a policing arm, because every inhabitant of the state would recognize the perfect justice and high ethics of the "Guardians" and so would give respect and obedience to their laws.

Nevertheless Plato himself was forced to recognize the difficulty of trying to apply pure theory to practical conditions. He refused to enter politics because he saw in individuals so much of self-interest and greed. He attempted to counsel Dionysius in the formation of an ideal state, and barely escaped with his life. Yet the theory of the perfect state has persisted and even today there are many who feel that a complete submergence of self-interest should be possible to all individuals, and that the interest of the whole state should be made the first consideration. I scarcely need to point to the recent expression of this viewpoint in Upton Sinclair's "Epic" plan for California.

For many centuries students of economics considered only its abstract phases and made no real effort to develop economic laws from the observation of actual circumstances. In the seventeenth century, however, many thinkers and philosophers began to see that the activities of men en masse, and therefore the activities of nations, were capable of interpretation, forming the bases for theories or systems. Such thinking and writing continued into the eighteenth century, where the economic theory of "mercantilism" was given a fairly clear expression. This was the theory that the best form of national economy was that in which the value of exports exceeded the value of imports, with the consequence that money flowed into the nation, serving to stimulate production and trade, and so leading to greater employment and industrial activity. It was a form of nationalism based upon a large development of international trade.

We may be inclined to think that no present day lesson can be drawn from the economic principles of the seventeenth century. Yet Othmar Spann, one of the finest of economic commentators, remarks—"one of the flaws in mercantilism was that its champions were often inclined to regard the mutual relations between the various national economies from the outlook of individualistic economies (cutthroat competition), assuming that for the sake of its own enrichment each nation must strive to outwit and overreach its neighbors, and fancying that life on such terms would be an enduring possibility! This is not a tenable view. Just as every national economy is a whole, dependent upon the fruitful mutuality of its parts, so the world economy is a super-whole dependent upon the fruitful mutuality of the national economies which constitute its parts. The essential characteristic of the world economy is not that one nation gains what another loses, but that both gain by mutuality."

From the time of Francois Quesnay (who died in 1774) and Adam Smith (who wrote his "Wealth of Nations" in 1776), there have been hundreds, even thousands, of writers and students of economics, who have attempted, from observation of facts, to develop sound explanations and theories of national and world economics, and until less than ten years ago many of the relations of cause and effect seemed to be fairly well defined and understood.

In the years 1925 to 1929, however, there began to arise in this country a new school of economic thought, formulating principally the theory that a new era had arrived, in which former economic disasters could not exist. It was hailed as an era of great productivity, of free and rapid flow of money, of high profits, of massive enterprises. Depressions could not occur because mankind had solved the former baffling economic problems. Poverty would be banished because of the perfection of production and distribution. The only disturbing voices were those of some real old-timers who believed that human nature, and therefore the actions and emotions of men, does not change thus rapidly, and that what had been, would be.

Presently, at the end of 1929, there came the stock market crash, which was more stunning than convincing. The theorists loudly insisted that the "New Era" was still with us and only required confidence and an attitude of "business as usual" to preserve the Utopia which had been gained. For almost a year industry and finance tried to stem and even to disregard the tide of economic disaster. Then the conviction began to creep in that this slump could not be explained away by any "New Era" economic formulae. By the latter part of 1930 there began the processes of retrenchment. Building programs were discontinued. Industrial output and working forces were curtailed. There began to be evidences of wage and price cutting.

From then on, until the spring of 1933, the whole nation lived more or less hopelessly and stoically, suffering from a process of deflation for which there seemed to be no remedy. It seemed to be a case of waiting for the storm to subside and praying that there would be something left alive when it lifted.

In this period there had at first been almost a complete economic bafflement. As time went on, it gradually became evident that the nation had incurred disaster by reason of previous excesses — excessive use and free flow of credit, excessive construction of capital goods, excessive accumulation of consumer goods, all resulting from the after effects of the World War. The truth came slowly that there had been no "New Era," but only a wild credit inflation in which all former economic warnings had been disregarded. There had been no new economic formulae, but only the usual working of human nature in its usual individual and social relationships.

Yet even this general view as to the cause of the collapse did not lead to any obvious means for promoting recovery. The feeling was that only time would serve to restore more normal conditions. In all previous depressions this had been true, and people were now, for the first time in two decades, beginning to accept the lessons taught by past economic history.

Then, at the darkest moments of the depression (marked by the country-wide bank moratorium), came the presidential declaration that there could and would be a "managed recovery." The first steps taken were those necessary to restoring confidence in the banks, to reopening sound banks and seeing that they were supplied with needed currency, and to securing congressional action on plans for revising the national economy.

In this period, no detailed plans were stated, and the frank admission was made that a period of experimenting would be necessary in working out various changes. Within a few months Congress passed approximately twenty acts, many of which could not be interpreted as to actual intention or probable final effect. Administration of these acts alone could tell whether they would be desirable, or would aid in bringing about recovery.

The immediate effect of such decisive action on the part of our chief executive was to inspire the nation with confidence, which, aided by certain inflationary moves, brought on a sharp industrial recovery. This activity has since been found to be somewhat hasty, although it served an excellent purpose at the time, and a recession became evident in August, 1933, which continued until November.

It is not necessary here to discuss the events which are such a recent memory to

204

all of us. Nor is it necessary or in fact possible to try to state which of these economic revisions may be wholly sound and desirable. Actually, even when this period has become history, it may not be possible to analyze the effect of all of the economic principles involved, because many of them will have been modified or dropped without being carried to the point of perfect application. There are men who now insist that if the only changes made had been those necessary in remedying the defects of the monetary system, the country would be further along the road to recovery. There are men who believe that the aim of industrial recovery has been lost sight of, and has been made secondary to efforts to secure social economic reform. Others no doubt believe that recovery alone, without curing the causes of depression, would be a useless effort. Still others claim that the whole period has merely been one of politics and experiment which is both mistaken and costly. For my own part I believe that much good will finally result from many of the principles which have been developed especially in that they have led to much thought and analysis in terms of a higher idealism, while some (such as the banking, securities and exchange acts) make it a little easier to do right, and a little harder to do wrong.

It is evident, however, that we are still in a period of uncertain economic thinking. Where six years ago there were many who blindly believed in the "New Era," so today as many blindly accept the promises of the "New Deal." When the present economic status is so confused in form, there would seem to be little basis for attempting to prophesy what may be the future of our economic system.

Yet in all this confusion of thoughts and actions, a few fundamentals seem to me to be more clearly accepted and understood than was formerly the case. Let me for a moment go back to a former quotation, "—as every national economy is a whole, dependent upon the fruitful mutuality of its parts—." That thought we as a nation are now more ready to accept than we were in the days of pre-depression prosperity. It has become evident that industry cannot prosper unless agriculture is profitable. It has become clear that capital suffers from the lack of purchasing power when large masses of labor are unemployed. The fact is generally becoming understood that I am my brother's keeper not alone from an ethical and religious viewpoint, but also because my brother's condition always affects my own. This perhaps was the thought in his mind when Mr. Justice Holmes remarked—"I confess that altruistic talk seems about equally unreal with cynically selfish talk. With all humility, I think 'whatsoever thy hand findeth to do, do it with thy might'—infinitely more important than the vain attempt to love one's neighbor as one's self—."

While it is necessary to be socially minded, it is an error to forget the individual and to develop theories based on pure altruism. As Mr. Justice Holmes indicated, we can only benefit our neighbors when we ourselves are "doing with our might" whatever there is to do. Until great changes have been made in human nature, it is important for each individual, each state and each nation to be working with a personal incentive and a viewpoint of personal gain, while recognizing the broad necessity for social coordination. Adherents of socialism or communism fail to recognize the need for personal incentive and direct personal gain, and their entire program is made faulty by the absence of those driving forces.

In recent years the necessity for being socially minded and for attaining social coordination has been increasingly important, due to the closer physical and industrial interlocking of all people, which in turn has been the result of improved transportation, increased specialization of the workers, increased interlocking in the affairs of nations, greater size in financial and industrial enterprises, etc. The world has been passing from the agricultural to the commercial era and so from the individualistic to the community basis of activities. World progress in the present and in the future will result less from pioneering than from the social massing of effort.

The more ancient pioneers were those who explored and exploited the great undeveloped areas and natural resources of the world. The more recent pioneers have been those who developed and exploited both natural resources and the new fields of large scale industry. It may be freely admitted that many of the recent individualistic pioneers have been somewhat ruthless and have weighed too greatly the factor of personal gains, yet it must also be admitted that the possibility of huge gain has led to a correspondingly great application of effort and initiative and has had a tremendous social value in the overall development of resources, invention and industry.

Now the more advanced nations are passing from the period of industrial pioneering to a period of broad utilization of the advancements which have been made along the lines of science, production and distribution. There is less requirement for further developments along these lines than there is for the technique of making these benefits available to all people. The necessary objective is not for the concentration of wealth and power as a driving force, but rather for the greater distribution of wealth and the spread of higher standards of living among the masses.

Because the world is thus passing from the old individualistic-capitalistic development stage into this new phase of broad social utilization, there has come to be considerable criticism of former motives and methods and a fairly widespread attitude that the "profit motive" of individuals and nations is no longer necessary or desirable. There is even a trend to regard it as outworn and perhaps unethical. Yet it should be recognized, as a fundamental precept of human nature, that all men, at all times and under all conditions, who accomplish things worthwhile, are actuated or stimulated by a profit motive. The student of the abstract may not desire a profit in the form of material goods, yet works for public recognition and acclaim. There are others who work hard only in order that their loved ones may enjoy more plenteously the material things of life. Sometimes profit is in the form of power, or of fame, or of scientific accomplishment. In my mind, all incentives may be described as the desire to attain a "profit." The present discussion of profit motives is too narrow in its conceptions and many who claim to oppose profits are merely opposing unjust profits or excessive profits, or profits whose attainment creates injury to others.

In the United States we have come to the realization of the social era somewhat later than other industrial nations, first because we have been undergoing such an intensive development of resources and industrial methods, and secondly, because the liberality and freedom of our principles have made us always partially social and democratic in our attitude. Moreover, wealth here has been the result of effort rather than of heredity, and so has been fairly well spread, and has constantly shifted to newer entrepreneurs rather than lodging permanently in a relatively few great estates. In addition, as the great single corporations have grown in their concentration of enterprise, the stockholdings of these units generally have been broadly distributed. These large businesses do not therefore represent individual concentrations of wealth and power, and rather rarely have formed the focus of any attack against capitalism, partly also because large business, as a rule, followed higher ethical principles and ideals than did the smaller, more individualistic enterprise. The larger a business becomes, the more need it has for a sound code of ethics and fair dealing, since its size makes it easier to be hit by any charges of unfair practice, and since its size is dependent upon the retention of goodwill.

While charges of exorbitant profits may be brought against large corporations, they are rarely proven. The public has found that lower prices and consequent greater availability of comforts and conveniences are often the result of massed enterprise, so here our large businesses have been an unconscious step toward socialization, rather than the strongholds of the property or profit system.

The general present result in the United States is that there never has been felt the pressure for a more radical socialization of our economic structure. We find on analysis that capitalism has been steadily and fairly perceptibly socializing itself. In the past thirty years the per capita wealth of the country has increased greatly, the working hours have lessened, the ownership of industrial corporations has become very widespread, living conditions have improved rapidly, participation in government has increased, the wealth redistributed by government has mounted rapidly, and in a broad way the country has attained the major benefits of socialization without any real declaration or conscious adoption of the usually proclaimed socialistic principles.

It seems to me, therefore, that the present furor of socialism is an indication of what has been happening rather than a forecast of what may happen. We see that the future is probably only to be a continuation of the principles which have become increasingly effective, and not any sudden dislocation based upon a repudiation of capitalism and individualism. The past success and prosperity of the country have been in part due to the encouragement of individual enterprise, and in part due to the gradual socialization of the principles under which individualism and capitalism have functioned. The future of our economic system, therefore, will probably be based on the following points:

1. That individual incentive and initiative should not be stifled.

2. That any blindly vicious personal viewpoint (cutthroat competition) cannot be tolerated, either individually or nationally.

3. That to accomplish the latter aim, some degree of broad social supervision and control by juridical rather than bureaucratic methods is necessary in order that vicious industrial practices may not persist, and that all efforts may be correlated to obtain the greatest mutuality of benefit.

A little reflection will serve to show that these elements have been recognized in the past and have at least partially been applied. Thus the capitalistic or property system, which has been so successful in this country in the past two centuries, allows for the maximum of initiative and incentive. The more vicious personal practices are partially restrained by the policing forces of municipalities and states. The more vicious industrial practices have been partially restrained by such factors of government as the anti-trust laws (the principles of which should be retained). Correlation of effort and practices has been partially provided in the monetary field by the Federal treasury and the Federal Reserve System. In transportation it has been provided by the Interstate Commerce Commission; in industry it has been provided by state laws, by certain national bodies such as the Federal Trade Commission, and by industrial bodies such as trade associations and trade practice committees. It is true that the administration of these various controls may not have been wholly effective, but the principle has been that of the common good. Their further development along judicial lines would be helpful.

It does not seem that a national economy, which has recognized and at least partially applied these basic conceptions, can be far wrong. So it does not seem to me that our future economic system, either needs to, or will, depart very much from the principles this nation has followed successfully from its inception.

This does not mean that I am advocating an attitude of indifference to change. That has never been the attitude of the industrial and political leaders of the past, nor of the present. Rather, there has always been on the one hand a real, even if not fully recognized, adherence to the fundamental principles outlined above, while on the other hand there has been a constant and conscious striving to devise a practical application of these principles to the changing industrial and political complexion of the nation.

So it may be expected that the present and the future also will see constant development along the lines of improved social co-ordination and a continual adaptation of methods to the changing affairs of this great nation.

For example, it has been felt that while the anti-trust laws were a necessary and vital control, when they were applied some thirty years ago, at present they may be an unduly restrictive control over industry. In my opinion these acts have performed a valuable function, and we should not depart too far from their basic principles. Nevertheless the search for a current modification of these laws has led to the application of certain portions of the National Industrial Recovery Act. This present method tends to permit a greater latitude in industrial control, placing on representative committees of given industries the burden of devising and enforcing trade practices which may be socially practical and which will prove neither unduly restrictive nor dangerously liberal. Naturally this process requires time, experience and experimentation and cannot avoid some period of confusion and dispute. If industry is not ready for this method of self-regulation, then perhaps some other form must be devised.

Another portion of the National Industrial Recovery Act deals with the problem of working hours. Few people realize that between 1900 and 1930 the average number of working hours per week had declined from 60 to 48. Possibly this natural process of shortening the working hours would have continued, and it may not have been necessary or desirable to apply a form of national control by means of federal legislation. This latter may, however, do little harm, even though it may accomplish little direct good. At least it focuses attention upon the factor of our rapidly increasing industrial efficiency in production, and the consequence of unbalance between the various portions of our national economy.

This matter of unbalanced production is dealt with more specifically in the NIRA and in the Agricultural Adjustment Act, both of which include provisions for the restriction of production in certain industries. It has generally been assumed heretofore that the law of supply and demand provided an automatic check on overproduction and overcapacity. Recent study, however, shows that this check is far too slow in its application and in some cases does not work at all, especially as regards the natural resource products. Too often the tendency has been to increase production as prices declined, in the hope that increased volume at the lower prices will provide the same gross financial return. Similarly overcapacity and overproduction may occur in the manufacturing industries, for one reason or another, but usually because the lure of large profits in a new industry induces a growth of production facilities far in excess of the immediate consumption capacity.

Apparently, then, some degree of overall control of industry in matters of production is admissible, as a means of avoiding economic waste. But I must express my doubt that any federal control can be established either rapidly or in detail, which may not prove more harmful than beneficial. It is true that a problem exists, but no body can be set up so all powerful, so large, or so intelligent that it will serve as a national regulator of all elements of production. The solution of this problem must be worked upon over a considerable period of time, and in such fashion as to avoid undue disruption and change.

More than any other phase of the national economy, the problem of money has been discussed and experimented with in the past twenty months. The matter is complex not only because the modern national economy is based entirely upon the functions of money and credit, but also because all national economies interlock with each other in the matter of standards of international exchange. This nation departed from a gold basis not because of any lack of metal reserves, but because a readjustment of exchange rates was essential if we were to participate in international trade, and because as a creditor nation our monetary problems were world problems. Before long it may become essential that there be a world adjustment of national currencies—call it stabilization if you wish—if all nations are to enjoy a mutuality of fruitfulness.

The drastic nature of this depression has focused national thought and attention on problems which have been growing for years, but whose importance had been obscured during a period of inflation prosperity. Among these are the matters of wage rates, of recognition of labor unions, of unemployment insurance and old-age pensions—in fact, of many of the elements of personal economic security, including the preservation of savings through the media of banks and investments. It is probable that the depression severity has led to an undue emphasis on these things, and that some of the recent regulations and conceptions go further than is either necessary or desirable along these lines. Thus the restrictions imposed by the Securities Act and the Securities Exchange Act appear to have a depressant effect on new investment or expansion of investment, and therefore in preventing a normal recovery in the capital goods industries. There would appear in this and in some other phases, to have been an excessive zeal for social economic reform, at the expense of economic recovery, and it is small wonder that industry grows restive and even a bit fearful under what may be the shadow of bureaucracy or even dictatorship. It has been very encouraging lately to note, on the part of the federal government, some recession from the viewpoint of pure theory and reform, toward the basis of less drastic interpretations, and toward a more practical application of recovery measures.

If this is indeed to be an era of reform, it seems to me that some of the more necessary and fruitful fields are being overlooked. For example, we need a more simplified and coordinated plan of state and federal governments, with an accompanying simplification of all plans of taxation. We need improved legal and court procedures and more effective action against crime.

However, the solutions to all problems of social economics and the development of a national economic plan are far too complex to be settled in any brief period of time. In fact there never is a long-time solution or plan, for conditions change steadily, requiring continual economic readjustment. If economics were a fixed science, with definite formulae, it would be logical to lay down principles of conduct designed to govern unborn generations. But life is never static, and human nature rebels against too much restriction, sometimes even when such restriction is provably beneficial.

Therefore it is my belief that our future economic system will have many of the characteristics of the past—that is, an adherence to the fundamentals of individual initiative and of social coordination and cooperation, constantly adapting the details of application, to be in line with the changes brought about by human progress. Greater progress would undoubtedly be made if more business leaders had the spirit of the trustee, and were honored not for wealth or power, but for capable administration. The world as a whole recognizes the necessity for social progress, but it has generally been the case that those who knew how to achieve that end, lacked the power of accomplishment; while those who had the power to achieve, lacked the will. The requirement now, even more than ever before, is for leaders who are industrially capable and who are socially minded. I believe that the coming generations will adequately develop the leaders and administrators necessary for these economic adaptations, and I do not think that we, in the present, should go too far in restricting our children's children with the dead hand of outworn theory. Nor can I feel that it is just or wise for us to try to achieve recovery from this depression at the financial expense of future generations, which we may be doing when we pile up untold billions upon an already large national deficit.

Just now there is a tendency for men to believe that, since the national government is the medium for emergency correction, it can also become a permanent godfather of good fortune, insuring us against the evil results of our own errors and excesses. There is a tendency, too, to believe that we have reached the limit of material progress and that there can be no further attainments, and no scope for individual effort and initiative. Actually, we as a country have only laid a foundation for future industry and accomplishment. We have established the possibility of certain goals, though we have not generally attained them, but they can not be attained solely through national paternalism nor governmental socialization.

I think that "security" for the country and for the individual is one of the broad goals which must be sought. By this I do not mean protected laxness and laziness or idle dependence. It has been said that eternal vigilance is the price of liberty and so also, initiative, effort and intelligence must be the means to security. The capable worker must be secure in his job and in the ownership of his property. The weak must be secure against any predatory aggression of the strong. Mankind must build security against the black fear of poverty, by having an incentive to work and a proportionate reward for his effort. All of these can be accomplished only through common effort and understanding. Neither capital nor labor should get something for nothing.

Of course it may be a long time before this principle of human security can be fully realized, and in the process of attaining security there may be some further loss of freedom of action to individuals and to businesses. But this has always been so. There could be no national and international security were it not for the policing restraint imposed by armies and navies, which to be sure, limit the entire freedom of action of individuals and nations, for the general protection and the general good of all peoples. In the same way, because we have laws, policemen and jails, many individuals find it wiser not to do some of the things they otherwise would. Therefore, it may also happen that in improving the economic security of all individuals and all industry, there will be some loss of individualism and freedom.

I would like to add that there is still room for great improvement in human relationships—there is too much of bitterness, jealousy, selfishness and cruelty. These traits in the individual cause much suffering and oppression, and in nations are the cause of wars. War is still a barbaric relic, a throwback to the tribal strife of the caveman. Until the world overcomes war, we cannot take any great pride in our human progress or achievement. Nevertheless, despite the recent world horrors and the present international jealousies, we probably are making some ethical and moral progress, and it is possible that new economic conceptions and changes may play their part in building a new status of international relationships.

In this period of change and modified principles, we must be careful not to go too far in the restriction of individual liberties and incentives, nor too far in new enthusiasms, along new and untried trails. We must not discard all of our old ideas, actions and principles merely because they are old; nor must we acclaim all new ideas merely because they are new. It is not well to try to achieve too rapid a change, when one is experimenting with the economic well-being and lives of 125 million people.

In the past we have done great things along the lines of production and transportation, and have made possible a great variety of good things for the human race. In the future we must develop the monetary phase of distribution which will make these things increasingly available to all people. If the barrier to distribution can be unblocked, we shall attain a volume of industry which now can scarcely be imagined, and which will lead to still higher technical and production developments. Whether this distribution will be attained through the medium of monetary revision, or through some leveling of the inequalities of wealth, or through some method of social insurance, I do not know. But the requirement is to unleash our productive powers to result in a more general availability of the possible higher standards of living and security.

Another thought, too, should be kept in mind, and that is the possible effect on mankind of an increasing degree of leisure and freedom from the anxiety and strife of living. If we are to attain a higher living standard with lessened hours of work, the question arises of how this leisure may be employed. The assumption is that it will permit of attaining higher cultural and intelligence levels. But there is a possibility of softness and degeneracy, such as has occurred historically when countries lived too easily. There is a necessity for setting up fairly definite goals on the cultural, mental and especially the spiritual side. We must guard against becoming wholly materialistic and self-indulgent.

Thus while I fail to see the necessity for any drastic change in the economic principles which have persisted in the past, I do believe that we are on the threshold of a better recognition of social principles in their relation to the everyday industrial life of mankind. I believe that the greatest economic rewards of the future will accrue to those who sincerely and honestly accept the task of making this world a better place for all people— a place of increased security, increasing intelligence and higher social and ethical ideals.

Our part today is to preserve an attitude of open-minded intelligence and to set for coming generations an example of "doing with our might the work our hands find to do."

Present day problems affecting the presentation and interpretation of financial statements

Before the American
Institute of Accountants,
Boston, October 15, 1935

*Permanent improvement in
accounting practices and
corporate reporting cannot
be brought about by legislation
or regulation, but
must flow from the efforts
of those who determine the
policies of corporations.
Professional accountants
can contribute to this
progress by insisting on
sound accounting principles.*

SINCE the beginning of the twentieth century, a little more than one generation ago, many volumes of extraordinary events have been written into the history of mankind. The world has seen wars, earthquakes, floods, famine, revolutions—and, on the other hand, has made great progress in the development and use of machinery and power. All of these things have been primary events. They have caused many further changes of a secondary nature which eventually may even more powerfully affect the history of the world. Among these are profound changes in international boundaries and relationships; changes in the social policies and governments of various nations; extreme disruptions in the economic and financial field; a tremendous growth of new industries; and the modification of industrial operations by reason of the trend toward larger and more widely-owned units of production. In all recorded history there has probably never been a period of time so crowded with swiftly moving events of such a vital nature.

It may be said that business, which is the mainspring of human living in the modern community, has felt the impact of all of these factors and has been forced to adapt itself rapidly to new and ever-changing conditions. In this country especially the rate of change has been great, for here individual freedom and initiative and individual reward have given an incentive to new developments of every sort. Corporations have increased in size and in complexity of organization, operations and finance. Completely new industries have started from nothing and have grown to tremendous size, such as those engaged in the production of motor vehicles, electrical power, electrical products, radios and airplanes. At the same time all business has been increasingly subjected to the elements of greater social control and mounting and burdensome taxation. Another problem has been the development of a completely new technique of finding the capital required for this industrial expansion. A further complication lies in the fact that the period of the World War changed the United States from a debtor to a creditor nation, with a suddenly new position in the matters of international trade and financial relationships. More recently new problems have arisen, as the deflation period necessitated changes in methods and even changes in the application of principles which had been considered entirely sound during the period of expansion. The latest problems are those caused by political changes which have definitely applied the principles of a broad social control over all industry.

These changes in the conditions and structure of business have multiplied the problems of accountancy. Where industry is concerned with matters of production, accounting is concerned with the determination of all the elements of cost, extending from the broad bases of accounting policies as to depreciation, maintenance and distribution of overhead down to the details of expense classifications, inventory controls and what not. Where industry has the broad problem of sales, accounting has the many problems of sales classifications, of branch-sales accounting, of territory analyses, of profits by classes of product, of selling costs, etc. Even more vital are the accounting problems in the field of finance, in which the problems of taxation, of bank credit, of long-term borrowing, and of preparation of annual statements for publication, call for the development of a specialized technique. As important general problems, accounting must deal with the matters of adequate reports to executive and administrative heads, with questions of budgetary control, with the effectiveness of the system of internal check, with the organization of the accounting department, etc. In other words, accounting penetrates into every phase of business operation, in the two aspects of: first, providing the bases for the establishment of broad principles of operation, and second, as the detailed recording of and control over all results of operations.

Thus, while accountancy may be said to be an integral part of business, in another sense it stands beside industry as a counselor and guide. In the one function it keeps pace with the requirements of industry in matters of current operation, but in the other function it must anticipate and interpret for industry the effects of the many economic and technological changes which have been taking place with bewildering rapidity.

When businesses were small and personally controlled, both of these functions of accountancy were underdeveloped and but little recognized. But the changes of the past half century have lifted accounting to the status of a profession. Actually it is the youngest and most immature of all professions, and is handicapped in its status not only by this lack of tradition but also by the necessity of being practical as well as technical. The older professions attain a dignity based upon the cumulative technique of hundreds of years, and upon the maintenance of a fair degree of mystery. Accountancy has thus far but little accumulated technique, for it is still in the process of steady development of fundamental principles. It cannot attain any high degree of mystery, for its methods and principles must be practical and understandable, and in step with the progress of industry and people. It cannot function merely as a code of fixed rules, for it is constantly modified by the principles which are developed as a composite of the best and most enlightened business experience.

Because accountancy is a profession rather than just another line of business, it must assume responsibilities which go far beyond those imposed by the business function alone, for it has long been recognized that the published financial statements of corporations are clothed with a public interest and that the accountant has a responsibility to the public as well as to his client. This responsibility is based on social premises; it exists regardless of legislation, which serves only to focus attention upon it. In the past decade this factor of the public interest has been of increasing importance, due to the tremendous spread of security holding by the public, the trend away from ownership operation of businesses, and recently, the economic slump and financial ruin which affected so many people.

Great portions of the public feel that they have been insufficiently informed or even misled in connection with past security issues, not alone by those in the management and control of industry and finance, but also by the public accountants, who have not fully met their professional responsibility. This viewpoint is not entirely justified, but the situation cannot be lightly dismissed as due to misunderstanding or animus. That the feeling exists, indicates that the profession is faced by very definite problems, the answers to which lie either in the province of education of both client and public, or in the correction of certain methods which, by force of circumstances, have existed to date.

Specifically, it would appear that the following problems exist:

1. The problem of providing more informative reports for the investing public.

2. The problem of educating the public as to the meaning of and fundamental limitations of accounting statements.

3. The problem of simplifying accounting statements.

4. The problem of more rapidly and accurately adjusting accounting policies to changing economic conditions.

These problems are not new. They have been with us for many years. But today they appear in the form of a direct challenge which must be met by definite answers.

A considerable part of the criticism that corporation statements are not sufficiently informative is due to failure on the part of the investing public to understand accounting phraseology. What is clear to the technician may not be clear to the layman. Yet this is true in any profession. No one expects a doctor, a lawyer or an engineer to have a vocabulary entirely free from necessary technical terms, or to be capable of explaining extremely complicated principles to the man in the street. An attempt at extreme simplicity of expression may be either impossible or misleading, and the accounting complexity of a modern business is at least as great as the complexity of our social laws, or of electrical and mechanical devices. It may be that the real answer to this problem is not one of "writing down" to the understanding of the general public, but instead, a necessity on the part of the public for acquiring some understanding of the principles which must be applied in safeguarding its wealth and interests.

A second rather general criticism is that many of the values and amounts shown by financial statements lack exactness. This also is due to the fact that the public generally is ignorant of the principles and factors involved. The man in the street cannot see why an item of $2,000,000 of plant assets in a balance sheet is not an absolute statement of value, true today, tomorrow and next year. To him accounting, if it means anything definite, means only a mathematical computation which is either right or wrong. If he buys a $1,000 mortgage bond which, according to the balance sheet, is backed by $3,000 of plant assets, he blames the accountant if, some years later, he realizes only $300 in liquidation. He believes the original statement of asset values must have been in error. He cannot credit the fact that there are different bases for valuation in a going business and in a liquidated business, or in the same going business under different economic cycles.

The correction of the misunderstanding which underlies this criticism must be founded upon a program for education of the layman. He must learn that the accountant is not an appraiser but that his duty is to report the basis of stating the value of assets in the balance sheet. He must understand that a balance sheet is not a statement of liquidating values, that many factors must be given weight in the valuation of securities, and that book value is of little significance unless considered in connection with the income account. He must realize that the determination of the values at which assets of a corporation are stated in its accounts is a function of the board of directors. It is the function of the accountant to describe the basis of stating such values. There have occurred errors due to faulty judgment or due to a lack of knowledge of all essential facts or perhaps to undue optimism. There are even errors due to an excess of conservatism. Yet corporate management is no more superhuman than the rest of the human race. During the period of expansion it was almost impossible to resist the idea that there had been definite economic changes which warranted a changed viewpoint towards property values. The business world commonly felt that the values of both tangibles and intangibles might in large part be based upon earnings and upon the high-price levels in existence at the time. This viewpoint naturally resulted in many an overstatement of values —as such values are now determined in the light of reduced earnings and deflated prices. Perhaps in the current period management may be subject to the error of undue pessimism and may determine values at so low a level as to damage the equities of security holders by understatement. The accountant should be particularly concerned with those write-downs which result in an obvious understatement of values. Such a practice is fully as objectionable as the practice of the writing up of values which prevailed in the years prior to 1930. Its immediate effect is an overstatement of future earnings, and dividends paid out of such earnings may in part represent a return *of* capital rather than a return *on* capital.

A third criticism is that financial statements are misleading because they fail to clearly reveal facts of which the accountant is fully aware. This criticism has frequently been directed at the accountant's statement of qualifications and disclosures. Broadly speaking, a qualification constitutes a statement of the accountant's reservation short of his full endorsement of a financial statement; a disclosure is the presentation of a material fact on a financial statement. Qualifications are objectionable; they tend to obscure the clear-cut presentation of facts and to destroy confidence in the statements to which they are attached. Unfortunately it is impossible in many instances for the accountant to state the actual monetary effect on the financial statement of a qualification or to state all material facts in terms of figures. Where the basic causes for the need of a qualification or of an involved explanation of facts can be removed by appropriate action of the board of directors such action should be taken. The accountant is powerless to act on his own initiative. He cannot make adjustments of the accounts excepting by authority of his client. He cannot and should not attempt to dictate the policies of a corporation, but he may and should use all means in his power to induce his client to adopt policies and to make those adjustments which will permit the presentation of the published accounts without material reservation. There is today a noticeable willingness on the part of corporation management to make those adjustments which will lead to the elimination of qualifications from the financial statements, a trend that is greatly in the interest of the investing public.

216

The need for more informative financial statements cannot be met by the addition of undigested and nonessential details. Intelligent presentation of financial statements requires a nice balance between clarity and detail. A balance sheet consisting of naked figures is not informative; nor is a balance sheet burdened with pages of footnotes informative.

The latter type of statement has been one of the unfortunate results of an excess of caution on the part of those who are subject to the statutory liability imposed by the Securities Act of 1933. It has become common practice to view the financial statements as a vehicle for protection against such liabilities. This viewpoint is not constructive. Fundamentally the financial statements are a vehicle for conveying information. If they are truly informative and if they are predicated upon a reasonable examination in conformity with duty and custom, the question of statutory liability will automatically be answered. When confronted with the necessity for a decision on a difficult question of policy with respect to financial statements the accountant should search his conscience rather than the statutes.

While accountants must strive toward more informative reports and statements, within the scope of their own work, and must in every possible way seek to further the knowledge of the general public in regard to the meaning of financial statements, a significant portion of the responsibility also falls upon the shoulders of management. The education of the public may be made easier as progress is made along the line of simplification of statements and reports. The statements will be complicated if the corporation facts and conditions are complicated, and they in turn are shaped by the acts, policies and decisions of management.

The audited financial statements of corporations are not inherently complicated. They sometimes become complicated because they must reflect the completed or uncompleted results of transactions which are so intricate that no simple explanation is possible, or because of the necessity of explaining a company's departure from recognized accounting practices. Neither of these causes is within the control of the public accountant. He may and should counsel his client as to the advantages of simplicity and as to the wisdom of adhering to recognized accounting practices, but the responsibility for taking definite corrective measures rests with the management including the board of directors. It has been my observation that during the past several years there has been a sincere and effective effort on the part of many boards of directors to bring the accounting policies of their corporations into line with recognized accounting principles and to improve the standard of corporate accounting.

There is also a distinct trend towards simplification of corporate structures and intercorporate relations but the efforts of management in this direction, particularly as to those corporations whose business is national in scope, are handicapped by the conflicting laws of the several states—laws which are to a large extent responsible for the holding company system.

The financial statements of a corporation are seldom really informative to the reader who does not possess a knowledge of the accounting policies governing their preparation. This is particularly true in comparing the statements of two or more companies in the same industry. In my opinion, the lack of information as to such policies is one of the real deficiencies in corporate accounting. A statement of the major accounting policies of a corporation has an importance equal to that of the financial statements themselves since neither is complete without the other. A corporation's published financial statements should be accompanied by a concise statement of its major accounting policies, such as those relating to the annual provisions for depreciation and depletion, valuation of inventories and plant properties, amortization of discount and consolidation of subsidiaries.

Since it is the duty of the directors of a corporation to pass upon the major policies governing its administration, the major accounting policies should receive the same scrutiny which is given to matters that are directly concerned with the administration of production and distribution. The accounting policies are important because of their bearing on the preparation and presentation of the company's financial statements. These statements form one of the means by which management may control the details of operations; which serve as a guide to aid the directors in determining the results of management policies; and which, in their published form, are almost the only source of information available to the investing public by which they may judge for themselves the success of the enterprise. Every board of directors should insist that its members be furnished periodically with a statement of the company's accounting policies and should insist also that all major accounting policies be submitted to them for formal approval.

In this connection it may be said that accounting policies may, to some extent, be shaped by the broad economic beliefs of the management and the board of directors. It will probably come to be increasingly necessary that corporate managements adopt a long-range viewpoint, that their plans be laid in advance to enable them to attain certain definite objectives. Managements that rely upon and follow principles which look only to what is immediately expedient without regard to any long-range objectives cannot hope to achieve a lasting success. At the present time it is possible to hold three distinct general viewpoints. First, that the country will shortly see a secondary reaction, during which the levels of commodity prices and industrial activity will fall far below current levels. Second,

that the present level may be relatively permanent, representing a reasonable and normal recovery from the extreme depth of the depression. Third, that the present level is far below the normal, and that there are periods of prosperity ahead equal to or more pronounced than those which prevailed in the past. Obviously, no man, be he an economist or financier, can look ahead and foretell with certainty which of these theories is the correct one, but it is equally obvious that the general and accounting policies of the management of an enterprise will be vitally affected by the school of thought to which it belongs.

In considering the problems of providing more informative financial statements and of simplifying those statements, it is well to remember the fundamental limitations in the scope of an accountant's work. An accountant is just what the name implies—one who is skilled in the construction, presentation, examination and interpretation of accounts. It is his function to determine facts; to determine whether or not the accounts have been kept in accordance with recognized principles and whether or not those principles have been applied on a consistent basis; to verify the propriety of the distribution of items as between capital and income; and to satisfy himself that the financial statements provide an adequate disclosure of material facts pertinent thereto.

The accountant is not an appraiser nor is he an engineer. He is not qualified to determine plant values, adequacy of depreciation, investment values, condition or value of merchandise, or similar matters. As to such matters he must confine himself to the determination of those facts which are within the scope of his recognized qualifications and to render his opinion within those limits. Thus the limitation of the accountant's responsibility as to the verification of the inventory is in good practice set forth in some such descriptive phrase as "Quantities and condition determined by the company—priced at the lower of cost or market." This means that the accountant has not verified and does not take responsibility for the determination of either the inventory quantities or condition but that he has satisfied himself as to the clerical accuracy and the basis of pricing. The accountant ordinarily should not take responsibility for the determination of quantities because in many industries this would require specialized knowledge outside the field of accounting and in most cases the expense of an independent verification is prohibitive. The accountant cannot determine the condition of the inventory because he does not have the special knowledge which would qualify him to undertake such work.

Again, the accountant is not a lawyer and is not qualified to interpret the legal effect of charter provisions, contracts, titles to property, and other legal agreements. He should, however, have a sufficient knowledge of law to recognize legal problems which have a bearing on the accounts.

Finally, a public accountant is not a forecaster. It is not within his proper functions to predict the future results from operations of a business nor to forecast the condition of a company's affairs at a future date. His opinions should be, and are commonly understood to be, based on his knowledge of facts and conditions existing at the time that his work is performed. This limitation should always be carefully observed in the preparation of pro forma statements used with public financing. Pro forma balance sheets giving effect to the application of proceeds from the sale of securities are on the border line between fact and fancy and should be avoided excepting in those cases where the exact effect of the financing can be determined in advance. The same principle applies to the preparation of pro forma income accounts. The once widespread practice of eliminating so-called nonrecurring charges falls within the field of forecasting and is, therefore, objectionable.

A considerable part of the public criticism against statements which prove uninformative because they are so complicated, has arisen in connection with the reports on the affairs of holding companies and their subsidiaries. Accountants have long recognized the limitations of consolidated statements, but have been inclined to emphasize their importance without reference to their deficiencies. There are certain points of limitation which if not recognized by accountants will serve to mislead the public. Thus, from a purely mathematical or technical viewpoint it is possible to add two and two and get four. But the sum of two apples and two oranges is not a definable four. So in accounting it is possible to sum up various factors to result in a consolidated statement, which, however, is only a fiction. The consolidated statement may not have a practical or applicable meaning in that its component parts are subject to the statutory restrictions of different states or countries, its apparent earned surplus may not be available for dividends, its stated asset valuations may represent the application of several different policies, etc.

In determining its policy as to the consolidation of accounts in the company's annual report, the board of directors of a holding company or any corporation owning subsidiary companies should be guided by the sound principle that the financial statements should be presented in that form which will most clearly reflect the financial position of the companies and the results from their operations. If this principle is conscientiously applied, the consolidated accounts will, in many instances, be accompanied by separate statements of the accounts of the parent company. This policy is now followed by the more progressive holding companies and there are indications that the practice will become more general in the near future.

Moreover, the current economic conditions have introduced other factors, such as the devaluation of various national currencies, which may prevent any practical interpretation of the apparent results. A generation ago foreign exchange rates moved between the rather narrow limits of the gold points. Since the World War, foreign trade has been faced with widely fluctuating rates of foreign exchange, a condition which has been greatly aggravated during recent years by the rise of nationalism accompanied by changing standards of value, deflation of currencies (including our own), government control of foreign exchange, and other artificial devices. A number of countries have established restrictions on the transfer of funds abroad which are so severe as to make the official exchange quotations meaningless. Under these conditions the consolidation of the accounts of domestic companies with the accounts of corporations kept in terms of foreign currencies does not appear to clearly reflect the facts. Certainly there is no sound basis for including in the consolidated income account of a corporation the earnings of foreign subsidiaries located in countries such as Germany, where strict regulation of the transfer of funds abroad is an effective bar to the conversion of those earnings into American dollars.

Problems inherent in the preparation, presentation and interpretation of financial statements thus arise from multiple sources—first, the lack of accounting knowledge on the part of the public; second, the complications introduced by the nature of the business and the attitudes and policies of management; third, the limitations imposed upon the accounting profession, both as regards the scope of its authority and its relationships with client and public; and fourth, the lack of precise and uniform principles within the profession. The accountant is an interpreter, but he also must be an educator. He discharges a vital business function and at the same time is charged with ethical and moral responsibilities of a high social order. He has the problem of his own education and adjustment during a period of rapidly changing world conditions—a period in

which the decisions and principles of today may be proven faulty tomorrow, either by a changed operating condition, a new legal requirement or a different economic cycle. Because he is integral with industry and society, he must strive to preserve an intelligent balance between the necessary principles and technicalities of his profession and the practical aspects and necessities of industry.

It is perhaps easier to make progress along the lines of correction of professional technique than to discharge the more intangible functions of industry advisor and educator, yet there are still many weaknesses within the working aspects of the professional functions.

It is not uncommon for accountants to be too technical—to accept figures as an end in themselves rather than as an interpretation of practical conditions. They are sometimes inclined to follow an orthodox form for setting up balance sheets, in complete disregard of special conditions which may exist. This is particularly true in cases where the corporation is in the process of reorganization under Section 77B of the National Bankruptcy Act. Another example of this failing sometimes occurs in preparation of earnings statements. It is obvious that in the ordinary course of business some items technically applicable to the operations of one year will be entered in the accounts during a later period. Overlapping items of this character which arise in the ordinary course of business should be absorbed in the income account of the period in which they are taken into the accounts and should not, except under extraordinary circumstances, be treated as adjustments of earned surplus. Obviously where overlapping charges or credits are substantial in amount they should be set forth as special items in the income account so that their effect on the operating results may be readily observed. The practice of making direct surplus adjustments for items of this character is in the nature of a bookkeeping approach that may easily lead to serious misrepresentation. In good practice the earned-surplus account should be virtually closed except for dividends and the balance of the net profit-and-loss account for the year.

It is equally important that the general and surplus reserves should not be used for the purpose of equalizing earnings of a corporation over a period of years. The practice of equalizing earnings is directly contrary to recognized accounting principles. The proper function of accounts is to record and report, as nearly as may be, the actual results of business transactions. If the nature of a business is such that its earnings fluctuate from year to year it is nothing less than direct misrepresentation arbitrarily to equalize them between years through the medium of what has been known as a reserve for "contingencies." There is no reason why most reserves cannot be specifically identified in the balance sheet as liabilities, as reductions of assets, or as permanent or temporary appropriations of surplus. The changes in these reserves are of considerable importance in the analysis and interpretation of corporate earnings and should be reported in connection with the financial statements.

It is, on the other hand, sometimes possible for the accountant to deviate too far from technical conventions thus losing sight of fundamental principles because of the urgency of some particular situation. Thus the accounting treatment of losses arising from a reduction of recorded values of assets of the corporation is too often decided upon the basis of expediency. As a matter of accounting principle such losses should be charged first against earned surplus, and only after earned surplus has been consumed should they be charged against capital surplus. Earned surplus should be the cumulative result of all income, losses, and distributions from all sources.

Another current problem which is of technical interest occurs in connection with the treatment of debt discount. Recent months have witnessed an increasing number of refunding operations through which corporations have taken advantage of the present low cost of money. It is characteristic of many of these operations that the new securities refund prior issues which in the ordinary course of business would not mature for a number of years and in most cases there is a reduction in interest rates resulting in a substantial saving in annual interest charges. In this connection the problem arises as to the proper disposition of the unamortized discount and expense on the bonds retired and the premiums paid incident to their redemption.

It is, of course, conservative practice to write off such discount and the premium against earned surplus at the date of refinancing. But there are many instances in which this procedure cannot be justified from an economic or business point of view.

Debt discount is properly chargeable against earnings of the debtor corporation over the period of years in which it has the use of money represented by the debt. To insist that all bond discount and premium applicable to refunded issues should be written off against earned surplus at the time of the refinancing would, in some instances, have the practical effect of preventing a refinancing which, if carried out, would effect a real reduction in the cost of money to the corporation and would be highly desirable on other grounds. After all, these costs may properly be spread over the years for which it can definitely be ascertained that an actual saving has been effected in the cost of money. In these cases, therefore, the unamortized bond discount and expense applicable to the issue retired and the premium paid in connection with such retirement should be amortized over the period of years ending with the maturity of the refunded bonds. The debt discount and expense applicable to the new issue should be amortized over the life thereof. This procedure would appear to be fundamentally sound as it limits the spread of the amortized discount and premium applicable to the refunded issue to those years which, as can be definitely determined in advance, will receive the benefit of the lower cost of money as a result of the refinancing.

*   *   *   *   *

We are living in an interesting period enlivened by changes of far-reaching effect. Our own profession has shared generously in this experience. The past few years have probably brought about more changes in accounting practices with respect to published reports than were experienced during the preceding generation. Most of these changes have been beneficial and no well-informed person would deny the need for them.

However, accountants must be alert to preserve the gains which have been made. The time is not far distant, perhaps, when reviving industry and optimism, and increased profits, may serve to abate the public outcry against uninformative reports which was so loud two or three years ago.

While no one may question the effectiveness of most of the reform measures which have been adopted, there is always the tendency for a healthy body to discard the precautions which have served to create that new vitality.

Permanent improvement in accounting practices and in methods of corporate reporting cannot be brought about by legislation or by government regulation. The regulations laid down by a governmental bureau serve a good purpose but can never successfully take the place of individual initiative, intelligence and courage. If any real progress is to be made towards continued improvement in corporation reporting, it must flow from the efforts of those charged with the direct responsibility of determining the policies of corporations. As professional accountants we can contribute to this progress by emphasizing the advantages of adhering to sound business principles, by seeking to establish more firmly the standards for accounting practice, and by having the moral courage to cling to these standards.

Excerpts from the remarks of Arthur Andersen to the partners and managers of Arthur Andersen & Co.

At their meeting in
Chicago, October 27, 1936

This firm owes its progress in no small degree to the fact that it has had a broad business viewpoint, broader than the mere checking of the figures.

As a preface to what I have to say, it might be well to indicate in a general way how I look upon life, facing it from here on. We are in a period of rather extreme and unsettled social and economic conditions. I do not become as concerned about that as do a lot of people.

Personally, as a practical matter, I do not believe it makes very much difference whether Roosevelt is re-elected or Mr. Landon is elected. I am still going to vote the Republican ticket.

It seems to me that the effect of study, travel, observation, and that sort of thing leads you, if it is done constructively, up one alley, and only one alley, and that is, you are better equipped to face life from then on. After all, there is very little that any of us can do as individuals to overcome some of these seemingly insurmountable difficulties. Indeed, I would say that unless you can translate all of your study and observation into terms of being better able to face life, you would be better off to live the life of the hermit in the hills of Kentucky.

The human race is being challenged in a way that we have never seen in the history of this world. So, therefore, if there was ever a time when young men, and I still class myself as a young man, should face life courageously in all of its relationships, it is now. This is no time for a pessimistic attitude. It is no time for anything but the most constructive approach that any of us can conceive of.

We are going to go through rather broad basic changes, I think, in our social and economic structure. I believe that capitalism, as such, is likely to survive, though not in its old form. The day is past, and rightly so, when men can be exploited by a group of other men for their own benefit. In other words, we are likely to have what I choose to call a socialized capitalism, under which there will be fewer millionaires and more people with average wealth, all of which I think will make for a happier civilization.

I think that the whole social and capitalistic structure, however, is very likely to be challenged. It would not surprise me very much if, in the event of a great war, you would find Great Britain and the United States lined up on one side against other nations which would have a very definite tendency of becoming communistic.

The philosophy that we must have is one of the greater good for the greater number. Without that we are not going to get anywhere. Basically it is difficult for me to believe that it is right that you and I, and some to a greater extent than others, should be assured of continuous employment, and of a return on our bonds and stocks during a period of depression, whereas the laboring man, equally willing to work, finds it necessary to get relief from the state or otherwise. The right to work is inherent on the face of this globe, and also the right of protection beyond the point at which a man can be expected to take care of himself.

So, we are going to come into a period where all social and human relationships, I think, are going to be more far-reaching than any of us can visualize. If you visit the Scandinavian countries and England, as I have on three different occasions, you can well understand that these broad basic changes are things that come in spite of everybody. In England legislation along the socialistic line began as far back as 1806, in Norway as far back as 1860. And, as one Englishman put it, the difference between our country and your country is that we choose to do things through the evolutionary approach, whereas you have done them through the revolutionary approach.

The election of Franklin Delano Roosevelt four years ago was in response to a great, broad, underlying current among the people of the lower classes in this country which demanded that there be a change from what had been done under the three preceding Republican administrations. I think, also, that a large part of the deficit of the present administration could, in no small degree, be charged over to the three previous Republican administrations. So, therefore, it is not a question now as to whether Roosevelt is re-elected or whether Landon is elected. It merely means that the principles of basic, fundamental security and less exploitation on the part of people who are in power, must be different from what it has been heretofore. All that would happen, and that may have its virtue, is that under a Landon administration the tempo would be slowed up, but the basic demand for these things, these changes, on the part of the people as a whole still exists, and will be multiplied as the years go on. So, therefore, we are all going to take our places in a gradually modified capitalistic order.

One of the largest places that will be taken in such a new day will be by the accountancy profession. It is, therefore, difficult for me to believe that this firm, or any other firm, should get itself into the mental attitude of routine auditing. Anybody who tells you that that is the place of an accountancy firm in the future just has no feel of the pulse, or has no conception of the responsibilities that lie ahead of us. This firm owes its progress in no small degree to the fact that it has had a broad viewpoint, a broader viewpoint than a mere checking of the figures, and if it goes forward it is going to go forward with that same thought in mind. I do not mean that in any sense we are going to undertake the old type of survey. There are many reasons why that should not be done, apart from the legal liabilities we might be assuming under the Securities Act.

But, to say that the profession should not continue to grow, that we should not draw bigger men into it who are capable of doing bigger things, is tantamount to saying that the profession has reached the end of its field of usefulness, and from here on we are to develop into just a lot of routine workers. It would be absolutely criminal to exact the fees that we do in certain instances, and submit nothing more than a balance sheet.

As far as the next generation is concerned, it rests very largely on the shoulders of young men who have come through, as the most of you have, in the last three or four years. The firm, as I visualize it, has never been in a stronger position than it stands at this moment. We have our weaknesses, sure. I hope the day never comes when we do not think that we have a lot of problems because, the moment we think we have all our problems solved, from then on we will go downhill so fast there won't be anything to talk about.

The firm's reputation is not only national, but it is becoming international. That places a responsibility upon us far beyond the conception any of us may have at the moment, and we have no idea, nor can we begin to visualize the standard of actions and contacts which are likely to develop over the next ten years. In other words, if this firm is guided right and it clings to fundamental principles, if it clings to honesty, if it clings to basic integrity, I visualize that its reputation in the next ten years will be broadened in a way that will surprise any one of us.

The whole profession has got to rise to newer and higher levels. It has got to stand for something. It has got to get away from the general idea of being a lot of pencil pushers. The very fact that this element exists in it, makes it, of necessity, a young man's profession, and, to put it another way, makes it an opportunity for young men.

I am rather amused that men should think, in this particular line of business, that the opportunities from here on as against the past are very limited. The world is literally starving for ideas, for men who can really throw live suggestions, constructive suggestions that we can cling to, and go forward on. Our organization in the twenty-three years of its existence has suffered more from lack of ideas than anything else. Generally, the man with ideas is worth ten times what the man gets who functions purely as a technician.

The profession in this country, as compared with England, is obviously on a much higher level. They measure ideas on their mass content and perform in a routine manner work such as was done a quarter of a century ago or longer. We have a very much higher conception of our responsibilities.

We have, of course, confidential relationships, which should be protected, the relationship of a professional man to a client, which is always sacred. But as far as having any fundamental policies or principles that we would be afraid to show to the world, we never have had and never will have so long as I head this administration.

And I think it is perfectly clear that the trend of capital, which in the latter part of the last century was from England to other shores of the world, will be reversed, and the trend of capital from here on will be from the United States into other parts of the world. That, obviously, will lead to a new inventory-taking on our part. We all know that the establishment of the accountancy profession in this country really arose out of the audits and investigations made for and on behalf of English capital, the latter part of the century. Well, from here on, as I have indicated, the reverse will take place. I do not mean by that that the English will be cut off from making investments of capital in other parts of the world. They will continue to do so. But we are now the creditor nation of the world and are likely to remain so, for many, many years to come.

Therefore, that changed situation necessitates a broader approach on our part. In other words, we cannot hope to retain or obtain large, substantial connections in this country, unless we are in a position to carry the same kind of service into other parts of the world, as other large firms, in the main, are now able to do.

The relationship to our present English representatives started out largely in an agency way. We knew literally nothing of what would happen. And it has proved very interesting and, in the main, very satisfactory because, after all, you have to bear in mind that their ideas have to cope with ours and our ideas have to cope with theirs. But, casting our imaginations ahead for a decade or two, and realizing that if this firm is to take its place among the other firms, not only in this country but in the world, we will have to establish connections of a character that will enable us to undertake work in practically any part of the globe. Negotiations are proceeding along rather interesting and instructive lines, and before the year is out we hope to be able to announce that there will be a new firm which will probably be styled, "Arthur Andersen, McAuliffe, Hope & Company." The exact title is yet to be determined.

That firm over the next three to five years will be equipped to undertake work in Canada, Continental Europe, South America, Australia, and the Dutch East Indies. In other words, we will so mould this machine that we will have an organization that will enable us to take care of work in any of these parts of the world that I have referred to.

We find that these people are not as progressive as we are. In England they have a tendency to be extremely conservative and to cling to the past, and the young men have little or no chance to develop rapidly. In other words, you have to be about fifty years of age before a junior partner can address a senior partner by his first name.

And, that is literally true. I am not overstating the situation at all. But, contrast that with the situation over here. The senior partner over here is just one more fellow. But over there he is "the works," and it is carried out to the point where it has really operated in the direction of a minimum opportunity for the men. But they are basically honest and they are basically capable; they are quite willing to learn. As I survey the situation, we made the best possible choice of any that were offered to us at the time. Charlie Jones and I went to England in 1930.

So, you see, out of all this we should place the firm on a sound, international basis, and the question of having foreign subsidiaries of large American corporations is nothing that should cause us to lose sleep, from here on.

We are going to have two classes of competition from now on. We are going to have, first, the competition of the routine auditing type of firm. From that point of view we will have no advantages against anybody else, for we are not any smarter than they. If we let ourselves become routine auditors, and if that were the policy of the firm, I would retire from it so fast that you could not hear my heels as I got out of this office. That holds no interest for me, none whatever.

The second type of auditing firm is the one that will do something more than the routine auditing. I realize that in every professional office, either lawyer, engineer or doctor, practically eighty-five percent of the work which is done is what might be styled mill-run, or routine. There are certain mechanical phases that you have got to go through in order to arrive at the point at which judgment can be applied and opinions expressed.

Now, we want to belong to that second class of firm, where we can measure our contribution more by the quality of the services rendered, rather than by whether we are getting a good living out of it. If it is just a question of making a good living out of anything, and the creative factors are absent, I can say to you honestly, looking you all in the eye, that I just have no interest in that sort of thing.

* * * * *

It was twenty-five years ago this fall that I made that famous refrigerator car investigation, which is just as good today as it was when written, and I was twenty-six years of age. But I did something some of you fellows would think inhuman to do nowadays. I took a room at the Hotel Sherman, and I stayed there for six weeks, but I got the report out.

* * * * *

We were all juniors at one time; very crude material at one time. The extent to which you have come through is reflected in no small degree by the approach toward not only yourself but primarily the other fellow. As nearly as possible, put your relationship to the men underneath you on the basis of merit, and merit alone. Then you will grow

and others will grow, too, and you will go ahead.

If any of you men, as partners or as managers, are doing work that someone below you could do just as well, you are not only curtailing your own growth and development but, worse than that, you are choking the man down below you. It is necessary to pass on as much responsibility as you can to others.

* * * * *

All I want to look forward to at all times is whether or not the organization is sound, whether the type of personnel we have is the right type of personnel, and are they all linked together, working for one common good, namely the success of the organization.

It is not altogether a happenstance that this firm went through the depression in the way we did, or that it came out of the depression with a larger and better reputation than it had when it entered the depression. There were elements of luck, but we clung to fundamental principles and a broad business approach, and these are, I think, the important factors in such success as we have had.

227

Introduction to the First Issue of *The Chronicle*
October 1, 1940

The introduction of The Andersen Chronicle marks another significant step in the continued progress of the firm. Its fundamental policy is to avoid dogmatism in all of its expressions. Indeed, it will be used as a vehicle to provoke thought and make for intelligent discussion of principles and policies. At no stage is it to be construed as stating firm policies on technical or other moot questions. It is intended to be a forum for the free and full expression of ideas of any member of the organization (regardless of place or position) who feels that a contribution can be made. The whole conception is born of a desire for closer cooperation and helpfulness in the realization that in this complicated and uncertain world, the problems confronting one member of the organization are the problems of all.

If we are to render broader and more effective service to our clients (which after all is the keynote of the success of any professional organization), we ourselves must continue to grow. Businessmen everywhere desire the advice and counsel of accountants who have technical sense and can use good business judgment in its application. It has been frequently said in our organization that good accounting flows from good business and not vice versa. There is no substitute for this fundamental approach.

Then, too, items of a personal nature involving members of our organization are of interest to all, not in a paternalistic sense, but, rather of understanding, interest, and helpfulness.

If this publication is to be continued, it will rest squarely on the response it receives from the organization as a whole. Let us dedicate ourselves to this larger purpose of greater devotion and loyalty to rendering finer service to society as a whole.

(signed) ARTHUR ANDERSEN

A layman speaks

Commencement address
at St. Olaf College,
Northfield, Minnesota,
June 3, 1941

Man must be moved by high moral and ethical concepts in all of his relationships and must believe in the ultimate triumph of right.

THE PEOPLE of the world appear to be drifting aimlessly. We have lost our way. Probably at no time has man been faced with such uncertainties, nor has he been so frustrated as he is today. Everyone is asking, "Whither are we going?" That there is a broad and worldwide economic, political and social change in the process of making (yet to reflect itself in concrete form) appears to be reasonably clear. Thinkers are searching the past for signs which will serve as a possible pattern from which deductions can be made. Many accepted economic theories have been upset and once established concepts are now being seriously questioned. This confusion in thinking has made it almost impossible to take soundings —much less to chart a course. We are living in a "Good Friday" world where the forces of good are apparently yielding to the forces of evil.

The plight of many nations grieves us deeply; that of Norway is especially heavy upon our hearts. The record of the Norwegian race cannot be read without recognition of the qualities that are present today in the hearts and lives of our kinsmen in that distant land. High morals and ethics have characterized our race for centuries. These people have believed more in the virtues of human cooperation than in the futility of human exploitation. They are a product of their soil and of the sea, and have been made strong through their struggle for existence in a stern and rocky land. Their basic qualities of being idealistic, courageous and intensely practical are a result of the difficulties present in their lives from birth. Each succeeding generation has recognized its responsibility to pass on as a heritage higher levels of living. That the democratic form of government in Norway had reached a higher level of relative perfection than in

231

any other nation was no accident—but came rather out of a better design for living. This has made for an independent and courageous race. Is it conceivable that such people can ever be conquered? No! — emphatically no. Freedom to them is as vital and necessary as the air they breathe. The Germans are in temporary possession of the land, but never, never will they conquer the free Norwegian soul which has been a thousand years in the making.

It is easy, far too easy, to take a cynical view; but, once again, hope and life will conquer fear and despair. One must endeavor in addressing young persons, particularly on the eve of their graduation, to present views which are at least intellectually honest. Moreover, we cannot take a short view, but must take a long view in the determination of sound principles that will remain unchanged through the ages. My experiences of many years, in the academic, religious and business fields, have led me to the inescapable conclusion that fundamental principles ultimately prevail.

Some years ago I read a book, written by a distinguished archeologist at one of the leading universities in England, entitled "A Challenge to Complacency." This book was intended to arouse the public mind everywhere to what appeared to the author to be an inevitable trend toward war, unless counteracting influences were set to work. To me it is a notable work; unfortunately, the condition foreseen has since materialized, probably far beyond the point the author thought possible.

In a broad and comprehensive manner, two major thoughts were developed and ably presented therein, namely:

1. Progress from one civilization to another is not cumulative, contrary to general and popular belief. However, the trend has always been definitely upward.

2. There are two main forces that govern the lives of all of us—the first is the economic or material; the other is the spiritual or intellectual.

It was further observed by the author that if either one of these two forces outstrips the other, chaos results, and that a balanced order exists only when the two forces are linked together in a spirit of cooperation, indeed, in a spirit of companionship. Is this not merely another way of saying—"by the sweat of thy brow shalt thou eat bread" and also "man cannot live by bread alone"? The world appears to be both morally and ethically bankrupt; no wonder, then, that the human race is without the spiritual foundation so necessary, not only for its preservation, but for its advancement. Man must be moved by high moral and ethical concepts in all of his relationships, and must believe in the ultimate triumph of right. Without this anchorage, he is indeed lost.

On a visit to Europe in 1934, it was my privilege to spend several hours with one of England's most brilliant men. Our meeting occurred immediately after the "purge" in June of that year when Hitler caused many leaders of an earlier day to be massacred. It was the opinion then that, as a result of this "purge," the possibility of war in Europe had been postponed for *at least* ten years. In other words, those in power in the major nations of Europe were already moving rapidly in the direction of inevitable war, instead of taking steps to avoid war. This is the price always paid by the human race when its affairs are governed by politicians rather than by statesmen. One would naturally ask (as I did then) how many more generations would have to come and go before man would awaken to the stupidity and futility of resorting to war as even remotely providing bases for settling differences. War has been going on ever since man acquired consciousness and probably will go on as long as exploitation of man by man, and nation by nation, continues. "Live and let live" will, we hope, be the fundamental premise from which all human relationships will ultimately spring.

Having indicated the major problem which confronts mankind on all sides, it appears appropriate to discuss the contributions I believe we can make toward the rebuilding of our civilization. If man cannot find his solution in the universal acceptance and practice of Christian principles, I know of no other road that can be traveled which will again restore the dignity of man and cause him to move toward higher moral and ethical levels. If this is not done, civilization will surely be lost. There are some persons who believe that the present crisis is merely evidence of the wrath of God. This view is not acceptable to me. It might better be said that man is inflicting punishment upon himself through his own grievous ways of living.

I say that unless we can see the evil of our ways in practising exploitation of our fellow men in an individual, national and international sense, as against cooperation in all human relationships, we have yet to find the road that will bring us out of our difficulties. This is the view of one who has been trained in the field of business, with less intimate contact with the religious and academic circles. I do not share the view that one group is more guilty than another. We are *all* guilty, and if the problem can be approached in that spirit, we are likely to find the common ground from which *all* groups can unite as one, to march forward to the realization of the Kingdom of God on earth. There are those who will say that two thousand years have already passed with little progress having been made along spiritual lines. Can it be that the saints and prophets of yore have lived in vain? Whatever may be said against the church, it must be acknowledged that it has kept the Christian spirit alive. While the church has not been able to bring about universal acceptance of Christian principles, it has made men mindful of what they must do if the manifold

problems which assume such large proportions today are to be solved. We would, indeed, be false to posterity if we did not enlarge upon and preserve the fine heritage which has been handed down to us by earlier generations. Life is an evolutionary process which should cause us to accept, as individuals, a challenge to do our part in trying to improve the lot of man. My father-in-law, who was a religious man, said to me a quarter of a century ago, "There may not be anything to religion. I believe there is, and that man is better off to go through life with that belief than without it." What a perfect statement this is.

Principles have a way of asserting themselves. They may temporarily yield to expediency but, actually, they are always lying close to the surface, constantly arising and often in least expected places. Expediency, on the other hand, is always in danger of yielding (as it ultimately does) to principles. To make a decision of any importance on the basis of expediency invariably means that the day of reckoning has only been postponed. If we could but make our decisions on principle rather than expediency, life for all of us would be much simpler. Continuity of conduct at a high level is too much to expect from frail human beings, but those who are more fortunately born, and who are imbued with a fine concept of what constitutes great underlying principles, in the end, prove to be the true leaders. Expediency never triumphs over principle—it may appear to do so, but it never does. It is this faith to believe that principles ultimately prevail, that distinguishes some men from others. The greatest statement of basic or underlying principles was made centuries ago; there are few who would enter into any discussion of the validity of the pattern of life given us in the "Sermon on the Mount." Too many men would say that the principles are sound, but they cannot work in a complicated civilization such as the one we live in. But, it has been proved that in the larger business units they have worked—and reasonably well. One does not mean to say that these principles have been applied in any universal sense, but insofar as they have been tried, without sentimentalism and emotionalism, experience unquestionably establishes the fact that man is more successful following principles than otherwise. Certainly he can live with himself much easier.

Although it is recognized that all men, to live fully and honestly, must be guided by principles, I shall confine my comments regarding their application to the businessman, the preacher and the teacher, since their interests are more directly allied with the activities of educational institutions.

The businessman is a much criticized individual because his activities are centered in trade and exchange of things tangible. Few people realize that the major activity of the world is that of commerce and that half of that activity springs directly from the soil or the farm. The constant struggle of men and nations in the field of trade and commerce is undoubtedly one of the basic causes of war. Trade restrictions, secret treaties, broken covenants, deliberate deception and intrigue, misrepresentation, and refusal of those in high places to recognize justice and fairness in international affairs have been, and are, taking their toll. The world is suffering from a dearth of statesmanship. Most businessmen in our nation (particularly in the larger units) are committed to the policy of considering the welfare of customers first, employees second and capital third. This is a bright hope, and indicates the acceptance of thinking in terms of principles. This approach, which avoids paternalism, makes for the development of a finer sense of social responsibility. It is in this same spirit that labor must take its share of fair dealing and adjustment. Both labor and capital must become more socially conscious and must recognize the common good as their primary objective.

The preacher reaches for the unattainable —he clings to the hope (and rightly so) that men and nations will accept and practice Christian principles. The preacher is well qualified through higher learning and more time for study and meditation, to point out the fallacies, by-passes, and "dead-end" streets to be avoided by *all* humanity. On the stage of life he is the prompter, certainly not the actor, nor a propagandist, and is in no sense a professional holy man. But, through his privileged position, he can be stimulating and helpful to his hearers and challenge them to carry into everyday life some of the fine principles, philosophy and understanding which all thinking men recognize as the true way. If man could but realize that no one stands between him and God, and that only he can save himself, it would make for a quality of individual responsibility that no earthly rulers could hope to contend with.

The teacher is, indeed, a fortunate member of society. The greatness of a college or university is not judged by its buildings and physical equipment (as necessary as they are) but by the quality of its faculty— men of character, finely trained, loyal and devoted, independent thinkers, inspiring and stimulating to the students, with a sacrificial attitude toward their social and intellectual responsibilities in their everlasting search for the truth, which is their life.

The opportunity for a college education imposes a great responsibility upon those who are privileged to drink at this stream of inspiration. If one could choose between a formal education without common sense, and common sense without formal education (and one can have common sense without formal education) the choice would certainly be the latter. But, if one is born with common sense and has had the rare opportunity to obtain formal education, he has indeed been raised to a level of great obligation to his fellow men. Those of us who ultimately move into positions of leadership through such privileged opportunities do not belong to ourselves, but, rather to those whom we endeavor to serve. There is a humanitarian compulsion to success that must be recognized.

There will be little progress if we accept the theory that only the successful and those in high places recognize and act upon the humanitarian impulse. Sacrifice is relative, and is usually inspired by deep devotion to ideals. This devotion may express itself both tangibly and intangibly. We need only to look about us to see tangible results. This institution, its high accomplishments, its fine physical properties, and its reputation, represents sacrifices from numerous sources and by people in many walks of life. Its buildings were not built by large gifts nor endowments, but by the cumulative sacrifices of many persons. These buildings were made possible because *you* believe in ideals. On my first visit to this campus, as I was being shown about by President Boe, I thought of each stone in each building as an individual expression of interest and loyalty to St. Olaf by some alumnus or friend. Loyalty to an ideal, broad understanding and courage on the part of the church, alumni and friends, have brought to full realization the vision of the founders of this college. More than ever will educational institutions have to depend upon the continued interest and support of their alumni and their friends.

This day marks another significant milestone in the history of St. Olaf College. Through application of sound principles and policies, and able administration, this institution has reached the coveted place of ranking among the foremost colleges of our country.

Today we shall witness the laying of the cornerstone of the new library building. It will not be the most costly nor the most elaborate library building on an American campus, but it will rise from the ground, dedicating itself to the preservation of culture, high ideals and fine traditions, as a living testimony that there is a God in the heavens; that fundamental and true values are still present in the hearts of men; and

that we still maintain faith and hope that neither war nor rumors of war can dispel. What a fine answer to those who fear the tomorrows!

A library houses the books representing the accumulated knowledge of the centuries and provides the principal workshop for students in their college years. Its halls provide the connecting link between generations where the scholars of today come to know and appreciate the good works of the scholars of yesterday. The wisdom of great teachers is thus made available to those who accept the responsibility of trying to make this a better world in which to live. Progress seems so fearfully slow in view of the two thousand years which have elapsed since man was given the pattern of life. Thinking persons will recognize this pattern of life as the only way likely to meet the never-ending difficulties which cause men to stumble and fall, then to rise again with new strength to carry on their determination to leave the world a little better than they found it.

Living with books permits us to partake of that intimate and friendly relationship with scholars, prophets, seers and saints who have pointed the way, all having contributed to the sum total of knowledge and wisdom which continues to guide and inspire men.

One's reading habits after graduation are determined greatly by the use which was made of the facilities of a library in the four-year stay in college, despite the fact that perhaps they should have been formed early in life. The library is literally the workshop of the student in cultivating and training his mind. The contact with old scholars, not only is made quite real, but, out of it comes an inspiration to keep currently informed on events in a swiftly moving world, and to think more deeply than most men and, therefore, to be better able to face problems as they arise. Reading also deepens one's insight into life, and while the deepest understanding will not overcome crises, one is in a better position to sense, see and adjust himself more intelligently and courageously than otherwise would be the case. The library is the silent companion of teacher and student alike. Next to the faculty itself, it offers facilities more likely to influence the course of the student's life than any other.

May I now refer to the action of St. Olaf College in providing the Norwegian-American Historical Association with a hall in the new library building. This is a most practical and gracious gesture and, as President of the organization, I express the deep thanks of our group for this thoughtfulness.

I know that in this gathering there are many persons of Norwegian extraction who will readily realize the importance of the work of our Historical Association. Our pride of race compels us to obtain and preserve records of the part our people have played in the development of this country, particularly these Middlewest and Northwest areas. Norwegian culture, tradition and philosophy represent a heritage which many of us here, possibly unconsciously, draw upon and live by. We cannot see this die nor melt away with passing years without making some effort to preserve it. The Norwegian-American Historical Association is the vehicle for the preservation of this heritage and for the recording of our achievements. It has been said by prominent historians that our group is the outstanding example of organized effort on the part of any national group in this country to preserve the records of its people. We must continue to justify this reputation.

When the invitation was extended to me to make this address, I readily accepted with a deep sense of gratitude and appreciation. My interest in education has always been profound, because it has been my privilege to have been identified with a leading university as student, teacher and chief administrative officer. I can see, and you will see when you occupy positions of leadership and responsibility, that the generation coming from behind is likely to do a better job than your generation did. It is this feeling that keeps alive the desire of man to constantly improve the quality of the human race. Therefore, for the next few minutes, I shall address myself primarily to the graduating class of this year.

Recently I saw a choice bit of writing that referred to the renowned psychiatrist, Dr. Alfred Adler, and his statement that there are four types of men:

The first type he terms as anti-social—this individual feels that the world owes him something and he promptly proceeds to get it. The gangster and racketeer are of this type, and also those who feel that their interests and those of society are not common ones.

The second type is that of the dependent. He does not think or act for himself. Without active and vital members of society, he would starve.

The third type is the hermit or isolated individual who can not quite square himself with the social responsibilities of life. He, therefore, withdraws to live by himself.

The fourth type is the contributor. He accepts life as an opportunity—as a challenge. He is constantly adding to the culture of life. He sincerely hopes that he will leave the world a little richer than he found it. This, Dr. Adler says, is the only survival type; he alone is capable of perpetuating society and culture.

Therefore, I express the hope that *all* of you will be of the contributor type. So far, you have had every opportunity to move into that classification. The place you are to take in society can be determined only as your talents unfold.

The broad underlying concept of the contributor type lies primarily in character and the ability to think impersonally. This is a rare quality of mind because one must detach himself from selfish considerations and rise to that of merit, sheer merit, with all factors surrounding the problem dispassionately reviewed. Such an approach, a level of human thinking and action which admittedly is difficult to maintain, would liberate you and develop more fully your potential capacity. Impersonal thinking compels growth and development and makes for relative peace of mind. It is the genuine mark of a truly big man in any field of endeavor.

And now, a *final* word to the graduating class of 1941 —

Shortly, this beautiful campus with its buildings will be but a memory to you. What you take out in spiritual and intellectual culture, training and inspiration will be part of your lives so long as you live. What use you make of these virtues in the years that lie ahead will be determined largely by your own attitude toward life. In its day, every generation is a modern one, and while you face what appears to you to be insurmountable difficulties, other men in earlier generations have experienced similar feelings. Adversity and understanding, not leisure and softness, bring out the best in all of us.

Truth, faith, honesty, honor, courage, devotion, tolerance, humility and loyalty are still the propelling forces in a well-ordered society. Cling to these fine qualities; hold them in a spirit of sacred trust; and you will come back to your Alma Mater again and again with your heads erect, proud to be numbered among the Alumni of St. Olaf College.

"Therefore whosoever heareth these sayings of mine, and doeth them, I will liken him unto a wise man, which built his house upon a rock; and the rain descended, and the floods came, and the winds blew, and beat upon that house; and it fell not; for it was founded upon a rock."